WALKING IN
PROVENCE

Baou St-Jeannet from village below

WALKING IN PROVENCE

ALPES MARITIMES, VAR, VAUCLUSE
(Luberon and Mt. Ventoux)

NORTHERN PROVENCE
including
Gorges du Verdon

by
JANETTE NORTON

CICERONE PRESS LTD
MILNTHORPE, CUMBRIA
www.cicerone.co.uk

ISBN 1 85284 293 8
A catalogue record for this book is available from the British Library

ACKNOWLEDGEMENTS

I would like to thank my many stalwart friends who came from Geneva and parts of England to accompany me on my walks in the various regions of Provence; Loulou Brown, Penelope Drew, Gilberte Furet, Lynn Mermagen, Ann Nicholson, Jill Robson, Isobel Shaw, Anne-Lise Van der Vlugt; my sisters Hilary Birch (from Nassau, Bahamas) and Julia Jamison (from Paris); my brother Adrian Leeming; my resident friends in the Alpes Maritimes region, especially Ingrid Berg, Margaret Blomberg, Angela Hemmings, Vi Matthewson, Elizabeth Reynaud, Sally Roessler, Akiko Takayama and Pete Tannahill.

A special thanks to Alexa Stace who came three times and gave valuable editorial advice; Janet Locke without whose map reading and compass directions I would still be wandering around the mountains of northern Provence; my husband who, as usual, read it all before it went to the publishers; my daughters Rebecca, Joanna and Tanya for criticism, advice and holding the fort in my absence; lastly, my son Angus for suggesting I write the book in the first place!

I am extremely grateful for the information provided by the Tourist Offices in the different regions, especially the director of the office in Dignes-les-Bains, the director of ADRI (Association pour le développment de la randonnée en Haute Provence) and the Geological Museum (both in Dignes-les-Bains).

Advice to Readers

Readers are advised that whilst every effort is taken by the author to ensure the accuracy of this guidebook, changes can occur which may affect the contents. It is advisable to check locally on transport, accommodation, shops etc but even rights-of-way can be altered.

The publisher would welcome notes of any such changes

Other Cicerone books by the same author:
    Walking in the Haute Savoie

Front Cover: The Verdon Gorge Photo: R.B.Evans

CONTENTS

THE WALKS

When two timings are given it means shorter and longer circuit. A + sign after the timing indicates that extra time should be allowed for visiting a historical site or village.

Introduction

My love affair with Provence is fairly recent - I never went there as a child or a young adult even though for years I lived within a few hours of the region. However, I have an early memory of my parents going to "the Riviera" and sending us postcards.

Provence at that time would have been quite different to what it is today. Tourism did not extend beyond the coast, where the towns were elegant resorts catering to the wealthier members of Europe only. Elsewhere was still a rural community of small peasant farmers living in primitive hill villages, where life was a constant struggle despite the bewitching landscape of hills and fertile valleys, rugged upland plains and a breathtaking coastline with the deep blue of the Mediterranean lapping the shores of unspoilt fishing villages.

The only facet of Provence my parents would recognise 50 years on would be the enigmatic bright light which sheds a luminosity over the landscape, making even the most humble of buildings glow enticingly. For hundreds of years it has attracted artists, sculptors, writers and more recently tourists, from all over the world.

I was introduced to the fascinating small roman town of Vaison-La-Romaine near Mont Ventoux in the 1980s because my husband was running a half-marathon nearby around the white jagged peaks of the Dentelles de Montmirail. This turned out to be a yearly weekend event, but instead of running the course I took to walking it. This was fine because there were tidy yellow flags at the side of the path to show me the way. My problems started when, armed with a map, I started to wander elsewhere. Often I got hopelessly lost or ended up in a farmyard being faced by ferociously barking dogs, the problem being that the walking routes are not well marked and sometimes go through private property. This is not welcomed by the independent French farmers.

The idea of writing another book was far from my thoughts but one day, when walking with my son, we took the wrong turning and after futile efforts to find our way, ended up hitch-hiking back to Vaison-la-Romaine late for our rendezvous. Meanwhile my husband was making enquiries of an indifferent officer at the police station, who was merely puzzled and surprised that anyone would want to hoof off into the surrounding hills, let alone get lost in them! With a classic Gallic shrug he dismissed the idea of an eventual search party, walking anywhere lengthy being completely foreign to the average Provençal.

Finally safe and sound over a drink in the bustling main square, Angus looked at me wearily: "I think this will have to be your next book Mum, otherwise I'm not walking with you again around here." He was quite right. I felt that in order to get to know all the diverse areas of this fascinating region and to be able to share my knowledge and enjoyment with others I would have to write another book.

This book has been a challenge but thanks to the support of many, and the friends who came to walk and inevitably get lost with me, the project has become reality. And of course Provence is now "under my skin" and I can't leave it.

THE PROVENÇAL REGIONS

If you drive down through France on the motorway aptly named La Route du Soleil (sun road!), you will notice that after Valence, south of Lyon, the landscape starts to alter and the light changes. Everything suddenly looks clearer, the sun is brighter, the sky bluer. The little red-roofed villages stand out on the hillsides, each with its distinctive iron trellised church bell-tower; where there were fir trees there are now pines and tall cypresses; placid cows, green pastures, maize and wheat fields give way to stony vineyards, rows of purple lavender, olive trees and broom.

You feel a certain indolence take hold; things that were stressful and important have taken on a trivial air. The air is warm and smells of pine trees and herbs; the people on the motorway *péages* (toll booths) actually smile! It could all be imagination or just the Mediterranean magic that has seduced thousands of tourists as they enter Provence.

Provence is situated in the south-eastern corner of France but the exact boundaries are an enigma. The well-known Michelin Guide, for example, excludes the Alpes Maritimes (Riviera) and also northern Provence, but includes the Gorges d'Ardèche (there are separate books for the other two areas).

Most other guides include five regions, namely the Alpes Maritimes, Var, Bouches du Rhône, Vaucluse and northern Provence. Officially the region Provence-Corse-Côte d'Azur was created in 1956, Corsica became independent in 1970 leaving Provence-Côte D'Azur, which then split into the five departmental regions in 1971.

For my part I have excluded the Bouches du Rhône which includes the flat Carmargue plain and split the Vaucluse into two areas, Mt. Ventoux and the Luberon.

When describing each area I have suggested a few towns and villages where the visitor might like to stay. There are dozens of excellent guides to Provence in English giving myriad places to visit, including architectural sites and museums plus lists of hotels, restaurants and campsites.

None of the walks I selected was more than an hour by car from where I was based. In the Alpes Maritimes I stayed in a friend's house in the village of Le Rouret, conveniently situated between Vence and Grasse. In the Var I had a cosy little cottage on a wine estate outside the village of Nans-les-Pins, south of St-Maximin-la-Ste-Baume, east of Aix-en-Provence. Saignon, a hill village above Apt, was my base in the Luberon and I stayed in Le Barroux, near Carpentras, for my walks near the Mt. Ventoux. Finally the larger town of Digne-les-Bains was my temporary home for the wilder walks in northern Provence.

Although France is well known for its long distance *grande randonnée* paths which criss-cross the whole of the country including the Provençal region, the markings on other paths were somewhat haphazard. This has changed recently as the local s*yndicats d'initiative* (information centres) have become better organised. In order to attract tourists many villages publish leaflets (in French) with maps indicating the various *boucles* (circular routes) that can be made around the village.

It should be pointed out that walking in Provence is often a lonely occupation - while the towns, especially on the coast, are thronged with people, the hills are often devoid of anyone apart from sheep, and it is easy to lose your way. Unlike the Alps there is rarely a cosy mountain refuge just around the corner or a handy walker to ask directions from. Walking for pleasure is foreign to the nature of the average Provençal who would rather sit under a tree and drink a pastis.

But the walking is magical and full of discovery - an ancient ruin, a tumbledown village, monuments, shrines, *bories*, *oppidums* and old canals - this is a countryside with a past and when walking in it you stumble on history! The attraction of Provence is its diversity - one day you can be walking on a remote plateau or windswept hill, the next down a leafy gorge. Wherever you are you feel you need to linger, to explore further and reflect on the hitherto hard life of the peasants who scratched a living from the stony soil, many to abandon their remote villages and move to the towns.

There are so many interesting diversions that walks often take longer than anticipated but the air is warm and fragrant with herbs - time takes on a new meaning.

When you finally arrive back there is hopefully that pastis waiting for you in a little café under shady trees in the main square of the village.

A SHORT HISTORY OF PROVENCE

The history of Provence is long and complicated as it has been the melting pot of different tribes and cultures over thousands of years. Nevertheless a few salient points are a help when walking in the region and visiting the larger towns whose architectural richness testify to the diversity of its origins.

During the Bronze Age the area was settled by primitive Ligurian tribes who made their fortresses on hill-tops away from the coast. The remnants can still be seen in the form of jumbled rocks called *oppidums* forming vague circles in now remote upland areas (see walk No. 6 for a good example). One marvels at the ingenuity of these people in creating such structures in a landscape so harsh and climatically inhospitable. The first *bories* are thought to date from this epoch. These are curious drystone huts made of local stone and built without any cementing mixture but of incredible thickness, with one low door for access. They can be found either in small clusters (see the *borie* village near Gordes) or standing alone all over the Provence area, but mainly in the Vaucluse region. Of different shapes and sizes, they were built and used up to the 18th century mainly as shepherd's huts, but earlier on also as places of refuge in troubled times.

From 8000 to 4000 BC came progressive waves of Celts from the north who intermingled with the existing Ligurian tribes without conquering them, and formed the basis of the indigenous population. The arrival of the Greeks around 800 BC was to play a large part in the civilization of the area. They founded the city of Marseille (then called Massilia) which became an important trading centre in oil, wine, salt, arms, bronze objects and slaves. This led to the establishment of other trading posts such as Avignon and Cavaillon. Meanwhile the local people, now called the Salian Franks, who had helped Hannibal cross the region in 218 BC, became more powerful and rose against the imperialism of the mainly Greek residents of Massilia.

In panic the Massilians called on support from the Romans who were happy to extend their domains. They easily conquered Entremont, the capital of the Salian Franks, and continued to expand their power over the whole Provençal region. They created the first boundaries of a new province named Transalpine, although Marseille remained independent until, as a result of supporting Pompey against Caesar during the Gallic wars, it was besieged in 49 BC. The Romans were responsible for the flowering of architectural masterpieces, such as viaducts, theatres and temples in the already important towns of Narbonne, Nimes, Arles, Fréjus and Aix-en-Provence. Vestiges of these impressive buildings remain to this day and are visited by thousands of tourists. Christianity came to the area in the 4th century with the conversion of the emperor Constantine, who made Arles his favourite city and contributed to its magnificent buildings.

With the fall of the Roman Empire the golden age of Arles was over. In 471 it was invaded by the Visigoths and from then on confusion reigned as waves of barbarian hordes poured into the region, pillaging and laying waste as one local ruler succeeded another. In the 8th century constant raids on the coastal towns were made by the Saracens (Moors) from North Africa.

Provence became part of the Holy Roman Empire in 1032 and the devastated towns started to expand again. The rural population huddled together in perched villages surrounded by walls for safety and governed by local counts. When Charles of Anjou married Beatrice of Provence in the 12th century it brought further stability to the region, and the building of many beautiful Romanesque churches and abbeys followed. It was also the time of the Crusades and the romantic troubadours, wandering poets who travelled through medieval Europe singing of the historical happenings of the times and serving as modern news media.

In the 13th century the most important town was Avignon, where the French bishop, elected Pope in 1316, decided to take up residence instead of in Rome. Papal supremacy reigned in Avignon for nearly a century, resulting in the building of an impressive papal palace and the expansion of the city within fortress walls which remain a tourist attraction to this day.

Disarray again hit Provence in the 14th century as the country was laid waste by brigands, famine and the plague. When King René, the youngest son of Louis II of Anjou, inherited the region in 1434 he managed to restore political and economic stability and was much loved by the people. He was a poet and the first person to attract artists to Aix-en-Provence which was the capital and cultural centre of the province from the 12th to the 18th century.

The Reformation spread through the south of France in the early 1500s and numerous abbeys and churches were ransacked by the Huguenots. François I finally retaliated and ordered the brutal massacre of 3000 people of the Waldenses Protestant sect in the Luberon area in 1545 and many villages were razed to the ground (for further details see Vaucluse chapter and walk No. 22). Protestantism continued to spread, especially west of the Rhône, and divided the people of Provence from those of the Languedoc-Cévennes region. The two regions were to clash again in 1702 when the Protestants fought back in the war of the Camisards and were again defeated.

The next tragedy to strike was the great plague in 1720 which originated from a Syrian ship docking in Marseille. Despite the building of a 28km plague wall to stop the people fleeing the city (see walk No. 21) the epidemic spread to the other major towns and in two years 100,000 people had died, half of them from Marseille.

During the French Revolution, Provence was stripped of its autonomy in 1790 and divided into three *départements* so that politically it no longer existed. In 1792 a group of national guards from Marseille marched through the city of Paris singing a newly written war song dedicated to the Battle of the Rhine. This was later called the *Marseillaise* and became the french national anthem.

On March 1st 1815 Napoleon Bonaparte landed at Golfe-Juan near Cannes from his exile on the island of Elba. From here he started his epic journey to Paris with 1200 men on what is called the Route Napoleon, now the modern N85 going from the coast up to Grenoble, which opened in 1932 (see walk No. 6).

The Industrial Revolution wrought great changes in Provence. The railway system, starting in 1843, enabled movement of people and goods hitherto unknown in such a remote region. The port of Marseille expanded, boosted by the Fench annexation of North Africa and the opening of the Suez Canal. The delights of coastal Provence were discovered, mainly by the English aristocracy, and soon hotels, casinos and fancy villas were being constructed for the rich and famous of Europe. The coastal areas prospered but inland the peasant agricultural way of life continued unchanged. Development suffered a setback when the first appearance of the deadly phylloxera disease appeared in 1868 affecting many of the vineyards.

The First World War halted expansion and changed the agricultural rhythm of life irrevocably as thousands of French peasants perished in the north of France. The carefully tended terraces were abandoned through lack of manpower, but it was only after the Second World War in 1945 that the real exodus to the cities took place. The German occupation of southern France is still etched in the memories of the older Provençal population, and monuments and plaques to the inhabitants of a village or a young Resistance group who lost their lives, dot the countryside and remind the walker of those difficult times.

Since the 1940s Provence has leapt ahead with industrialisation and the modernisation of its agriculture such as market gardening, wine, oil and fruit. Rivers have been harnessed to produce hydro-electricity and nuclear power stations have been constructed. The biggest expansion has been in tourism as the coastal strip has become the playground of the masses rather than the elite few. The airport at Nice is now the second largest in France and the construction industry has boomed as even more hotels, supermarkets and apartment blocks continue to rise, mainly in the Alpes Maritimes.

But tourism has also brought culture to the region as the larger towns are the hosts to well known music, art and theatre festivals. Small towns and villages vie for the tourists by reviving local customs and festive days with colourful processions, flower festivals and folk dancing. There are also thermal baths at many places including Aix-en-Provence and Digne-les-Bains.

Happily in some regions ecologists have also woken up to the fact that if they do not protect the landscape now there will be precious little to protect in the future. Areas such as the Luberon and the Mercantour have been made National Parks and walking in summer has been banned on certain mountain ranges due to fire hazard (see 'Flora and Fauna' - page 19).

History marches forward, and if industrial progress and tourism have overtaken the old traditional way of life, drawing the population away from agriculture to the cities, they have also enabled the Provençal people to have a higher standard of living in an area which by its geographical position, beauty and climate is the envy of many other regions.

Information from: *Histoire de la Provence* by François-Xavier Emmanuelli (Hatchette, 1980).

WALK EXPLANATIONS AND SIGNPOSTING

WALK GRADING: None of the walks in this book goes higher than 2000 metres and many of them are considerably lower. They are generally within the capability of an averagely fit person and are graded Difficult, Medium or Easy. The comments after the grading should give a good idea whether this walk is suitable. Many people suffer from different degrees of vertigo and where this could be a problem, it is indicated. Under *'Observations'* are historical anecdotes about places visited or seen on the walk and any other information to interest the reader.

TIMINGS: The timings correspond to the average walking pace of a reasonably fit person but this is very approximate as everyone has a different rhythm. It is also important to leave plenty of time for stopping to look at the views, taking photos and for a picnic.

As a rough guide, you can expect to walk 3km in one hour if there are no excessive gradients. Four centimetres on a 1:25,000 scale map equals 1km (for quick measuring put three fingers sideways on the map - this equals roughly 4cm which is 20mins walking).

HEIGHT GAIN: When reading the walk details look carefully at the altitude gain. Extra altitude equals extra walking time and steep gradients can tire you very rapidly if you are not used to it. Only a few walks in this book have a significant altitude gain but, as a guideline, with a light rucksack (6 to 7kg) you should be able to climb 400m in one hour (250 to 300m with a weight of 15kg). The descent is quicker, namely 500m in one hour. When climbing, especially in southern climates, the heat and humidity will slow you down (see 'When to go' - page 16).

MAPS: Although each walk is accompanied by a sketch map it is recommended that you buy the listed IGN map. The walk will be clearer on the 1:25,000 scale than on the 1:50,000.

The numbers on each sketch map show key reference points, especially where there are major changes in walk direction. However, please read the instructions carefully as there may be additional turnings that are not numbered but where the path is not clearly indicated, even on the IGN map. Unfortunately many maps are out of date or inaccurate and the jeep tracks and paths taken are not shown on the map. The Série Bleu series are particularly poor and are being phased out, to be replaced by the Top 25 series.

HOW TO GET THERE: Directions to find the beginning of each walk start from a specific town. Where possible the walks start from convenient points where there is a car park or good roadside parking.

SIGNPOSTING: This gives an indication as to how well the walk is signposted and whether you are following a *Grande Randonnée* path or a local path with its own yellow, green or red splashes.

If you see white and red horizontal paint splashes on your route you are on one of the long distance footpaths (*Grandes Randonnées*) which go all over France and are usually well maintained. Look at page 15 for illustrations of the signs and remember that a cross instead of a splash (of the colour you are following) means that you are about to go in the wrong direction! Some of the local walks join these paths for a while but then break away to circle back to the starting point. Local walks have different coloured splashes but in some Provençal areas these are rather arbitrary and can suddenly disappear for no reason. In others there are so many colours that one gets bewildered!

Follow the walk directions carefully as often bushes can hide markings or the signposts have been torn down. Another feature of Provençal signposting is that the local tourist office may have decided to re-route the walk without eliminating the old signs or splashes.

One important hazard to watch out for is that you can be walking along quite happily and then suddenly find the path fenced off with a large notice *Propriété Privée!* All readers or viewers of Marcel Pagnol's *Manon des Sources* will understand that this attitude towards ownership of land is rooted in the Provençal character, though why a walking path should cross private land without preliminary permission is a mystery - perhaps there has been a change of ownership without warning? Whatever the reason, remember that you cross private property at your responsibility unless you have explicit permission, so be prudent and stick to the main pathways. Many farms have a couple of fierce dogs which are trained to discourage intruders and it is not pleasant to be confronted by them.

GUIDELINES FOR WALKING IN PROVENCE

- Read the walk description carefully and look at the map before you go.
- Make sure the walk is within the capacity of you and your companions.
- Give yourself plenty of time by setting off early. If a walk says 5hrs allow at least 2hrs extra for looking at things, reading the walk description and eating.
- In Provence, especially in the summer, you will need to take **plenty of water and sunscreen** - wear reliable sunglasses and a hat.
- Avoid deviating from the marked path - if there is a short cut it is usually shown.
- If you are lost go back the way you came if possible.
- If you are climbing be careful not to dislodge stones or boulders - they can gather momentum as they roll down the slope and hit other walkers.
- If you choose to walk alone be aware of potential dangers and always tell someone where you are going.
- Don't go beyond any barrier indicating *Propriété Privée* unless the walk description indicates that this is permitted.
- Even if the day looks hot and fine take waterproof clothing as Provence often has sudden storms. Also the cold *mistral* wind can strike at any time, especially in spring.
- Please take your litter home with you and leave the wild flowers for others to enjoy.
- Don't light matches or make a fire, especially when it has been dry. FIRE IS A DANGEROUS HAZARD IN THIS PART OF THE WORLD. Many fires which have swept this region have been caused by tourists.
- Remember to walk on the **left**-hand side of the road to face the oncoming traffic.

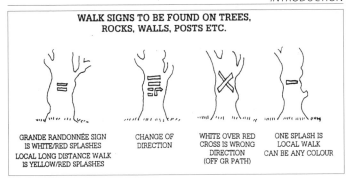

**WALK SIGNS TO BE FOUND ON TREES,
ROCKS, WALLS, POSTS ETC.**

GRANDE RANDONNÉE SIGN
IS WHITE/RED SPLASHES
LOCAL LONG DISTANCE WALK
IS YELLOW/RED SPLASHES

CHANGE OF
DIRECTION

WHITE OVER RED
CROSS IS WRONG
DIRECTION
(OFF GR PATH)

ONE SPLASH IS
LOCAL WALK
CAN BE ANY COLOUR

TRAVELLING TO PROVENCE

BY CAR: It is not possible to reach many of the walks in this book without
a car. If you come by train or air all the big car hire firms operate from stations
and airports and information about rental can be obtained before you leave.

If you take your own car, the easiest route to the South of France is to
take the direct motorway from Calais via Reims, Dijon and Valence which
avoids the tiring journey round Paris. The motorways are refreshingly empty
in France compared to Britain, except on some busy holiday weekends, and
have excellent stopping areas. There are motorway tolls to pay which can add
considerably to the cost of driving from Calais to Nice.

BY RAIL: The English office of the French Railways - Rail Europe, 179
Piccadilly, London W1V OBA. Tel. 0990 024000 (hot line) - will, on request,
send an informative brochure outlining the different ways to get to France
by rail, including timetables, cost, car hire, travel insurance information,
special hotel/rail packages for short and medium breaks, cross channel fares,
Interrail information for the under 26s etc. For ticket booking Tel. 0990
848848. Fax 0207 6339900.

It is possible to travel by Eurostar to Lille or Paris where you change and
take a direct train to Avignon and Marseille (change in Marseille for Aix-en-
Provence). It is easier to change in Lille than Paris, where you have the hassle
of crossing the city from the Gare du Nord to the Gare du Lyon. For
information and reservations contact Eurostar (U.K.) Ltd, Eurostar House,
Waterloo Station, London SE1 8SE. Tel. 0870 6000785.

BY BUS: The most economical way to travel to the South of France is by bus
from London Victoria Station. For information and booking details contact
Eurolines Tel. 0990 143219 or your local National Express Agent. The bus to

Nice stops off (amongst other destinations) at Avignon and Aix-en-Provence. It leaves London at 18.00 arriving Avignon at 12.00 the next day, Aix-en-Provence at 13.45 and Nice at 18.00. The return bus leaves Nice at 08.45, Aix-en-Provence at 13.30 and Avignon at 15.15, arriving in London at 8.30 am the following day. These times are subject to change and are an indication only.

BY AIR: There are direct flights from London to Marseille and Nice. British Airways: Heathrow/Nice four times a day. British Airways: Gatwick/Marseille three times a day. There are also daily flights from Manchester and other regional airports. EasyJet also have flights from Stanstead, Luton and Liverpool.

WHEN TO GO

Provence is renowned for its temperate climate, low rainfall, clear light and days of bright sunshine. This agreeable climate together with an attractive landscape is why the region is inundated with retired people who wish to escape the rigours of winter in northern Europe.

This does not mean there is no seasonal change. The climate is governed by the land relief. The coastal areas, particularly the Alpes Maritimes, have a mild, dry sunny winter but inland the climate is harsher and in the mountains there is a considerable amount of snow. The dreaded *mistral,* which is a cold north-westerly wind sweeping down from the Massif Central and funnelling down the Rhône valley, can cause a sudden drop in temperature causing havoc to crops. This wind can blow up at any time in winter or spring, lasting for days or merely for a couple of hours. It is often succeeded by still bright periods when the clarity of light is exceptional.

Spring and autumn are the rainy seasons, though compared to other climates the rainfall is comparatively low (23.5in annually). From mid-September to early December there can be violent thunderstorms. In spring the rain is less violent and there are brighter, sunnier days. It is the four months of summer which bring in the highest influx of tourists to the coast where the average temperature is a delightful 24°C and there is constant sun and no rain. Inland the heat is more overpowering - life slows down as the population retreats indoors during the day, emerging in the evening to eat and socialise.

ACCOMMODATION

All regions in Provence have good accommodation facilities ranging from first class hotels to primitive campsites; it is all a matter of choice and how much you want to spend. The walker has the advantage that it is really too hot to walk in July and August when most places are full and the campsites are cheek by jowl. It is much easier to find accommodation in May, June and September, when there are fewer people about and prices are lower. It is always advisable to book in advance though this is not essential. If you plan to walk in the winter months it is best to check that the hotels are open as this is when the hotel owners take their holidays. Most camping and caravan sites are only open in the summer months. Below is a list of the different types of accommodation available:

Hotels in France are typically less expensive than in England and are great value - the only thing missing is the tea facility in the bedroom and of course the hearty breakfast - you pay extra for this in a French hotel. Most rooms have en-suite bathroom or shower and WC. The choice is wide but below are some recommended hotel chains:

Logis de France: This is a nationwide network of hotels which offer comfortable accommodation and excellent food at reasonable prices. The hotels are graded from one to three-star according to their degree of comfort (look for the distinctive logo which consists of a yellow fireplace on a green background). The Logis de France book listing all the hotels available, with additional information regarding facilities, is available from good bookshops or the Maison de France shop in Piccadilly.

Campanile Hotels: These hotels tend to be on the outskirts of towns rather than in villages. They are usually modern and functional, catering for the family market. For further information and a free booklet (only partially in English) tel 0208 569 6969 in the UK or 01.6462.4600 in France.

Châteaux and Independent Hotels: If you want to go upmarket there is a book with a list of lovely looking châteaux (often with the owners acting as hosts) and independent hotels available all over France, with a description in English and a photo. Prices of the rooms and meals are clearly marked. Some of them are not at all expensive for what they offer! The book is available from Châteaux et Hôtels Indépendents, 12 rue Auber, 75009 Paris. Tel. (33) 140.07.00.20. Fax (33) 140.07.00.30. Internet: http://www.chatotel.com E-mail: chatotel@chatotel.com This is also a reservation centre - English spoken.

Gîtes de France: Very popular with the English, these are country cottages which are available for a weekly rent all over the French countryside and are very good value. They can vary from extremely comfortable to quite basic, so read the small print beside each photo in the guide carefully! It is a good idea to pick an area of Provence that appeals to you and then rent a gîte in a central position for the walks indicated in this guide. Gîte de France holidays are now run in conjunction with Brittany Ferries. For a free booklet outlining the gîtes available (in English), with photo and full explanations, tel. 0990.143.537 (24hr).

Gîtes d'étape: This is a type of youth hostel, usually without a warden, but open to people of all ages. They can be reasonably comfortable with good beds, showers and a well-equipped kitchen but they can also be quite basic and are mainly intended for cheap overnight stops by walkers and cyclists.

If you prefer not to cook your own meals there is often a café/restaurant in the vicinity. In the high season they can be uncomfortably full but are a wonderful way to get to know fellow-travellers and share a convivial evening. Out of season you often have the place to yourself. The only snag is that you may have to hunt for the person responsible in the village or nearby (usually posted on the door) to get access to the gîte.

A complete guide to the gîtes d'étape all over France is available from good bookshops, Brittany Ferries or the bookshop at Maison de la France.

Chambres d'Hôtes: This is the English equivalent of bed and breakfast, though often the breakfast is not included or, if it is, is limited to coffee and bread (croissants if you are lucky). The number of these establishments is increasing all over France (look for the Chambre d'Hôte sign or enquire in the local café or shop). The degree of comfort varies tremendously but, unlike British establishments, you will rarely get a TV or beverage-making facility in your room. Most rooms have their own shower/toilet but you could be sharing with the family.

The book *French Country Welcome* is available from the French Travel Centre (see below) or can be bought direct from their shop.

Youth Hostels (Auberges de Jeunesse): These are rare in France outside the main towns, but for a complete list called Guide des Auberges de Jeunesse en France contact the Youth Hostels Association, Trevelyan House, 8 St. Stephen's Hill, St. Albans, Herts AL1 2DY. Tel. 01727 855.215. Fax 01727 844.126. Also available - Hostelling International Europe, Information and Addresses of hostels all over Europe. Don't forget you have to be a member of the Association to stay in a hostel (reductions in membership fees for under 18s). Most hostels provide breakfast, packed lunch and an evening meal. Many of them have kitchens where you can cook your own meals.

Camping: Campsites are graded from one to five-star and range from those offering shop, hot showers and swimming pool to sites with basic washing facilities.

Camping *à la ferme* is cheap and popular though the facilities are minimal - remember some toilets in France, especially on campsites, are still of the squat variety!

The local tourist offices (Appendix B) have a complete list of campsites. Most of them speak English and will gladly send the information. Otherwise telephone Maison de la France (see below).

For information concerning Provence contact:

Maison de la France,
178 Piccadilly,
London W1V 0AC. Tel. 0207 399 3500.

There is also a shop selling a wide range of books in English and French. French Information Line: Tel. 0207 399 3531 (affiliated to Maison de la

France). Open from 8.30am to 8.00pm Monday to Friday. 9.00am to 5.00pm Saturday.

CLOTHING AND EQUIPMENT

When one thinks of the South of France one imagines that the sun never stops shining and it is always agreeably warm summer and winter. Unfortunately even in Provence it can turn cold, the *mistral* will blow and there are sudden storms. In the summer it can be unbearably hot so dress in layers you can put on and take off depending on weather and altitude. In winter and springtime the fierce cold *mistral* will suddenly sweep down so even if the weather looks good take a good windproof jacket. Avoid the nylon type which does not breathe and makes you hot and sweaty. Even in late spring and early autumn the sun can be extremely hot so sun protection is important. Remember that if you like to wear shorts there are lots of prickly bushes such as gorse and broom in this region and you can get quite scratched. Walking in Provence is not comparable to walking in the Alps so many of the walks could be done with a pair of stout training shoes with serrated soles, however it is preferable and more comfortable to have a lightweight sturdy pair of boots with plenty of ankle support and good grip on rocks. As none of the walks described exceeds six hours, a light to medium weight rucksack is quite adequate. A special outside strap for a water bottle is useful for Provence where you must take lots of water. It is always wise to carry a compass and altimeter, provided you know how to use them! They are not essential for these walks but can be very helpful in bad weather.

The following is a suggested list of essentials for your rucksack for a day's walk in Provence: maps (1:25,000 or 1:50,000 as stipulated); compass, basic first aid kit; insect repellent; survival blanket (useful if you get lost or hurt); high factor sun cream and lip salve; sun hat and sunglasses; woolly hat and gloves - winter only; vitamin tablets such as vitamin C - useful if you begin to flag; Swiss Army knife with as many attachments as possible; cape or poncho that goes over everything, including your rucksack - useful when it is really pouring, and for sitting on; a lightweight sweater; a lightweight wind and waterproof jacket; water bottle - **it is essential to take lots of water, especially if it is hot,** but do not drink out of streams or dubious village fountains; picnic - buy a crusty *baguette* at the local bakery before you set off and eat it with fresh cheese or ham. Optional extras: altimeter (useful but not essential); camera, binoculars and reference books; mobile phone.

FLORA AND FAUNA

FLORA: Since the summers are so hot most flowers blossom in springtime with often a second flowering in autumn. But Provence covers a wide area and the vegetation differs widely from the mild coastal region to the high mountains of the north. In the warmer coastal regions the spring flowers, such as primroses, violets, periwinkles, snowdrops, crocuses, and daffodils are already appearing in early February when the mountains behind are still covered in snow. Many villages have special flower festivals: Tourettes sur Loup in the Alpes Maritimes is known for its violet festival in February (violets are cultivated here and sent all over France) and there is a mimosa festival in Mandelieu near the Esterel. But spring does not linger in Provence even at altitude and much of the vegetation is specially adapted to resist drought.

There are the various species of evergreen oak trees, such as the kermes (often called shrub oak which has prickly leaves) and holm oaks which are bushy, thickset and with glazed leaves which retain water. Cork oaks are taller, with a distinctive thickly ridged bark which is stripped every 10 years leaving a smooth reddish brown trunk. The bark is principally used to make cork wine stoppers.

The white or downy deciduous oaks favour the valley bottoms and more humid mountain slopes. They are the haunt of the truffle hunters whose dogs or pigs dig beneath their roots to find the highly prized fungus which is harvested in winter when it is ripe and odorous. In some places the oaks are planted in rows called *truffières* and it is possible to become the proud owner of one of these fields of oaks - truffle hunts are now part of the tourist scene! The Mediterranean oaks cannot be compared with their impressive counterparts in more temperate climates. Nevertheless there are forests of oaks in many parts of Provence and particularly in the Luberon area.

There are four species of pine to be found: the maritime pine which has a purple-red bark, the umbrella (or stone) pine which can be recognised by its shape and grows mainly on the coast, the Aleppo pine with a twisted grey bark, and the tall sombre Austrian pine which is not native to the region but is planted for timber - there are considerable forests in northern Provence.

Forest fires, the scourge of the whole region, break out with increasing frequency during the summer months and have reduced the once proud forests, especially in the Esterel and Maures region, to shrubland,

Tall cypress trees are often planted in lines as windbreaks, plane trees utilised for

Red helleborine - Gorges de la Nesque

shade and limes for bordering avenues and for making tea. Beech trees flourish on the Sainte Baume in the Var (see walk No. 13), chestnut trees in the Maures range, cedar trees on the Petit Luberon and larch in the northern ranges.

Groves of olive trees are part of the scenery and mark the limit of the Mediterranean climate. They were brought to the region 2500 years ago by the Greeks and have flourished ever since. Provençal olive oil is highly prized the world over for its very special taste and high quality.

Exotic trees and shrubs have been introduced from other countries and flourish, especially along the coast; lemon, orange, bougainvillea, various species of palm, and flamboyant yellow mimosa and eucalyptus, brought from Australia, are a feature of the Esterel region (see walks Nos. 8-10). The almond tree, whose delicate pink blossoms brighten up the landscape in February, was imported from Asia as early as the l5th century.

Walk in the hills and you will encounter juniper bushes, whose berries are used in flavouring gin and poultry, yellow-flowering gorse and broom which set the slopes ablaze from April through the summer, carpets of purple and white cistus and pistachio scrubs with red berries ripening to brown. Many of the flowering bushes which we cultivate so assiduously in our gardens are running wild in the countryside - white flowering viburnum and amelanchier, climbing honeysuckle and clematis amongst others.

Particularly prevalent in the Esterel region is the the strawberry tree (*arbutus unedo*) which has white bell shaped flowers often fluted with pink, in drooping clusters flowering from October to March, followed by bright red berries. In earlier days it had many uses - the wood was made into charcoal, the leaves and bark used for medicinal purposes and the sour berries, which have a high vitamin C content, to make an alcoholic drink. The Esterel is also known for its variety of tall white heathers and majestic asphodel lilies (*asphodelus albus*), which have delicate white flowers resembling the alpine St. Bernard Lily. They blossom at the beginning of March and are most plentiful on the slopes of the Pic d'Ours.

Asphodel lily - Esterel

21

Another plant evocative of Provence is lavender which grows wild in the hills. It has been grown commercially since the second half of the 19th century, reaching its heyday in the 1920s. Most of the lavender cultivated now is a hybrid called Lavendin, which is more productive but less fragrant. The Valensole plateau is famed for its lavender fields and it is worth going to see the bright carpets of purple flowers in June. The lavender is mainly used for the cosmetic industry and is best picked under a hot sun which flavours the lavender aroma. Since 1970 the picking has been mechanised.

Mention here should be made of the *garrigue* which means an area of rocky limestone which has very sparse vegetation consisting mainly of herbs such as lavender, thyme and rosemary interspersed by thistles and stunted bushes such as gorse and broom. *Garrigue* is often the word a local person will call an area which has been decimated by fire and which is now covered by shrub, although this is not technically correct.

Of all the areas in France, Provence has the greatest density of butterflies. The commoner varieties such as the red admirals, tortoiseshells, brimstones, fritillaries, cabbage whites and tiny meadow blues abound. But you will also find the graceful creamy and brown swallowtails (the author has even seen the rare whiter variety), the purple camberwell beauty with its striking cream border, the clouded yellow, the black veined white and the now protected Apollo with its distinctive red rings, which lives on wild scabious and thistles.

Suggested book: *Mediterranean Wild Flowers* by Marjorie Blamey and Christopher Grey-Wilson (Harper Collins). This is a complete guide with over 2000 illustrations. It includes illustrations of the different pines, deciduous trees and bushes to be found in the area.

FAUNA: The ecology movement has been slow to take off in the Provençal regions, hunting and bird trapping being part of the old peasant mentality. Nevertheless an awareness of the need for conservation is growing among the younger generation.

The first national park, called the Mercantour, was opened in 1979 and consists of 68,500 herctares covering seven different valleys. Here the animals are protected, including *bouquetins* (ibex), *chamois*, *mouflons* (a type of mountain sheep originating from Corsica), and about 30 couples of royal eagles. Added to this are marmots, mountain hares, wild boar, grouse, the rare *Tétras Lyre* (capercaillie), partridge and ptarmigan. These are all found in the alpine regions of northern Provence and the higher ranges further south such as the Luberon, Mont Ventoux, the Lure and the Sainte Baume.

Walking in the lower and hotter south one is constantly alerted to the frequent rustling in the undergrowth. This could be attributed to the thousands of tiny lizards which abound everywhere, a grass snake or a viper which are rarely seen, or a huge iridescent green lizard which at 60cm long is the largest in Europe. The air is alive with the rasping noise of *cicadas* (crickets) and other insects. One of the more fascinating is the praying mantis, a long green insect which does look as though it is praying, but has the reputation of eating its mate!

Different species are endemic to specific vegetation. Wild boar favour the evergreen oak forests such as the Luberon and in this type of vegetation you will also find owls, pigeons, blackbirds, jays and nightingales. Bright green metallic beetles, whose lava eat the wood of the oak, abound here. Deer prefer the deciduous oak forests as do the woodpeckers, nuthatches, woodcocks and sparrowhawks.

In the gorges and on the cliffs will be found crows, eagles, vultures, swallows and swifts, while down by the rivers are kingfishers, dippers, wagtail and inoffensive grass snakes which live off fish.

The *garrigue* is a favourite haunt for all sorts of lizards, vipers, tiny shrews, weasels, red partridges and birds who love semi-arid surroundings.

On the open high grasslands are birds of prey such as buzzards and eagles which feed off the voles which are prevalent in the area, butterfies, particularly the Apollo variety, and the *vipère aspic* which is a special species of viper.

In the pine and conifer forests are the hanging cocoons of the Processionary pine moths. The caterpillars eat the leaves of the tree which eventually kills it. They are also poisonous to dogs and cats and cause skin irritations in humans (see walks Nos. 4 & 25). Flocks of little firecrests and goldcrests which are the smallest of European birds also live in the pine forests.

Each species of animal and bird has adapted itself to the vegetation and climatic conditions of the diverse Provençal terrain - you might even be lucky to see a rare tortoise though there are only a few left (so I'm told) in the dense cork woods of the Massif des Maures in the southern Var.

PROVENÇAL WRITERS AND ARTISTS

No book can be written about Provence without including some mention of the incredible number of writers and artists who have been native to the region or have made it their home. This is undoubtedly due to that indescribable "something" in the atmosphere that is conducive to artistic development. For painters it is the light and colour which has a clarity and perspective seen nowhere else in Europe; for writers, perhaps the indolent climate, the stress free way of life, the diversity of scenery and the timelessness of the quaint huddled villages.

In no other region are there so many art galleries, *trompe l'oeil*, pottery and glass workshops, not to mention sculptors, wood carvers and metal workers. Artists like to flock together for inspiration and companionship but a more mundane reason for the diverse cultural output in the present day is the influx of tourists who are more likely to buy while on holiday or staying at their country houses.

In the 12th and 13th centuries, it was the troubadours singing and recounting tales in the ancient Provençal language called Occitan, who were the first perpetuators of Provençal culture. Already in the 15th century the French language was taking over for administrative and official communication and the original language was dying out.

The last person of note to write exclusively in his native tongue was Frederic Mistral, born in 1830. He became a member of the Félibrige, a society committed to keeping alive the Provençal language and culture (Daudet of *Lettres de mon Moulin* was a member).

In the present day there are English translations of Jean Giono (1895-1970) born in Manosque (Vaucluse) and Marcel Pagnol (1895-1974), born in Aubagne, near Marseille (see walk No. 17 for further information). Both writers evoke a magical picture of their native soil and the changing rhythm of peasant life across two European wars. Giorno is a more serious, reflective writer while Marcel Pagnol's lighthearted books about his childhood holidays in the country have been made into popular films. Henri Bosco (1888-1976) born in Avignon sets his novels in the Luberon.

Interestingly, Emile Zola went to primary school in Aix-en-Provence where he lived in poverty after the death of his father, before moving back to Paris with his family in his early teens. He was a boyhood friend of Cézanne.

French writers, amongst them Guy de Maupassant, Colette and more recently Antoine de St. Exupéry, Albert Camus and Françoise Sagan all spent time getting inspiration for their writings by sojourning in the Provençal countryside. Not all of them were enthusiastic about the area. Prosper Mérimée (1803-1870), who was nominated Inspector of Historical Monuments, made a series of journeys around France, notably in the Vaucluse. He describes Apt as *un trou abominable* (a dreadful hole!) and he didn't appreciate the climb to the Fort de Buoux (walk No. 22), although he does admit that the site is interesting!

When the Riviera became fashionable it was almost taken over by English and Americans writers, like Somerset Maugham, Katherine Mansfield, Scott Fitzgerald and Ernest Hemingway. More recent residents are Anthony Burgess, Graham Green and Lawrence Durrell. Finally Peter Mayle's lighthearted tale about *A Year in Provence* (translated into a myriad languages including Japanese) has catapulted the Luberon into the forefront of international tourism and, say many inhabitants, "ruined it for ever".

Of earlier vintage, but on the same lines, is *Perfume from Provence* by the Honorable Lady Fortesque. Dedicated to her husband Monsieur, she tells of the trials of renovating a house in the Alpes Maritimes before World War II - her attitude towards the workmen is one of a colonial officer to the natives under his jurisdiction! "I had grown to love these excitable emotional men of the South and to regard them as my children - as they were little more"!

As early as the 14th - 15th centuries schools of religious art flourished in Avignon and Nice. In the 16th century Pierre Puget was famous for his sculpture, and examples of his works can still be seen in his birthplace Toulon. Grasse-born Jean-Honoré Fragonard (1732-1806) is perhaps the most typical of Provençal artists as his paintings are full of flowers. There is a museum and exhibition of his paintings in Grasse and a perfume factory named after him!

It was only in the 1800s that the Impressionists, discovering the unique quality of light and colour which inspired so many of their works, moved in and started painting. Native born Paul Cézanne (1839-1904) spent much of his later years trying to perfect his painting of the Mont Ste. Victoire (see walk No. 16), which never satisfied him despite more than 60 attempts to depict the enigmatic white glow of the mountain.

Vincent Van Gogh, Paul Signac, Jean Cocteau, Marc Chagall, Henri Matisse and Picasso have all left the marks of their stay in art galleries, museums, and churches throughout the region. Artists are still trying to capture this incredible Provençal light and who knows which one will go down in the annals of history with the great names already mentioned.

REGIONAL SPECIALITIES

Picture a typical Provençal village - the huddle of houses and sinuous alleyways leading to the church and cobbled central square. A little restaurant with gay umbrellas, the dancing sunlight filtering through the branches of a huge plane tree and a strategically placed menu outside with the mouth-watering *plat du jour* (today's special) costing little more than £5. A "foodie's" paradise? - for most people Provence fits the criteria, not just for the food but also the idyllic surroundings it can be eaten in.

Read any guidebook on Provence and there will be a long chapter consecrated to the culinary delights of the region and the large selection of local wines with recommended restaurants and specialities. Far better, however, to venture forth in a village or town and see what you can find for yourself without reading about what has already been discovered! This is just a short resumé of what to expect when looking through a typical Provençal menu.

Provence dishes are based on fish, meat (mainly lamb), tomatoes, aubergines, peppers, onions and, most important of all, lots of garlic, olives, fresh herbs and oil. It has to be remembered that until recently the area did not have good public transport and people relied on local produce to make their dishes. Much of the population lived in rural communities and ate only what they grew or could barter for. Little meat was available, so to compensate for this the food was flavoured with garlic and herbs, with emphasis on the vegetables which could grow in a hot arid climate.

On the coast fish was the main diet and although the variety of fish to be caught is declining, the famous speciality *Bouillabaisse* is as popular as ever. This is basically a fish soup consisting of rascasse (the spiny red hog fish) mullet, monk fish, conger eel and anything else freshly caught that the cook wants to throw in! (it could be mussels, crab or lobster etc). This is boiled with each individual chef's secret spices and is not, as many people think, a fish stew. Traditionally the broth is served first with a *rouille* - a paste of peppers and toast, then the fish is eaten separately afterwards.

In the arid hinterland where flocks of sheep roam the hillsides, lamb is a favourite dish, eaten as a roast or grilled on a barbecue and flavoured with rosemary which grows wild everywhere. It is often accompanied by *ratatouille*, a mixture of courgettes, aubergines, onions, tomatoes and peppers sautéed in olive oil which originated in southern France but is now known the world over. Beef stew (*boeuf en daube*) is another speciality, especially in the northern regions when the winters can be chilly - it is traditionally cooked in a large earthenware cooking pot called a *daubière* with the usual Provençal vegetables and, most important, a couple of glasses of wine. Cooking takes the whole day and the longer it simmers the better it tastes!

Mushrooms are a common ingredient in Provençal dishes, and you will often see them for sale in the markets. Truffles are a great delicacy and very expensive but omelette stuffed with truffles is not too drastic on the purse strings and is worth tasting if you can find it. Look out for rabbit dishes which are often cooked in mushroom or tomato and garlic sauces. In season, game dishes such as wild boar, hare and partridge will be offered. What is more original are the various purées, perhaps originating from the locals' love of sitting around in the evening and drinking the local wine - they had to have something to nibble! *Tapenade*, a delicious olive, anchovy and caper paste, *l'aoili*, consisting of mayonnaise, lemon juice and mashed garlic (careful - you will smell to high heaven after eating this) and *brandade de morue*, salt cod, cream and garlic, are just three of the delicious appetisers to choose from as you sip your aperitif and scan the menu.

And what about desserts? These are much the same as you find in other parts of France although homemade lemon tart is a particular favourite. Go for the fresh fruits, especially the melons (see under '*markets*' below) or the ice-cream. Lavender ice-cream is often freshly made and has an interesting flavour. Delicious Nougat comes mainly from the Vaucluse and Apt is famous for its crystallised fruits.

Provence does not produce a wide variety of cheese but it does have small round goat's cheeses, often spiced with herbs. One interesting cheese is *Banon* which is goat's cheese wrapped in chestnut leaves.

The first vines to be cultivated in Provence were introduced by the Greeks in the hills around Marseille and later in the lower Rhône valley. The main regions which produce wine are the Vaucluse and the Var. There are excellent wines to meet all tastes but it is a good idea to try the local vintage and the restaurant will usually sell you a carafe of the house wine which they get from a local supplier. It is rarely undrinkable, sometimes surprisingly good but always good value!

The local supermarkets sell excellent wines, local and otherwise. In the

Vaucluse region try the Côtes de Mont Ventoux or the Côtes du Luberon (neither are expensive but very drinkable). When you are walking the Dentelles de Montmirail (walk No. 31) leave time to visit the local *domaines* (wine growers) to taste the reputed red "Gigondas". Baumes de Venise, a village not far from Gigondas, also has a reputed light Muscat wine. The only serious wine growing in the Alpes Maritimes is in the hills behind Nice where they produce a wine called Bellet. Bandol and Cassis wines come from the Var.

MARKETS

The markets in southern France seem more alive and fascinating than in any other region. There is everything on offer from the traditional Provençal fabric with its colourful motifs of flowers, grapes and vegetables which tourists love to take home to brighten up the winter days, to the famous *faïnce* (ceramics) and pottery, irritating imitations of crickets in wooden boxes, old and new clothes and of course an enormous range of vegetables and food.

The local produce is worth buying: pots of honey (lavender, rosemary, thyme and oak), packets of *Herbes de Provence* which smell so enticingly, and the different types of olive oil, and crystallised fruits (particularly in the Apt region), lavender products such as soaps and water, not to mention objects made from olive wood.

If you can visit a local market before you go walking, pick up a local goat's cheese or some delicious paté. The fruit is fresh and delicious depending on the season - melons, cherries, nectarines, peaches, apricots and apples.

The French take their food and shopping seriously - all the vegetables, fruit and mushrooms come in from the local farmers and it is fascinating to walk around listening to the vibrant conversation and good humour as each person touts their produce with verve and passion.

In Dignes-les-Bains I bought some delicious *chanterelles* mushrooms from an old lady who was telling the whole market how she had got up at 5am to pick while the dew was still on them (apparently this is important but I couldn't find out why!) and how she had discovered them growing under a hedge and been watching them mature for days. Her enthusiasm for her story was fascinating - even passers-by turned to admire the chanterelles and murmur *"magnifique"*, as though they were a beautiful picture! I watched her sell them all with an incredible reverence for an astronomic sum per kilo!

A list of market days in the principal towns and villages is given in the Appendix C. Most markets start early in the morning and continue until 1pm. There are exceptions but then this is Provence! There are countless special markets (for antiques, fish, organic food, local arts and crafts etc.) - the local Tourist Office will have all the current information.

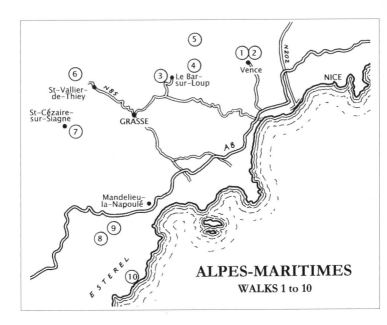

ALPES-MARITIMES
WALKS 1 to 10

Alpes Maritimes

WALK Nos. 1 - 10

Better known as the French Riviera or Côte d'Azur, this was the first region of southern France discovered by intrepid Victorian travellers and artists as they did their epic tours through Europe, almost a rite of passage for many a wealthy young English gentleman. First drinking in the cultural delights of Paris, they then struggled over the alpine passes (easier ways being excluded as this was a must for the average European tour), to arrive exhausted on the shores of the Mediterranean. They sojourned in the then sleepy fishing villages enjoying the rich food and wine, the endless sunshine and above all the slow uncluttered way of life of a peasant community before attempting the difficult journey home. Some, mainly artists and novelists, were completely seduced by the way of life and never returned. It was mainly the British who first fell in love with this coastline, instigating the transformation of the fishing villages to fashionable resorts for the rich and famous.

Nowadays the coast from Menton to Cannes is a continuous urban sprawl, one resort merging into another, a succession of hotels, apartments, restaurants and supermarkets. There are still many palatial mansions and exclusive areas, well barricaded with high fences, and it continues to be a place where the wealthy end their days, tottering along the famous esplanades of Nice and Cannes. Nevertheless, it has lost some of its allure for the young "jet set" who can afford to go further afield.

Despite all this it remains incredibly beautiful and there are pockets of tranquillity. I have picked oranges in February in a sprawling seedy garden in Juan les Pins with the sea winking beyond in that luminous light which is typically Provençal, the palm trees rustling in a peaceful silence, and felt that it has not entirely lost that famous atmosphere which made it so glamorous and exciting in the early half of this century.

But the Riviera, stretching from the Italian border a few kilometres east of Menton to St. Raphael, is only the coastal stretch of the Alpes Maritimes. Inland is a landscape of pine covered hills where the little villages clinging to the hillsides with their huddled houses and sinuous narrow streets were, until the 1940s, a hubbub of noise and activity; barefoot children running down the dirty cobbled streets, donkeys braying under huge loads of hay, chickens scratching in the dust and ragged dogs everywhere as the farmers emerged every morning to tend their nearby terraces covered with vines and olive groves. With the passing of peasant farming most of the young people moved to the towns, the houses crumbled and the streets fell silent.

Now these quaint villages have been renovated and given a new lease of life as artists and retired people have moved in to escape the congestion on the coast. In many instances they have been prettied up so much that they appear sterile and lacking in atmosphere, especially where too many residences are owned by people overseas and for much of the year the windows are shuttered. Still, it has enabled some descendants of the original families to remain, earning their living by owning handicraft shops, art galleries, cafés and restaurants.

In the 1970s a mini French equivalent of "silicon valley" called Sophia-Antipolis, near the village of Valbonne (behind Nice), was created. It has attracted a number of well-known American companies and with them a vibrant young international population needing special schools and adequate housing.

This surge of people has rejuvenated the area and created a building boom. There is now a proliferation of houses covering the pine-covered slopes around the villages in all directions, leaving less and less open countryside.

Two notable small towns in this area are Vence and Grasse. Vence, 10kms from the sea between Nice and Antibes, is a picturesque market town, population 15,000, with a history dating back to the Romans. It is one of the rare places to have conserved its ramparts as, in the 15th century, the inhabitants were allowed to build their houses right up against the walls. Inside the old town is a fascinating labyrinth of cobbled streets with many art galleries and boutiques.

Because of its sheltered location amongst lush hills Vence has long been a popular retirement spot and a haunt of writers and artists. D.H. Laurence died here of tuberculosis in 1930 and Henri Matisse decorated the little Chapelle de St. Rosaire between 1947 and 1951 to thank the local Dominican nuns who nursed him when he was seriously ill. The local church has a mosaic by Chagall dating from 1979. A little Anglican church serves the popuation of retired English.

Grasse, 25km to the east of Vence, is another old town stretching over the foothills of a limestone plateau. In the last century it was a popular winter resort. Somehow it has escaped being "prettied up" and remains delightfully authentic which may be because it does not rely entirely on tourism. In the 12th century it was a minuscule republic and was once renowned for its tanneries and leather work, especially glove-making. In the 16th century Catherine de Medici introduced perfume making from Italy and so began the growing of jasmine, roses, mimosa and lavender in the warm valleys rolling down to the coast. Today much of the actual flower growing has disappeared and synthetic essences are used. It has caused considerable unemployment and to try to combat this the industry has diversified into food flavourings.

Northwards, the pine covered hills give way to the rough limestone plains carved with deep gorges where the *mistral* whistles across in springtime and the little villages cling to the barren slopes. Gone are the tourist shops and the renovated houses - few people want to live in this inhospitable climate and it is a world away from the busy coastal strip in economy and outlook. But it is wonderful walking country and in winter it is popular for skiing with resorts such as Gréolières la Neige, north of Cannes, and Isola 2000 in the Tinée valley behind Nice and Breuil-Valberg, south of the Mercantour National Park.

The Estérel

The Estérel is technically in the Var but since I have included the walks in the Alpes Maritimes section, a description of the area is more applicable here.

The jagged red cliffs of the Estérel hills plunge into the Mediterranean on the coastline between Cannes and St. Raphael, called the Corniche d'Or (golden scenic route) - a breathtaking area of rocky promontories, narrow creeks and hidden sandy coves. The contrast of volcanic rock thrusting out of bush-covered slopes to plunge into the deep blue Mediterranean is incredibly beautiful - a kaleidoscope of green, red and blue, enjoyed by thousands who take the narrow winding coastal road perched between sea and mountain (though try to avoid it in high season). And yet only a stone's throw from this busy coastal road are quiet inland tracks where you will meet hardly anyone!

The Estérel is made of volcanic rock (porphyry) which was forced up during the Hercynian folding causing a concertina effect of jagged peaks which erosion has fashioned into the weird shapes you see today.

The hillsides used to be covered in pine and cork forests but the greatest enemy of this region is fire. The first major fire was started by Charles Quint in the 16th century to flush out the brigands who were hiding in the hills and terrorising the local population, the second by the Germans in 1943 and since then nearly every summer part of the region is swept by fires. Now the hills are mainly covered in bush (lavender, gorse, strawberry trees, cistus and heather) and few old trees remain. Slowly the National Forestry Office is trying to reforest the area but the threat of fire is constant.

The area has been inhabited for thousands of years, first by primitive man and then by hermits such as Saint Honorat (see Walk No. 10). The Romans skirted the massif and created the Via Aurelia round the northern edge, which was one of the main arteries in the Empire stretching from Rome to Arles. They mined blue porphyry from the nearby village of Agay to construct their buildings in the area (modern sculptures from this stone can be seen on the coastal road).

It was here, in the 18th century, that the highwayman Gaspard de Besse operated; a Provençal Robin Hood, dashingly dressed in red, he harassed travellers on their way to Italy and robbed them. It is said he then distributed the spoils to the poor and became a local hero. In 1781, at the age of 25, he was caught and his head nailed to a tree so that passing travellers knew that the danger was over!

In 1787 the well-known Genevese naturalist De Saussure explored the region but it was not until 1875 that Auguste Murtese (Inspector of roads and forests) opened it up and built a number of roads and refuges, with huge water tanks placed at strategic intervals in order to fight the frequent fires.

Where to base yourself when walking in the Alpes Maritimes:
Seven of the walks are in the hills behind the coastal plain and three are in the Estérel which is about an hour from Grasse. Both Vence and Grasse are good places to base yourself if you like towns, and between these two there are many villages such as Le Bar-sur-Loup, Tourrettes-sur-Loup, Chateauneuf and Prédu Lac. For walking in the Estérel the little coastal villages between Cannes and St. Raphael would be a good choice, though often expensive.

Walking in Estérel *(Walk 10)*
The village of Tourrette-sur-Loup in the Alpes Maritimes

Directions:

(1) Walk down the road in the direction of Vence. *On a rock just before the fenced off parking is a memorial slab commemorating victims who were killed by the bombing in August 1944 when Vence was liberated. On it are mentioned 5 Frenchmen, 4 American soldiers, 2 Frenchwomen and one boy of 14.*

Ignore the signpost indicating a steep path to the Croix du Baou but continue down the road following yellow splashes. *As you pass attractive rows of olive trees on terraces to the left, you will see on the wall right another memorial plaque.*

(2) You pass the former monastery and just before the first corner you will see a narrow turning down to the right (10mins) indicated by yellow splashes and opposite a house with a letterbox No. 2094.

(3) This is just a short cut and shortly after you reach the road again where you turn right and then almost immediately hard back left on the Chemin du

Riou. This road has houses along it but it is pleasant to walk along as it is flat and there are extensive views over the town of Vence down on the right with the Mediterranean beyond if it is a fine day. The Baou Noir and Baou Blanc tower over you on the left.

(4) Shortly after passing the auberge/hotel Lucanny (25mins) continue straight on the Chemin du Riou at a small crossroads. The road starts to deteriorate with the outskirts of the town still down on the right as you pass under the wires of an electricity pylon (40mins).

Now you can see the dramatic rocky outcrop of the Baou de Saint Jeannet which at 800m dominates the little village of St-Jeanette beneath it and is the highest and most imposing Baou in the region. *(When I did this walk at the beginning of February, people were spreading blankets and plastic under the trees to collect the olives.)*

(5) Continue on the road round a left corner and past a sign saying *chutes de pierres* (rock falls)/*circulation interdite* (no entry/danger) (45mins). The path is now a stony jeep track fringed with bushes going parallel to the side of the hill. Be careful to go left where the path forks (the right goes down to a private house). The path passes between two impressive rocks called Les Portes des Canons and would eventually take you into Cagne gorge and the source of the Riou.

(6) Look for a wooden sign to the left indicating Baou des Noirs/Baou des Blancs No. 58 (55mins) onto a narrow steep path up the side of the hill. In one place you need your hands to clamber up a patch of rock but there is no difficulty.

(7) After 5mins you come to a T-junction on a jeep track where you turn left and then left again after a bend onto a narrow path - **careful**, this is easy to miss although there is a yellow splash. The path winds up medium steep and you get a good view of the Baou St-Jeanette to the left and on the horizon are the ruins of Le Castelet. *The slopes here are covered with cistus bushes which look rather like wild sage and have lovely pink and white flowers from April to June. These are intermingled with wild thyme, yellow broom and gorse bushes with higher up the occasional Euphorbia (spurge).*

Halfway up the hill the path flattens out (1hr 10mins) which is a good place for a breather. Continue upwards through tall cistus bushes following yellow splashes. Higher up the path gets rockier. There is another wooden sign indicating Baou des Noirs No. 59 (when the author did this walk in spring 1998 this signpost was a mere wooden post!).

(8) At the summit (677m) there is large iron cross (1hr 35mins) and extensive views in all directions, particularly of the Baou de St-Jeannet across the valley on the left.

(9) Retrace your steps to the wooden signpost No. 59 and take the path bearing left which should say Baou des Blancs. Later on you pass a green signpost (these are obviously the original ones which have been replaced by fancy wooden ones but not yet taken down!).

Follow the defined path which goes along the top of the wide ridge and then curls round the inside of the hill which is like a bowl with a crease in it. You are following the tumbledown walls of the ancient terraces which have now deteriorated so considerably that you hardly notice them. There are the occasional stunted oaks and a beautifully proportioned evergreen oak tree standing dramatically against the bare stony hillside. Keep an eye open for the occasional yellow splashes so that you do not wander off the path. After curling round and up the hill you reach an area which has numerous piles of stones in all directions and another signpost at les Blaquières (2hrs 15mins).

(10) Bear left along the path on the top of the hill towards the Baou Blanc. The path goes gently down and under an electric pylon by another signpost. Continue straight following the brighter yellow splashes carefully; on the wide open hillside with no trees and bushes it is easy to go off in the wrong direction. Some of the surrounding mountains look as though they have a powdering of snow but it is because they are covered with small stones.

(11) You reach another signpost (2hrs 30mins) saying Baou des Blancs straight (this is the signpost you come back to on your return) . Here the path goes down into a crease or shallow valley in the hills (there is a green sign indicating left Baou des Noirs) and then continues up again towards ruins at the summit.

(12) Almost immediately at a small T-junction turn up left (there is another sign here) - to the right would take you steeply down to the road where you parked your car *(note - this is not the recommended way back)*. You can see the road snaking down from the Lubiane valley behind.

Nearing the top bear left passing a high ruined wall and continue on an obvious path past other vestiges of habitation - there are numerous tracks from here to the edge of the Baou so it can be quite confusing. This used to be the monastery of the Penitants Blancs (see *'Observations'* above).

(13) The summit at 673m (note 4m lower than the Noir!) is a picnicker's paradise with smooth green grass and lots of rocks and niches as well as civilised benches (2hrs 45mins).

There is another big iron cross and if you peer over the edge another cross dotted with electric bulbs - obviously it would look impressive lit up at night standing high above Vence. Also a stone slab showing the names of the villages below and the coastline but the view is so magnificent that the names seem immaterial - behind are rolling mountains and in front to the left is the town of Nice with the Cap Ferrat beyond; straight ahead is the Cap d'Antibes; to the right the Isles des Lérins shimmering in the sea with Cannes behind and the mountains of the Estérel on the horizon. At your feet is the opulent town of Vence with its countless swimming pools (I counted 39 without really trying) - it is a view which takes your breath away and you can't stop looking.

Retrace your steps down the hill and into the shallow valley past two signposts and up to the one at the top of the further hill (11 on walk map). Follow direction D2 Vence left on a path that goes down the hill (yellow markings) to the road which is clearly visible below. The path becomes quite a wide track as you descend.

(14) At a sign *Chiens interdit - Bergerie* take the narrow path up right (yellow splash). Keep on this narrow track which descends to the road (there is another signpost here).

(15) Turn left down the road to the parking area opposite the quarry (3hrs 30mins).

Walk No. 2
BAOU ST-JEANNET AND THE RUINS OF CASTELLET - Alt. 800m

Difficulty:	Medium - some uphill climb.
Time:	3hrs 45mins.
Height gain:	500m.
Maps:	Cartes IGN 3642 ET Top 25 Vallée de L'Estéron 1:25,000.
	Editions Didier Richard No. 26 Pays d'Azur 1:50,000.
Depart from:	Parking at entrance of St-Jeannet.
Signposting:	Good - GR51 red/white splashes and yellow splashes.
	The numbers on the signposts correspond to numbers on the map (Vallée de L'Estéron map only).

Observations: The Baou St-Jeannet is a sheer cliff, 400m tall, which towers above the village beneath. It is a favourite place for rock climbing. This is an interesting walk with maximum views and if you get tired you can go to the end of the Baou and back though it would be a shame to miss the spectacular ruins of the Castellet. It is a good idea to stroll around the village of **St-Jeannet** (population 3188).

It has a history dating back to the 13th century when a handful of families were living on the site of the present cemetery, situated between fertile slopes and the mountain caves where they could flee from attack. They called the area Castrum de Sancti Johannes. In the 14th century there were already 1000 inhabitants! The village prospered during the 17th and 18th centuries even though it is near to the Var region which at that time marked the frontier between France and the territories of the Dukes of Savoy. It continued to develop during the 19th century with around 1300 inhabitants and was renowned for its production of high class wine and oil from the 20,000 olive trees planted on the slopes around the village.

In 1876 running water was installed and in 1902 electricity but after the First World War the population started to decline. In 1946 it had sunk to 759

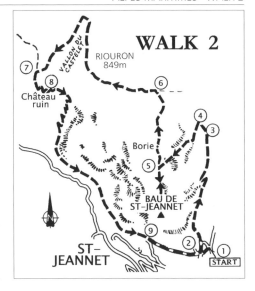

people. But in the late fifties and sixties the growing of flowers such as roses and carnations was established and more important, tourists started to flock to the south of France. St-Jeannet, a typical Provençal village, surrounded by orchards and vineyards and clinging to the base of an imposing cliff, became a tourist attraction. It now faces problems of urbanisation and growth but let's hope it manages to retain its unique charm and tranquillity.

How to get there (from Vence):
Take the D.2210 signposted St-Jeannet/Col de Vence and then bear right signposted St-Jeannet (straight ahead is the D2 Col de Vence). Go along this road for 8kms and at the entrance to the village park your car in a large parking area which is clearly marked.

Directions:
(1) Go up the steps out of the car park and facing you is a smart signpost indicating left Baou St-Jeannet/Le Gros Chêne/Baou de la Gaude. Walk into the quaint medieval village and opposite the war memorial turn up right to the Place St. Croix where there is an iron cross. This leads into the Rue de la Croix.

(2) Shortly after turn right into the Rue Romeguière where there is a sign indicating straight Baou St-Jeanet. The narrow road goes up in a series of widely spaced shallow steps. Go straight and then right following signs Les Baous. There are red/white splashes as you are now on the GR51. Continue up fairly steeply and soon the road becomes a stony jeep track. Follow directions to Baou St.Jeannet at signposts. The path eventually levels off before going gently up again along the side of the Parriau valley.

(3) At signpost No. 3 bear left on the GR51 signposted Baou St-Jeanette/Le Castellet/Vescagne (30mins) - straight goes to the Baou de la Gaude. Follow the red/white splashes on a narrow defined stony path which winds medium steep up the side of the mountain (avoid an undefined path also left). *At weekends this is one of the most popular walks in the region.*

(4) At signpost No. 4 (35mins) leave the GR51 and go left following yellow splashes. The path goes up medium steep past a big tree with the view opening up as you get higher. The path levels off momentarily and then goes up again. At the end there is a bit of rock scrambling but nothing difficult.

(5) At the top (45mins) there is a good view behind you of the Baou de Gaude. You are now walking along a wide ridge towards the end of the Baou. At a fork take the right path following the yellow splashes. At signpost No. 5 (50mins) continue on the path with yellow splashes as there are tracks in all directions. It takes you past a clump of low trees and through a natural stone wall. Pick your way over the rocks until you come to the end of the Baou (1hr 5mins). *Here there is a concrete helicopter pad and an Orientation Table which shows all the landmarks from this magnificent viewpoint: the village of St-Jeanette spread at your feet and the whole coastal region from the Cap Ferrat, Nice and the Var River on the left to the Cap d'Antibes on the right with the Estérel mountains on the horizon. It is interesting to note how built up this coastal area looks from above with houses, roads and lots of long greenhouses, the glass shimmering in the sunshine. Back from the coast west is the Pic de Courmettes and the Puy de Tourette. North are rolling hills and the high Cheiron ridge - a view worth climbing up for!*

Retrace your steps to signpost No. 5 (1hr 15mins).

(5 cont.) Follow the sign to Le Castellet left along an easy path (do not go straight which seems the more obvious way). On the left is a shallow valley-*this is one of the many depressions (called dolines) you see in this region which were cultivated by the ancient Ligurians. They fenced in with rocks any land worth cultivating which had water near it. Living in the hills for safety they never went down to the coast for fear of pirates. The stony remains of their ancient habitations (called oppidums) are scattered all over the Provençal hills (see 'Introduction: Short History of Provence').*

The path goes down nearer the valley (north) where there are lots of broken down walls. At a fork (1hr 25mins) with yellow splashes both ways, take the more defined path to the right which will take you painlessly back to the GR51.

Alternatively take the left fork which leads to an ancient Borie. *These circular stone edifices were built by the shepherds as bivouacs and they always faced south to get maximum sunshine. Many of them have fallen into heaps of stone but this one has been reconstructed so it is quite interesting to see.* The path curls round the top of the shallow valley by an old stone wall, if you can make it out amongst the piles of stones in all directions. Make for a large pile of rocks on the left (north) which has white stones on the top and as you get nearer you will see the Borie. Bear right by the Borie and follow the yellow splashes back to the GR51 by a small stone wall (1hr 40mins) and signpost No. 6.

(6) At this T-junction turn left following sign Le Castellet (if you go right you can get back to St-Jeanette in 45mins). The defined path goes along the right side of another stone wall with red/white splashes and curls around the Le Riourun hill. You can now see the Cagne valley down to the left (also Source de Riou) which has some interesting rocky waterfalls. Left across the valley are the Baou des Noirs and Baou des Blancs. There is also a good view of the Castellet ruin which looks very impressive as it stands out on a promontory over the Cagne gorge. The path goes down and skirts round the head of the narrow Castellet valley - do not go right where there is a red-white cross on stone. Cross the valley where there are old terraces and tall bushes of broom (2hrs) and then turn back up along it on the other side into denser vegetation including juniper bushes and evergreen oak trees. Keep straight as the path undulates along the side of the valley.

(7) At signpost No. 7 go left signposted St-Jeanette/N.D. des Champs. The GR51 goes right (north) to Vascagne and Coursegoules. You are at Castellet though you cannot see it from the signpost! Go straight and almost immediately it comes into view (2hrs 15mins). *It is an impressive old farm (though Castellet is French for small castle). You can still see the long sheep pens attached to the side with the old beams. The living area is square and high but it is all in a state of disrepair, ready to tumble down at any time. Apparently a mad monk lived here until fairly recently. There is a great view of the surrounding countryside and an old wall going out to the edge of the mountain.*

(8) Go to the front of the ruin and opposite the tall dwelling part of the building take a path to the right marked with yellow splashes. From now to the end of the walk follow these yellow splashes which are quite frequent. If you go straight on past this right turn you will arrive back at the signpost.

The rocky path winds fairly steeply down the mountain into the valley. There is a yellow cross telling you not to take a left fork. The path crosses the valley and follows it down contouring the Baou St-Jeannet. It flattens out high above the Cagnes River and you can hear the waterfalls and see the odd habitation in the valley bottom. You come to a signpost No. 7A (3hrs). Continue towards St-Jeanette (sharp right goes steeply down to the river). You can see the Vence-St-Jeanette road and a bridge ahead to the right. This is a pleasant undulating path going round to the south side of the Baou and eventually between two tall rocks (3hrs 15mins) - the one on the right has rolled off the mountain at some time! Rock climbing is taught here and it is quite interesting to pause and watch.

The path now goes up gently round the front of the Baou (ignore the left fork with a yellow cross) passing a concrete bunker with terraces on the left.

(9) You reach a paved road and the first houses on the outskirts of the village. Continue upwards round the last corner to reach a crucifix on the left (inaugurated 13 September 1992) with an area in front for religious services. Next door is a little chapel with lots of plaques commemorating men who died in the Mountain Rescue Service. The chapel is called Notre Dame de Baou and it is quite quaint inside with a number of rather simplistic statues, lots of artificial flowers and two plaques to young men who died in the mountains.

The path comes out at the end of the village. Go straight through on the Avenue Notre Dame towards an ancient turret which is part of a house. This is an extremely quaint old village with tiny winding streets and lovely old houses, all renovated of course. Keep right past the old covered washhouse and continue till you reach the war memorial at the start of the walk (3hrs 45mins).

Walk No. 3
LE CHEMIN DU PARADIS -
from Bar-sur-Loup to Gourdon

Difficulty:	Medium - it is a stiff climb up but on a very defined path. You can either retrace your steps or take a longer way back.
Time:	2hrs 30mins or 4hrs (not counting time to explore the village).
Height gain:	460m.
Maps:	Cartes IGN 3643 ET Top 25 Cannes/Grasse 1:25,000.
	Editions Didier Richard No. 26 Pays d'Azur 1:50,000.
Depart from:	Le Bar-sur-Loup.
Signposting:	Good on the way up - less good on the return. Some yellow splashes.

Observations:

The Chemin de Paradis is a classic walk but fairly tough in terms of uphill climb. The village of Gourdon, originally built by the Saracens, is one of the most famous of the Alpes Maritimes hill villages, perched like an eagle's nest on top of a high cliff more than 500m above the River Loup. The views all around are magnificent with the Alps to the north and the vast coastline from the Estérel to the Cap Ferret to the south. The village is entirely devoted to tourism - there are shops selling glassware, Provençal pottery, materials, perfumes and postcards (yet not a single grocery store or baker!).

How to get there (from Vence):

Take the D.2210 towards Grasse. Entering the village of Bar-sur-Loup leave your car opposite the restaurant La Jarrerie in a large parking area left.

Directions:

(1) With the restaurant at your back go left and walk along the viaduct to the Chemin des Bosquets (the name of the street is at the top of the hill). Turn down right and walk along this road which is flat and has houses each side- you can see the village of Gourdon perched on a cliff up to the left and it does look a long way up! You cross another viaduct in a few minutes. From La Jarrerie you are on the old railway line until you turn up the Chemin du Paradis.

(2) Continue round the corner and look for a narrow road going back to the left with a green sign on the wall indicating Chemin du Paradis (20mins). *This is a path which looks as if it has been walked for generations - it is stony and cobbled going steeply upwards, initially through private properties with delightful gardens - orange and lemon trees, bay trees, the inevitable olives, all delightfully haphazard and overgrown.* Keep going up on the main path and avoid the temptation of various off-shoots which go to private houses. You are soon out of the built-up zone and into woodland and stony terraces passing in front of a mission cross dated 1858 (35mins) - there is a little house here, all shuttered up when I went by. *The path narrows and becomes very Cornish looking with old stone walls covered in vegetation and masses of dry oak leaves underfoot - in Cornwall of course they would be damp! There are long narrow steps in places and you have to watch your feet as the path is always stony.*

(3) You arrive at a crossroads (left goes over the Canal du Loup aqueduct). There are blue and red arrows in all directions but no signpost (50mins). Continue straight following blue arrows and after 10mins (1hr) you come to the Canal du Foulon which is an enormous metal pipe taking water to Grasse. Below is a little fountain and as the water comes from the pipe it is drinkable. *This is where the GR51 crosses on its way from the Italian border to Grasse, through the Estérel and finally joining the GR98 west of Toulon.*

(4) At the top of some steps there is a smart wooden signpost No. 101 indicating left Grasse and to the right Canal du Foulon, Sauts du Loup, Bramafan. Continue straight signposted Gourdon Chemin du Paradis. When you arrive at a welcome flat stretch you can see above left the first buildings of the village but it is another 10mins of more winding upwards before you arrive (1hr 40mins). *Give yourself time to explore the village and have a rest before you start down again.* Retrace your steps.

Longer route back

(5) Take the road down out of the village, crossing the D3 from Prédu Lac to Cipières (there are two cafes here), and go straight up the D12 signposted Caussols. Go up and round to the left to a wooden signpost.

(6) Go left to Chapelle St-Vincent/L'Embarrier (right indicates Col de Cavillore). You are on a wide path curling round an open hillside (direction west) with sweeping views all round, including Gourdon perched on its summit. You pass the occasional house.

(7) At signpost No. 106 (1hr 55mins) go straight on following indication to the Plateau de Caussol. Up to the right is the recently restored Chapelle de St-Vincent. A few minutes later the path goes by some animal feeding troughs before reaching signpost No. 107 at an intersection where there is a water tank.

(8) Go left signposted Bois de Gourdon (straight on is the Plateau de Caussol) and cross a little stone bridge. You are on a wide rough track with scattered bushes around - there is a good view to the left of the Pic de Courmettes and the Puy de Tourette. The track veers left of the wide gorge past a high natural stone wall which is part of a quarry. Up on the right is a large stone white cross. Continue across an open area and then through a barrier intended to stop motorised vehicles. You are now coming closer to the gorge and the woods, mainly oak, of the Bois de Gourdon.

(9) *Careful* - watch for a narrow path going off left which is quite difficult to see. It is just after the wide path curves to the right. There is a small oak tree on the right with a red/white/red flash on it (this is a forestry sign and nothing to do with the *Grande Randonnée*) and also a yellow splash on a flat rock on the path (2hrs 10mins).

If you look at the map you are at altitude 785m. This is a short cut so if you miss it and continue on the wide track it is not a disaster!

For a few minutes the path goes parallel to the road before traversing through scattered woodland (direction south). In a clearing right there are a number of beehives. Soon after it crosses the jeep track (2hrs 15mins) and then another intersection. The path becomes narrower and stonier, dropping gently. Continue down towards a signpost Le Bar (2hrs 30mins). Turn right when the path meets the jeep track again (yellow marks on the trees) into a clearing where there is another water cistern to the left and a big forestry signpost. You can see the paved road beyond (the D3).

(10) Cross the road and take the path down (yellow splash). A few minutes later look for a deep rocky hole to the right. This is La Garagai Gouffre - *some people have pushed their old cars into it though how they got them there is a mystery!* **Careful here** - shortly afterwards go right at a yellow signpost (2hrs 40mins). About 50 metres later go right again (yellow splash on a tree). The path winds down fairly steeply through bushes and stunted oak trees and meets a road to a new house up on the left (signpost here Bois de Gourdon). Follow the signpost down right to Le Bar on a winding road till you meet the GR51 at a crossroads.

(11) Continue straight following the red/white splashes of the GR51 and the sign Le Bar as the track goes steeply down some hairpin bends. After about 10mins the GR51 goes off to the left where there is a wide concrete pipe which is the continuation of the Canal de Foulon. You leave the GR51 here, following a further sign right to Le Bar (3hrs 5mins) - Note: if you go straight on you arrive at the entrance to a private house. As you go down you can see a large food essence factory over on the right. The track reaches the road at a sign Bois de Gourdon (3hrs 15mins).

(12) Cross the road and continue straight on another wide track *(if you follow the road down you will arrive at the village).* You are now on an easy flat balcony path (direction east) with a large pipe visible from time to time. Soon you can see the outskirts of the village of Bar-sur-Loup down on the right. Ignore two small paths down to the right and continue past a water cistern to high cliffs and you pass under a Baou.

(13) *Careful* - as you go under the Baou look for a stony path going down to the right (3hrs 35mins) with yellow and green markings. Continue down this narrow steep path past a tall green fence and an old stone wall, and then bearing left to reach the road and a sign saying Belvedere du Loup (3hrs 40mins). The road passes a shrine on the left and then a cemetery behind a low wall which looks extremely neat and tidy!

The road (Chemin Bessurane) continues past a parking area into Yorktown Road (looks like an American road sign!). Bear down left past the school to Chemin Bosquet. Go back across the viaduct to the large parking place (4hrs).

Walk No. 4
PIC DE COURMETTES AND PUY DE TOURETTE - Alt. 1268m

Difficulty:	Strenuous - quite a bit of climbing and the way is not obvious. A compass would be helpful but not essential. Do not do this walk in poor visibility.
Time:	5hrs 30mins (including visit to Village Negre 25mins).
Height gain:	700m.
Maps:	Cartes IGN 3643 ET Top 25 Cannes/Grasse 1:25,000. Editions Didier Richard No. 26 Pays d'Azur 1:50,000.
Depart from:	Village of Courmes.
Signposting:	For part of the way there are signposts - you are on the GR51. Where the map shows a red unconnected line it means that there is often no defined path.

Observations:
This walk is rewarding but you have to be fit and with a good sense of direction! **Courmes** is a tiny village in a 250m curve over the Gorges du Loup

and dominated by the Pic de Courmettes and the Puy de Tourettes. Perhaps due to its smallness and relative isolation, it seems to have missed the renovation of many of the other villages in this area.

How to get there (from Vence):

Take the D2210 towards Grasse through Tourette-sur-Loup to Pont du Loup. At Pont du Loup take the narrow D6 signposted Cipières/Greolières/ Courmes (10kms), which is a twisty turning road down the gorge. After about 10mins cross over the River Loup at the hamlet of Bramafan. Almost immediately take the narrow turning up right on the D903 which winds up to the village of Courmes high above. Drive past a charming looking auberge (inn) and park your car by the telephone box in the middle of the village.

Directions:

(1) Walk upwards through this cute little village, crossing the small square (Place de l'Eglise) which has some lovely old houses. There is a small church on the left. Turn left at the back of the church and walk up to a signpost (5mins) where there is an iron cross on the right.

(2) Turn right following indication Domaine des Courmettes, Pic de Cour-mettes (signpost No. 82). This is a narrow rocky path going gently upwards. A few minutes later continue over a crossroads following the GR red/white splashes. There are evergreen oak trees, juniper, giant hellebore, broom and gorse bushes by the side of the path. This is an ancient mule track with worn shallow rocky steps as you walk along the side of the hill (eastwards) - there is a stream down on the right.

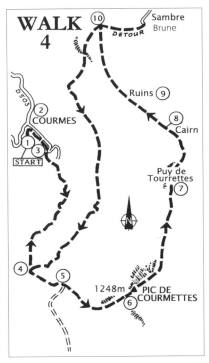

(3) When the path meets a wide jeep track (15mins) bear right at a signpost indicating Domaine des Courmettes/Pic de Courmettes and then a few minutes later, by a large oak tree on the right, bear right again where there is a red/white GR splash on a small tree.

    The small path goes up gently, past a concrete square water cistern and then up medium steep past the wall of another water cistern on the left. Cross a dry watercourse before the path bends to the left (look for the GR splash) on widely spaced shallow steps, a characteristic of all these ancient pathways which connected the mountain hamlets. The path goes round the contour of the hill through beech and oak trees. Look back and you can see the summit of the Tourette, left is the Cheiron range and to the right the Pic de Courmettes. The path goes past a tumbledown wall (there is another path the other side of the wall) and piles of moss-covered stones (probably old terraces). You meet the path which was on the other side of the wall (30mins) at a crossroads where you go straight on. There are faded GR signs along this path and on the stone wall to the left. At another crossroads go straight (35mins) - here the woods are quite thick and there are pines amongst the oak and beech.

(4) The path comes to a T-junction by a GR splash - this is where you come in from the left on your return journey. You are now off the GR51 as you turn up right to a barrier and a panel which says Domaine des Courmettes with lots of signs underneath indicating no dogs, no bikes, no cars etc. Go through the barrier to another signpost (45mins) and follow sign No. 81 upwards past another water cistern on to a wide, smooth jeep track with a good view of the Pic de Courmettes in front. The jeep track narrows amongst wild rose bushes, brambles, holly bushes and pines and goes up medium steep to a signpost (the directions had been ripped off when we did this walk). This is an open area and it is a good idea to take a breather here and enjoy the view (1hr). With your back to the signpost the village of Gourdon is perched in front on its incredible rocky summit, while behind is the Haut Mont and the white dome of an observatory, the Plateau de Calerne. Down below is the Gorge de Loup and the outskirts of the village of Bar-sur-Loup. To the right is the Mont Cheiron and to the left is the Mediterranean coastline.

(5) At the signpost turn up abruptly left (no markings). There is a little landslide but you get on to a grassy track. *In early spring look out for the cocoons of the processionary pine moth hanging in the coniferous trees (see 'Introduction: Flora and Fauna'). In the pine trees there also small flocks of firecrests, the smallest of European birds, who can be distinguished by their yellow and orange crowns and constant high twittering.*

    The path bears east, not well defined so look out for occasional cairns and orange splashes as it rises steeply with more boulders around. As you

View of snow-capped mountains, Pic de Courmettes

turn to the left (northwards) there is a lovely view of Courmes village below
(1hr 10mins). The path steepens further as it goes through bushes and
stunted trees, and then over rocks and boulders to a false summit with a
cairn. Continue upwards on a steep shoulder with lots of tree roots, small
rocks and pine trees dotted around. At another hump bear down to the right
by two small cairns through green oaks - be careful as this is not easy to see
(1hr 30mins). On the left is a substantial hill of white rocks which has to
climbed to get to the summit. Careful here - don't go up to the left where
the climb is steep but go round the mountain and then up. There are cairns
but they are difficult to distinguish from the rocks and there is a sort of path
but only really visible when you look downwards. In the valley below you can
see the buildings of the Domaine des Courmettes which is a spiritual Buddhist
centre.

Keep going to the top following the cairns - from halfway up the ridge
on a fine day you can see as far as the island of Corsica! The going is tedious
as you have to pick your way up the steep slope over the boulders but it is
not difficult.

(6) At the summit (1hr 45mins) there is a brown geometric edifice. The views
all round are magnificent. You can see the snowy summits of the southern
Alps and the Mercantour to the north as well as the impressive Gorges du
Loup from a higher angle. Go straight over the crest towards the Puy de

Tourette hump ahead and then down (northeast). There is no defined path but keep nearer the edge of the mountain. You reach a new green sign saying Domaines des Courmettes and a defined path which then peters out! As you pick your way down the stony slopes there are lots of box bushes here (reminds one of English suburban gardens) and lavender. Down on the right is a ruined *bergerie* (sheepfold). If you are not on a defined path make for this and you will hit the path which dips down to a low pass in the hills where there is a cairn (2hrs 10mins). You get another good view down to Courmes village and beyond, up on the right, the village of Cipières with Gréolières behind. Take the defined path to the top which takes you to a wide flat ridge (the actual Puy de Tourette itself is a jumble of rocks over to the left). Although the Tourette is 20m higher than the Pic de Courmettes it is not as dramatic, perhaps because the northern side is flattish - nevertheless the views from the ridge are magnificent (2hrs 35mins).

(7) *Careful* here as there is no clear path over the top so make for a tall cairn you can see to the right (north). Note: if you have gone to the top of the Tournette instead of to the ridge it is straight ahead. There is lots of lavender and thyme along this ridge. At the tall cairn look back left and you will see a smaller cairn. Make for this, skirting round a depression to the left (west) which often has a large pool of muddy water in it.

(8) At this second cairn you will see others which indicate the path down (2hrs 40mins) - they are difficult to see as there are so many other stones so the author and friend helped to build them up higher! On the horizon is the desolate plateau of St. Barnabé with one lone house on it. Make for a depression and ruins visible below with trees growing out of them. Skirt to the left following an undefined path which becomes clearer as you pass larger ruins with long tumbledown walls.

(9) There is a defined track to the left of the ruins which joins a T-junction (3hrs). Turn right through a stone wall down to a small plateau and then descending again over rocks to another plateau. You eventually hit a stony path which leads you to the bottom of the mountain at the Plateau de St. Barnabé and a jeep track where there are signposts - left to Courmes, right to La Baisse/St. Barnabé (3hrs 25mins).

DETOUR TO THE VILLAGE NEGRE (25mins there and back)
For an interesting detour turn right on the jeep track to visit the curiously sculptured rock formations caused by limestone erosion (marked Sambre Brune on the map). It is called "the African village" because the shapes are reminiscent of conical African huts. Go past an isolated modern house towards an electricity pylon. About 100m before the pylon turn right and, keeping the pylon on your left, make your way across to the rocks on the horizon. Go back the same way (3hrs 50mins).

(10) Turn sharp left on the GR51 which will take you all the way back to Courmes. This is a pleasant balcony path undulating round the southern edge of the mountain and is never really steep. There are lovely open views of the surroundings and the Loup valley to the left. Initially you go round the bare hillside, then through tall broom bushes and brambles with some slopes of scree. You can see the Courmettes peak looming ahead and it is difficult to image that you have climbed to the summit! The path goes into woodland with an old stone wall on the left. Ignore a wide jeep track coming in from the right by some ochre coloured boulders (4hrs 30mins). Shortly after you come to an old stone fountain on the left. Continue on the main path following the GR signs igoring all branches off, until you meet the original route you came up from (indicated by a cairn) just before the barrier and panel Domaine des Courmettes (4hrs 45mins).

Retrace your steps but be careful at the two junctions and the fork on the way back (not so visible on the way up) just after the second water cistern. Also remember the turnings by the oak tree (5hrs 30mins).

Walk No. 5
LE BAOU SAINT-JEAN - Alt. 943m

Difficulty:	Medium - the climb to the Baou is medium steep but not long.
	Note - if you do the walk in winter there are often icy patches along the Vallongue valley path as it is at the bottom of a north facing slope.
Time:	3hrs 30mins.
Height gain:	500m (note starting point 976m).
Maps:	Cartes IGN 3642 ET Top 25 Vallée de L'Esteron 1:25,000.
	Editions Didier Richard No. 26 Pays d'Azur 1:50,000.
Depart:	On the D2 at the Croix de Jubilé (small iron cross on the side of the road) 16km from Vence.
Signposting:	Good but be careful - there are yellow splashes on more than one path so you can get lost. The numbers on the signposts correspond to numbers on the Vallée de L'Esteron map only.

Observations:

An attractive walk and a climb to another, less frequented Baou. It is worth strolling around the village of Coursegoules, which is perched at the foot of the south face of Mont Cheiron above the ravine of the River Cagne. From

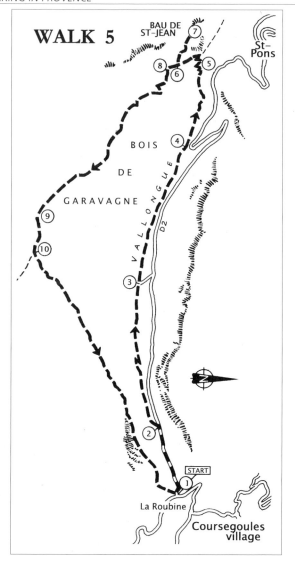

WALK 5

BAU DE
ST-JEAN

St-Pons

BOIS

DE

GARAVAGNE

VALLONGUE

D2

START

La Roubine

Coursegoules
village

afar its huddle of tall white houses stand out against the bare mountainside. With a population of only 300 people it remains a traditional Provençal village.

How to get there (from Vence):
Take the D2210 signposted St-Jeanette/Col de Vence and shortly after, where the D2210 bears right, go straight on the D2 signposted Col de Vence. This road winds up over the Col de Vence and is called Chemin des Evêques (the road of the Bishops!). After passing the turning to the right going to the village of Coursegoules there are two bends - just after the second one you will see a parking area on the left and a smart signpost La Roubine. There is a small iron cross just beyond on the righthand side (Croix de Jubilé).

Directions:
(1) Do not follow the signpost No. 150 at the parking direction left to St. Barnabé, La Baisse, Courmes, Bois de Garavagne, Bramafan as this is the return path. Instead walk left up the D2 direction Gréolières past a ruin on the right. Behind is the hill village of Coursegoules and on the right, behind a lower hill, the impressive ridge of the Cheiron with its highest point the Cime de Cheiron at 1778m. The road is flat and straight, bordered with boxwood bushes and stunted oak.

(2) About 8mins later turn left off the road at signpost No. 177 direction Le Tourounet par Vallongue. This is a wide jeep track with a sign saying *interdiction absolue de fumer, camper ou allumer du feu* (no smoking, camping or lighting fires) and a yellow splash. On the right is a low wall, bushes and trees with a field beyond and then the road (D2) which runs all the way along this valley, called the Vallongue, to the hamlet of St. Pons. Behind the road is a long ridge. This is an easy undulating path which dips down towards the valley and then around the side of the hill on a low balcony path. Watch for icy patches in winter.

(3) When you round a corner ignore a path to the right and stay on the main one (yellow splashes from time to time) which goes down parallel to the road again with fields on the right and a number of pines. Cross a dry river bed (40mins) into a narrow stony gully where you pick your way amongst the stones.

    Careful - at a corner (50mins) go straight down a bank into a dry river bed and up the other side (the more obvious path to the right leads to the road).

(4) At a T-junction (55mins) where the road is very near on the righthand side, branch left on a wide jeep track and continue gently down ignoring various forks to the left. Looming up in front is Baou de St-Jean which looks deceptively high.

(5) At signpost No. 176 (1hr 5mins) go up left to Bois de Garavagne, St. Barnabé and Bramafan (strangely this signpost does not indicate Baou St. Jean). The wide jeep track snakes up medium steep. At one bend there is a good view of the hamlet of St-Pons and the road going down the valley. You reach a flat plateau where the path curls round the side of the Baou.

(6) *Careful here* - look for a narrow path over to the right (1hr 15mins). There is a red splash on a stone but it is not obvious (if you get to the signpost No. 170 5mins beyond you know you have gone too far!).

Go up this narrow, very bushy path following the red splashes very carefully as they are not clear. It winds up fairly steeply. There is a lookout spot where you can see back down the valley, with the road alongside. You can also see the path where you will continue down on the right.

(7) After 15mins you arrive rather suddenly at the top on to a rocky ledge (with a precipitous drop beyond!). Here you have a magnificent view of the villages of Cipières (left) and Genolières (right) on the other side of the Loup valley (1hr 30mins). You can see the Baou on which the village of Gourdon is perched, on the southern horizon. It takes another 5mins to pick your way through bushes and over rocks to the end of the Baou as there is no defined path - there are oppidum ruins here (the fortifications of the ancient Ligurian people) and an impressive wall of rock forming part of the Baou which it looks impossible to reach. *This is the ideal spot for a picnic and, unlike the other Baou overlooking Vence, it has no concrete helicopter pads or orientation tables.* Retrace your steps to the jeep track (1hr 45mins). Turn right on the jeep track and after a minute you reach signpost No. 170.

(8) Take the left turn towards the Bois de Garavagne and St. Barnabé. This is a wide stony track climbing up gently through oak woods following spasmodic yellow splashes. The track moves round the hill through continued oak woods (the Bois de Garavagne) and you can see the Baou de Gourdon ahead.

(9) Keep on the main path and ignore a path going down to the right (2hrs 30mins) which has yellow markers. It levels off and reaches signpost No. 152 10mins later.

(10) Bear left following the sign to La Roubine and Coursegoules. Over on the left is a large building which looks like a *bergerie* (sheepfold) except that it is fenced in. Nearby is a Borie, *(see 'Introduction: Short History')* which has not been reconstructed. The path undulates over an open rather windswept looking plateau - the Vallongue valley is down on the left and you can see the serrated ridge on the other side of the valley. After a while it starts to go down slowly, at first through boxwood and attractive pine trees, then steeper as it comes off this hill with more good views of the high Cheiron ridge on the left and the village of Coursegoules, a huddle of white, on the far hill. Pass a small house on the left before reaching signpost No. 151 indicating left La Roubine/Coursegoules and a little later on the original signpost No. 150 at the parking area (3hrs 30mins).

Walk No. 6
LA ROUTE DE NAPOLEON

Difficulty:	Medium - mainly along the side of a valley.
Time:	3hrs 15mins.
Height gain:	496m.
Maps:	Cartes IGN 3543 ET Top 25 Haute Siagne 1:25,000.
	Editions Didier Richard No. 26 Pays d'Azur 1:50,000.
Depart from:	Parking area beyond the Chapel of St. Jean 8.6km northwest of the village of St-Vallier-de-Thiey.
Signposting:	White/red markings on the GR510. Then yellow splashes.

Observations:
The Route Napoléon is the road taken by the Emperor on his way back from exile in Elba. He landed at Golfe-Jean on 1st March 1815, mounted his horse

Route Napoléon

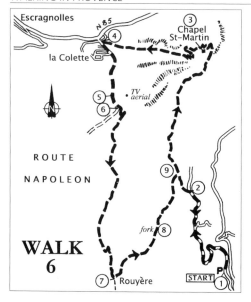

Tauris and with around 100 men and a cannon stopped briefly in Cannes before marching on to Grasse. From there he continued by mule track through St-Vallier-de-Thiey, Escragnolles and Seranon, reaching Castellane on 3rd March, quite a feat as even today the countryside is bleak and rugged. He then continued on to Digne, Sisteron and Grenoble, eventually reaching Paris on 20th March.

This is a delightful walk with historical connections and not too long or strenuous - to think that Napoléon trod the same stones is rather romantic!

How to get there (from Grasse):

Drive to the village of St-Vallier-de-Thiey which is 6.9kms northwest of Grasse on the N85 (Route Napoléon). Just beyond the parking area after the church, take a left turn by a wooden sign on a wall saying Route Napoléon. Go down this long narrow road called Chemin de la Siagne along the side of a valley for 8.6kms ignoring all roads branching off. Then, at a fork after 8kms, go left (not up right on the Chemin des Sources) which leads to a parking area on the right.

Directions:

(1) From the car park, facing the mountain, go right (north) which is the original route taken by Napoléon with 100 men and a cannon in March 1815. It is also the GR510 so look out for the red/white splashes. The wide jeep track is initially flat with a high green fence on the left. The path undulates along and you can hear the gurgling of a stream down in the valley on the right. This is the start of the Siagne River which has its source further up the valley; it gets wider as it flows southwards to the Mediterranean at Mandelieu La Napoule near Cannes.

After 5mins you cross a bridge over the stream which is very beautiful with limpid pools and a tiny waterfall. Ignore any other paths branching off as you walk up this wide ancient track and look for the GR splashes. You are entering the Briasq forest which consists mainly of evergreen oak trees so the hillsides are a bright shade of green even during the winter months. The track passes a rather run-down farm with falling fences and a rusty car on the left (called Léchen on the map) and then a ruin before coming to the gates and driveway of a large house (Les Figueirets) which you can see in the valley below (25mins).

(2) Turn up left (GR splashes here) and continue steadily upwards through delightful woods. Ignore a left fork at two small cairns (30mins) - this is where you will come out on the return journey (9). As well as being Napoléon's route to Paris this was also an ancient walkway to the nearby village of Escragnolles (Napoléon took a rest there) and the town of Castellane. At this stage the valley opens up and you can see the stream winding below and a few houses dotted about.

The man-made track (you can see the clever terracing they have made to level it as much as possible) has low stone pillars (chasse roue in French) at frequent intervals. These served as pulleys for the ropes attached to the carts so that they could be pulled up without slipping backwards. On the descent the ropes stopped the carts from rolling out of control down the track!

In front is a high wooded ridge which appears to be the end of the valley, though as you get nearer you see that it does not end but forks into two subsidiary valleys. The track goes steadily upwards through pine trees, giant broom and the odd juniper as it nears a white rocky outcrop which is the Baou Mourine.

After crossing some scree there is a rocky spur on the left which opens up a wide view of the valley. The track gets stonier and there are boulders on the hillside amongst the scattered green oaks. You can now see the cars high up on the right, going along the new Route Napoléon (opened in 1932) which goes from Grasse to Digne-Les-Bains. There is another rocky spur with a telephone pole on it which of course spoils the effect (1hr) but not the view! Through a gorge in front you can see a stream running down the main valley beyond, called the Vallon de St. Martin. The track continues northwest on the very edge of the hillside around the big boulders of the Baou Mourine with sharp drops down, towards the little ruined chapel of Saint Martin. As you go round you see the main road and the hamlet of Bail tucked cosily into the hillside.

(3) Walk past the chapel (1hr 5mins) (nothing much to see inside) and go left continuing on the GR510. This really looks like an ancient cart track as you might expect on the Route Napoléon. It turns west along the side of the Baou through rocky terrain with a scattering of pines, getting nearer and nearer to the road. After a cleared area to the right with animal watering troughs you arrrive at a crossroads with a scattering of houses and a fountain called La Colette. The N85 is just over on the right (1hr 25mins). Not far down the main road west is the village of Escragnolles where Napoléon went to see the mother of one of his generals who was killed in Egypt during the 1798 campaign.

(4) Go left on the road south leaving the red/white splashes of the GR510. As you go past a gravel clearing there is a fork (actually a garden of a house with a hedge) but bear left. Yellow splashes start here which you follow till the track hits the GR510 again. The paved road quickly becomes a jeep track. You are turning round the Baou, going back parallel to the track you came on and climbing steadily through pines.

(5) Just before a TV aerial turn up left and walk on the top of the Baou till you come to the broken down walls of an Oppidum *(see 'Introduction: Short History')*. Note: there is no defined path but it only takes a few minutes to get there. To get the best view you need to go right to the edge of the Baou. Retrace your steps to the jeep track (1hr 40mins) and turn left, direction south, still following yellow splashes.

(6) At a signpost which says Forêt Communale de Briasque (chemin de Briasq and Escargnolles is signposted right) go off the jeep track to the left signposted Rouyère (1hr 45mins). The track drops steadily crossing a number of *clapiers* (a word meaning rocky mass but in this case more like scree). Continue along the side of the mountain on a long easy path from which you can see down into the valley of the Siagne from a higher vantage point. Keep on the main track which goes down in wide zigzags. *Note: there is a steep short cut down left (marked with a yellow splash) which comes out just before the ruins of Rouyère. It then continues down but it is advisable to keep to the main track*. As you get lower you can see the attractive cluster of ruins called Rouyère (2hrs 20mins) where the track goes right through the tumbledown buildings which must have formerly been a big farm with outbuildings (ignore the chain across the path).

(7) After the ruins do not continue on the jeep track which turns down right but take the second path left (watch for the yellow splash) on a narrow raised path going initially through woodland with a wall on the lefthand side. This feels like the wrong direction, heading back up the valley to the north-east! The path descends steadily and goes through a broken down wall.

(8) At a fork (2hrs 35mins) bear down right (be careful, there are yellow splashes on both paths). As you get lower the woods become dense again with mainly green oaks.

(9) The path eventually arrives at a T-junction which is the Route Napoléon and the path taken on the outward journey (2hrs. 50mins). Bear down right and retrace your footsteps to the car park (3hrs 15mins).

Walk No. 7
LA VALLEE DE LA SIAGNE

Difficulty:	Medium walk down and along a delightful gorge - there is a climb in and out of the gorge but it is not difficult.
Time:	4hrs.
Height gain:	About 200m down and up.
Maps:	Cartes IGN 3543 ET Top 25 Haute Siagne 1:25,000.
	Editions Didier Richard No. 26 Pays d'Azur 1:50,000.
Depart from:	Parking area in the village of St-Cézaire-sur-Siagne.
Signposting:	Occasional signposts plus red/white GR splashes and yellow splashes.

Observations:
One of my favourite walks in the Alpes Maritimes region. It can be done at any time of the year but would be ideal in high summer as there is lots of shade and that magnificent river to swim in!

Information on the Siagne River: Its source is around Escragnolles, near the Route Napoléon, and it reaches the Mediterranean at Mandelieu (near Cannes). This gorge and valley opens a passageway between the coast and the hinterland. The Romans used this access to carry goods to Fréjus which was an important port for war and commerce. They created a large agricultural area on the north side of the Siagne introducing olives, wheat and vines. St-Cézaire has two claims to fame regarding its name - it was named either after a Roman emperor who halted there on his way to Pompei or after a man called Cézaire who was a monk on the island of Lérins and then later the Bishop of Arles in 503.

How to get there (from Grasse):
From Grasse take the D13 through the villages of Spéracèdes and Le Tignet to St-Cézaire-sur-Siagne (15kms). Make for the parking area as indicated.

Directions:
(1) Go left out of the car park towards the village and then up left past the old bath-house on the right. You arrive at a square and the church which you

Old bridge on the Vallée de la Siagne walk

pass on the right. Take the Rue d'Egalité up left. A hundred metres up this street turn right again down some steps. Bear left at a T-junction and you come to your first signpost No. 134. (5mins).

(2) Follow signs indicating Pont des Tuves/La Siagne/chemin de Montauroux/ Chapelle St. Saturin/Les Veyans. There is an extensive view here of the Var region to the west with the wooded slopes of the Siagne gorge in the foreground. You are now on the GR510 so watch for the red/white splashes.

You are on an old mule track which linked the village of St-Cézaire with Mons and Callian on the other side of the gorge. It starts down through terraces planted with olive trees but as the path descends south the vegetation changes to cistus, juniper bushes, lavender, wild asparagus, different species of broom and green oak. After 20mins you get your first view of the river glinting in the sunlight far below. The path undulates down the side of the gorge, often in shallow wide steps, without ever becoming too precipitous.

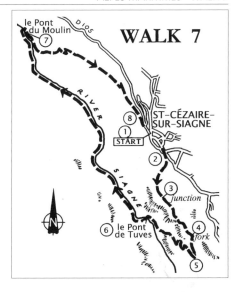

(3) At a junction there is another signpost; take the second path down to the left (not the upper one), signposted Chapelle St-Saturnin/Les Veyans (30mins). You pass an old *lavoir* (wash trough) on the right - did they really have to walk all the way down from the village to do the washing! The path becomes narrower and bushier as it approaches the gorge through predominantly green oak woods.

(4) At a fork turn right by a GR sign and ignore a branch right a few minutes later (GR cross on stone). Down in the gorge you can see a concrete watercourse and an aqueduct. The path reaches a narrow canal by a quaint little bridge (45mins). Here the GR510 continues left down the gorge to the Chapel of St-Saturnin which takes approximately 1hr there and back (the author did not do this).

(5) Cross the bridge and turn right along the lefthand side of the canal following yellow splashes. The path is raised up along the top of a wall which goes down left so that you are walking level with the tops of the green oak trees. *The canal is flowing swiftly through sloped concrete walls and looks extremely clean. It was built in 1868 to bring the Siagne water to Cannes and is still an important water supply for the villages further down the valley. Flowing south of Grasse it continues to Mandelieu (a suburb of Cannes) on the coast where it ends up in the Mediterranean.*

Where the canal goes under a huge rock the path temporarily goes down to the left but soon you are walking again on a narrow wall but with an iron barrier for support so the drop on the left does not seem so bad. Pass by another three little bridges till you get to a bigger bridge (the fifth in all) when

59

you get off the side of the canal and bear down to the left. *The sound of the river nearby is quite loud now and through the trees you catch glimpses of the water which is an incredible aquamarine.* The path winds down through giant white heather, wild verbena and plum, all in bloom in late February. Avoid a path down to the left (yellow cross on stone). After two small ruins and a cave you get back to the river bank. *Here you can appreciate the beauty of this river which is shallow in parts and crystal clear with the brown stones glistening through the water. As you walk further along there are numerous waterfalls and stretches of white water interspersed with deep aquamarine coloured pools; it is a swimmer's paradise with inlets of sand and rocks which would be blissful to swim from in the heat of the summer. Yet with the overhanging branches of trees and bushes there is a wildness about the river which makes it even more enchanting.*

(6) The path reaches an old roman curved bridge called Le Pont de Tuves (2hrs) but to cross it you have to go under a mini waterfall which falls on to the path creating a rivulet of water. After crossing the bridge be careful as there are numerous diversions with yellow splashes in all directions, some to little sandy beaches on the river. Take the path to the right which is the one closest to the river - do not go straight up past an old ruin, and continue along the river through stunted trees and bushes. Where the river widens you get your first glimpse of St-Cézaire high up over on the right. Follow the yellow splashes carefully keeping to the main path through dense vegetation with several ruins of watermills. *In 1907 St-Cezaire was one of the first villages in the region to be electrified but then the mills were abandoned after the first World War.*

A little further on, almost buried in vegetation, is a larger ruin, originally a papermill which was abandoned around 200 years ago. There is a short sharp climb above the river and then the path undulates through dense vegetation before descending to a little holiday house on the left called Le Chêne, a very apt name as it stands behind an enormous gnarled oak tree. The land to the right drops down in terraces to an open grassy patch by the river bank, probably part of their garden. *If you look up here you will notice that the vegetation goes through three stages - the jungle by the river bank, the green oak woods higher up and pine trees near the top of the gorge.*

(7) Shortly after you come to a junction (3hrs). Be careful here as both left and right have yellow splashes! Go right across another bridge called Le Pont du Moulin, a much newer one built in the 19th century, and then right again heading southeast towards the village. The path winds up till it meets the canal again at a bridge which you cross following a yellow splash. On the sides of the mule track you see occasional low stone pillars of the chasse roue (see Walk No. 6 for explanation).

Continue between ancient terraces and olive groves leading to a paved road and a signpost (rejoining the GR510) at the entrance to the village. *Look back for a good view up the valley, the glint of the river far below and to the south the forested hills of the Maures and Estérel with the sea beyond on a clear day.*

(8) Turn right and straight on where there is a no-entry sign and yellow splashes. Continue through the medieval archway of the Rue St. Ferréol (do not follow the yellow splashes left) and then through the quaint narrow streets of the village to the Place de la Tour and the church. Turn up left and to the parking area (4hrs).

Walk No. 8
TOUR OF MONT VINAIGRE (Vinegar) - Alt. 614m

Difficulty:	Medium - no steep climbs. Some road walking.
Time:	3hrs 45mins.
Height gain:	400m.
Maps:	Cartes IGN 3544 ET Top 25 Fréjus/St. Raphaël 1:25,000.
	Editions Didier Richard No. 26 Pays d'Azur 1:50,000.
Depart from:	Pont d'Estérel.
Signposting:	Adequate though not always obvious. Some of the time you are following the red/white splashes of the GR51.

Observations:
A classic walk in the northern part of the Estérel region with magnificent scenery, if somewhat marred by installations and roads. In summer and at weekends this walk is very popular. For information on the Estérel region see the description of Alpes Maritimes.

How to get there (from Cannes):
Take the N7 to the Pont d'Estérel, which is 16kms east of Fréjus and 12kms west of Mandelieu. This is on a corner where there is a large signpost saying Parc Residentiel de L'Estérel 550 hectares. In front is a small area for parking but be careful not to block the barrier giving access to the forestry road. Otherwise there is another parking area further on to the left.

Directions:
(1) Walk through the barrier and up the wide forestry jeep track towards the TV aerials you can see perched on the high rocky ridges on the horizon - you can hear but not see the Estérel stream to the right. *The scenery reminds me*

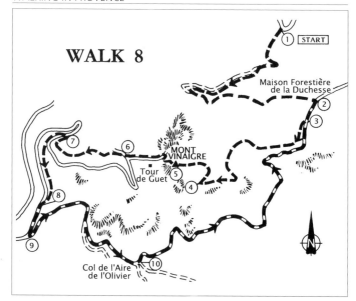

of Australia with its reddish earth and the smell of Eucalyptus trees. You are
passing through woodland, mainly olive trees, cork and holm oak,
Mediterranean pine and eucalyptus trees. The banks are covered with tall
white heather (also called tree heath) and strawberry trees (see 'Introduction:
Fauna and Flora') which are characteristic plants of this area.

Keep to the main track ignoring any paths going off. You are gaining
height gently as the track curves to the left and then does a wide righthand
bend. As you go higher there is a good view left of the small villages on the
north edge of the Estérel region with mountains behind.

(2) You arrive at a T-junction called la maison forestière de la Duchesse, alt.
389m (35mins) where there is indeed a forestry house behind a row of trees
in front together with a large white milestone indicating that you are on the
Route des Cols. The GR51 comes in here from the left and you should now
continue to watch for the red/white GR splashes.

(3) Turn right and walk down the track 100m. Just after a track going down
to the left take a narrow path up to the right (this is indicated by red/white
GR splashes but is not very obvious). Initially it is moderately steep and you
come quickly to another T-junction where you turn left (right leads to a yellow

building which is apparently a reservoir). Ignore any offshoots and keep following the GR red/white splashes as the track rises pleasantly through ferns, broom, clumps of very tall heather, bay, wild thyme and mint. There are also different varieties of pine, juniper, strawberry trees, eucalyptus, holm and cork oak - the smell of the sultry south penetrates your nostrils even in February when the author did this walk! You can appreciate the lovely vistas of the rolling tree covered hills topped with red jagged rocks which are a special feature of the Estérel region. On the horizon are the TV antennas of the Pic de l'Ours and the Pic du Cap Roux.

(4) Keeping to the red and white splashes you go briefly across some scree before arriving at a beautiful viewpoint (55mins). *Take a few minutes to enjoy your surroundings - to the north the Crête de Ferrier, the pre-alps of the Haute Verdun, northeast the Alpes-Maritimes (covered in snow in winter), to the south the whole of the mountainous Estérel region which plunges to the edge of the Mediterranean with the town of Fréjus and the bay of St. Raphaël. It is a breathtaking sight.*

Continue on this cindery track through some scree and boulders as you wind your way up Vinegar hill - the bushes get more stunted and close in on you for a while. As you go higher the views become spectacular - you arrive at a shoulder from where you can see the top above a jumble of large boulders. After clambering over these boulders to the summit (614m) you are surprised to find that it is a smooth round concrete slab with an antenna and an unattractive white container cabin - what a disappointment! Nearby to the west is another antenna called the Tour de Guet (watch-tower), with a square concrete building beside it - further over is another TV aerial surrounded by satellite dishes. Despite this the surrounding views are stunning (1hr. 15mins).

It is a good idea to get off the summit and perch yourself on rocky boulders nearby where, although you can still see the aerials, you feel you are in more natural surroundings - a good place for a picnic.

(5) Starting again from the summit, face the Tour de Guet and take the obvious path down following the GR signs by a rocky path down to a T-junction on a narrow paved road (1hr 20mins) which is the road to the watchtower where it says access interdit (no entry) to the left. Turn down right to another T-junction and then left, following GR splashes. This takes you underneath the watchtower which is perched on very attractive craggy rocks. You pass a barrier onto a helicopter landing pad which is also a car park (1hr 25mins), with a road coming in from the left.

(6) Avoid the wide jeep track on the right and take the narrow paved road going up with the barrier in front of it (there is a GR sign). Follow GR splashes left after about 50m, just before you get to the TV aerial. At a flat open area continue down a wide rocky path (the only way to go) which gets narrow and attractive through a dry stream bed and lovely pine and oak trees.

(7) The path meets a road (1hr 40mins) which you cross diagonally left to another path (GR splashes). As you descend there is a good view of Lake Avalon down on the right and the N7 road.

(8) You meet the road same again where you turn left (this is where you part company with the GR51), and 50m later reach an "aire de détente" (recreation area). Continue down the road (leaving the GR going off to the right) till you come to a junction (2hrs 5mins).

(9) Take the road going sharp left with a sign saying cul de sac, 1800 metres. This leads round the other side of the Mont Vinaigre to the end of a valley creating a sort of horseshoe effect. Go straight on when you come to a barrier across a jeep track heading down to the right; there is another white stone road marker here indicating that you are still on the Route des Cols (back to St. Raphaël 13kms, ahead Les Trayes 22kms and left Cannes 23kms). The road continues to a parking area at the Col de l'Aire d'Olivier (2hrs 25mins). *There is a plaque on a rock to the memory of August Muterse, Inspector of Water and Forests 1851-1922 who was responsible for much of the conservation work done in the Estérel region. He also supervised the building of the extensive network of roads criss-crossing the area to enable the firefighters to penetrate and keep the constant bush fires under control.*

(10) Go through another barrier to the left onto a narrow road which deteriorates to a jeep track with lovely views unfolding over the Maraval valley to the right (flowering verbena bushes here in February) as it circles round the flank of the hill. At another junction, keep to the upper main track. Ahead is a striking ochre coloured rock which is called "the phantom" (it really does look like one if you use your imagination). This part of the walk is the prettiest as you get wide vistas of the whole of the Estérel and the jagged rocks rear up ochre coloured above the green forest. The path passes where you set off earlier on the GR51 (No. 3 on map) and brings you back full circle to the forestry house of La Duchesse (3hrs 15mins). Retrace your steps back to the car park at the Pont d'Estérel (3hrs 45 mins).

Walking towards the Grotto of St. Honorat (Walk 10)

Sainte Baume *(Walk 13)*
On the cliffs of Sainte Victoire *(Walk 16)*

Walk No. 9
ESTÉREL - WALK TO LAC ECUREUIL
AND OVER THREE PASSES

Difficulty:	Moderate/strenuous - this is a long walk, much of it on jeep track. A short cut reduces the length by about lhr.
Time:	5hrs 45mins.
Height gain:	300m.
Maps:	Cartes IGN 3544 Et Top 25 Fréjus-St. Raphaël 1:25,000.
	Editions Didier Richard No. 26 Pays d'Azur 1:50,000.
Depart:	Near Mandelieu, west of Cannes.
Signposting:	Few signposts but much of the time the way is evident. Red/white splashes on the GR51.

Observations:
This walk gives an overall picture of the Estérel region with its fascinating rocky crags and peaks. Although the walk is long and much of it on road, there are possible short cuts. The reddish colouring of the rocks makes it especially beautiful. In February the mimosa trees add brilliant splashes of yellow to the green slopes - like the eucalyptus they originate in Australia and have been specially planted here. The blooms are exported all over Europe. In March the slopes are dotted with lovely white asphodel lilies. For further information about the Estérel see description of the Alpes Maritimes.

How to get there:
From the town of Mandelieu, west of Cannes, take the N7 for 3.4kms (distance from the roundabout with iron golfers on it) to a signpost saying Trois Termes on the lefthand side of the road by a cemetery. Drive up the road past the cemetery to a parking area just before a barrier (there is also a helicopter landing stage here).

Directions:
(1) Don't go up the main road but take the road on the left which says Piste des Oeufs de Bouc (translated this means goat's sperm track which sounds rather dodgy!). Down on the left is the Vallon des Trois Termes. This is an easy wide jeep track winding gently upwards - on the right you can see the N7 going towards Fréjus and the village of St-Jean-de-Cannes. Beside the track are olives, cork oaks, Mediterranean pines, tree heaths which looks like tall white heather, strawberry trees, and, further down in the valley, mimosa trees which have fluffy yellow flowers in February. You are walking up a wide

65

shoulder and the higher you get the more magnificent are the views in all directions. To the left is a panorama over Cannes with the Lérins islands beyond. This is in fact the only time you see the coast during the entire walk. On the horizon to the north are the high peaks of the Mercantour National Park.

You come to citerne No. 3, the first of a series of large water tanks found all over this area as it is very prone to forest fires in the summer. Cisterns 4 and 5 are before the top of the shoulder and after number 6 (15mins) the track goes slightly down (direction south). Up on the right are the curiously serrated reddish rocks which are so typical of the Estérel region. Keep on the main track, passing cisterns 7, 8 and 9 where you can now see the road coming up from the right to meet your jeep track. At citerne 10 (three tanks) in a clearing, fork right

WALK 9

START ①

les Oeufs de Bouc

②

Maison Forestière des Trois Termes

③

⑫ Col des Suvières

la Grosse Vache ▲

Baisse de Mathieu

⑪

Baisse de la Grosse Vache

Baisse de la Petite Vache

Mamelon des Aulnes ▲

④ Lac de l'Écureuil

⑩ Mamelon de l'Écureuil ▲

ford

Col du Perthus

⑨

⑤ ▲ Pic du Mal ▲ Infernet

⑧

Pic du Baladou ▲

⑦

Gué (ford)

Col de Belle Barbe ⑥

Ravin du Grenouillet

to the southwest (30mins). Go straight gently downhill before levelling out to reach number 11 with a fascinating rock behind.

(2) Continue down round the corner and join the main road (40mins) by a barrier. Turn left up this road to another barrier by a sign saying Forêt Dominale de L'Estérel (55mins). *There used to be a big parking area just below the Col des Trois Termes, which was accessible by car from the N7 until the barriers were installed in 1966. It is possible to reach it from the Pointe du Trayas at the expense of a long drive. There are a number of eucalyptus trees here which are not indigenous to the Estérel but have been planted because they are very fire resistant, as are the cork trees. You will find these trees around many areas where roads, parking areas or quarries have been built.*

(3) At the crossroads here don't follow the sign straight indicating Pic de L'Ours and St. Raphaël Agay, where you can see a house on the horizon (Maison Forestière des Trois Termes) - you will come back this way. **Be careful** - ignore the first and second roads to your left. Between the sign saying "Route Forestière Pic de L'Ours" and another saying "en cas d'infraction amende" there is an unmarked rocky path to the left of a eucalyptus tree, easy to miss as it looks like a dry watercourse. Head down south on this which is badly rutted by erosion. It goes along the side of a bushy ravine called Ravine des Trois Termes getting lower and lower until it reaches a recently made dam with lots of rocks and newly turned earth. This will eventually be a reservoir (1hr 15mins). Cross the dam and follow the path down the valley with the stream on the left (still going south). As you progress along the stream flows lower down on the right and you are walking along the hillside on a flattish path which then goes down again to cross the stream before it flows into a lake called Lac d'Ecureuil (Squirrel Lake).

(4) You reach the lake at a junction which meets the GR51 (1hr 40mins). Turn right onto the GR51 (no splashes) and continue along the righthand side of the lake ignoring a track to the right. This lake is attractive and elongated, obviously man-made. Over to the left a rivulet flows in from the Ravin de la Couche de L'Ane (plenty of names for ravines but not for streams!). There are two interestingly shaped rocks which are called Mamelon des Aulnes (alders) and Mamelon de L'Ecureuil (*mamelon* meaning nipple).

On the other side of the lake there is a curious small promontory which looks almost urban with short grass and very domestic looking pines - someone must have planted them. Behind are tall serrated rocks so it looks very romantic. The lake is separated in two by a narrow piece of land like a bridge (there is a sign here) but the other side is very swampy. Keeping the swamp and river on the left, you pass a dam which looks almost natural with a huge rock and water cascading down on the extreme left. A few minutes later the track crosses the river by a concrete ford (*gué* in French) with round stepping stones to the left (fun to jump along even if there is no water in the ford!) - 1hr 55mins.

Ignore a path to the left at a sign saying Réserve Biologique de Mal Infernet. Along the track there are views of interestingly shaped reddish rocks which rear up behind the Ravin du Mal Infernet, the name of the gorge you are now walking along with the river down on the right. You pass an interesting cave which could have been a sort of shepherd's refuge in ancient times.

(5) The GR51 goes off to the right (2hrs 10mins) - cut across this way to point (8) if you want to shorten the walk by about one hour. Otherwise continue down the ravine. On the left is an old fountain with a cute little basin of stone under it and then the river on the right traverses a weir with a natural cascade of water flowing over greenish coloured rocks on one side. Further on you come to a larger fountain dated 1935 with three pipes sticking out of the natural rock and a trough underneath. The wide track is very flat and easy to walk along and the river continues down on the right. Ignore a path to the left and cross another ford, exactly like the first one. The jeep track comes to a big clearing which looks as though it is a crossroads but isn't! Go straight (2hrs 25mins). The stream is now far below on the left in a wide gravelly ravine, the reddish pebbles reminiscent of Australia; this is the Ravin de Grenouillet (Solomon's seal, which is a common wild plant) and the river widens here.

(6) The track arrives at the Col de Belle Barbe where there is a barrier and a parking area. Careful here: this is a sort of T-junction but before you get to the road by a notice saying En cas d'infraction FF.900 turn up right (2hrs 45mins). This is a narrow path with no splashes or indication. After about 100m there is a possible short cut straight on, otherwise follow the main track to the right, going up fairly steeply and becoming rocky. There are bushes of tall white heather, young pines, lavender and broom and a beautiful view on the right of the Estérel in general, rather scarred by the complex of roads, with the tall TV tower of the Pic de L'Ours on the horizon. You can still make out the contours of the ancient terraces. This is a delightful path along the top of a hill with a good view of the ravine and the previous track to the Colle de Belle Barbe down on the right. As you turn eastwards the path flattens outward and then goes up again to the top of the hill, with an area over on the left which has been completely cleared.

(7) Soon you change direction, bearing round the hill to meet the short cut coming in from the left (3hrs 5mins). Behind you can see the Pic de Baladour. From here the path bears down towards the large cleared area that is on the left.

Walking in Estérel (Angela)

(8) At a crossroads on the Col Aubert, where the GR51 comes in from the right, go straight, not down to the left (3hrs 15mins). Look for the GR red/white splashes again as the path begins climbing steadily north.

(9) At the Col de Baladour (3hrs 25mins) you can either follow the road or continue on the grande randonnée up a narrow track to the left (do not take the wide jeep track). The GR takes you along the edge of the cleared area and you have to be careful to follow the marks on the side of cork trees which are the only ones left on the bare hillside. The road is visible below on the right. This is a narrow, obviously quite unused path but most attractive as it winds down to the Col de Perthuis (3hrs 45mins) - the Pic de Perthuis is over on the left and on the horizon are the twin peaks of the Mont Vinaigre. Cross two small patches of scree with a road and a river down on the left.

(10) The path meets the unsurfaced road at the Baisse de la Petite Vache (dip of the little cow) in a large clearing (3hrs 55mins). Leaving the GR51 which goes off to the left, turn right over the open area and then left to follow the road all the way to the Col de Trois Termes. You are now on a very wide jeep track with another good view of the Pic de L'Ours on the right and ahead are the serrated rocky peaks of La Grosse Vache (large cow) which are particularly beautiful. You reach a large open crossroads (4hrs 10mins at the Baisse de la Grosse Vache - cows must have done something special in this area!).

(11) At a further intersection called Baisse de Matthieu ignore a left branch as the road bends to the right (west) to circle below the peaks of the Grosse Vache.

(12) Go straight on at the Col de Suvières, a sort of forest roundabout with eucalyptus in the middle, and a road on the left with a sign saying Réserve Biologique des Sauvières. The track passes some tall eucalyptus and a steep drop on the right. You can see the Maison Forestière des Trois Termes long before you reach it as the road meanders with many interesting rocky peaks all round. You pass an open area on the left with a tall cliff behind which could be an abandoned quarry.

The road climbs slowly up to the Maison Forestière (4hrs 55mins), a large house which looks surprisingly suburban with a cultivated garden and orchard, hedges, stables and chickens! From the parking area at Les Trois Termes you can see the path you took on the outward journey, down the gorge on the right (No. 3). Continue straight down the road passing the track you came in (No. 2) to the right. There are lovely views on the left (you can see the N7 quite clearly) and, in February, rivers of yellow mimosa trees in blossom in the gorge and on the Tanneron mountains behind. Continue to the car park (5hrs 45mins).

Walk No. 10
PIC DU CAP ROUX - Alt. 453m

Difficulty:	Medium/strenuous - there is quite a bit of uphill.
Time:	4hrs 30mins.
Height gain:	453m.
Map:	Cartes IGN 3544 ET Top 25 Fréjus-St. Raphaël 1:25,000.
	Editions Didier Richard No. 26 Pays d'Azur 1:50,000.
Depart:	Corniche d'Estérel, at Cap Roux on the N28.
Signposting:	Some signposting and splashes but not always evident. Read the walk explanations carefully as not all the paths and turnings are marked on the map.

Observations:
A classic walk in the Estérel and an absolute must. The views of the coast and Estérel region are the best you will find. (However, avoid it at weekends and holiday times if you don't want to share it with too many people. It would also be too exposed and hot to do in the summer months.)

The Estérel region is an ancient volcanic area (porphyry) and the weirdly shaped, vividly red rocks are the result of the fissures which have solidified.

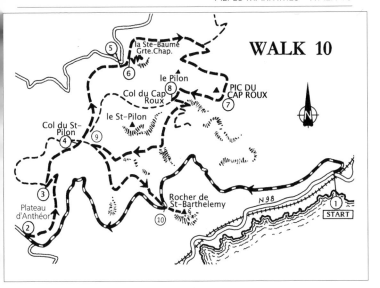

WALK 10

Constant erosion over hundreds of years has created a jumble of jagged rocks and deep ravines, a place of great beauty, as its precipitous red mountains tumble into the intense blue of the Mediterranean, with minute sandy beaches, rocky inlets and tiny offshore islands.

Towards the coastal village of Agay there was a mine which provided very hard rock called Estérelite (a grey/white colour). This rock, which was mined in Roman times, can be found in statues as far away as Alexandria and Egypt and the difficulty they must have had in mining and transporting it to such far lands is unimaginable! There are statues in the villages along the corniche (shore-line) made of this unique stone (for more information on the Estérel see description of the Alpes Maritimes).

How to get there:

From the town of Mandelieu, west of Cannes, take the N28 which is the well-known coast road round the Corniche de L'Estérel. This spectacular route winds through the coastal resorts of Théoule-sur-Mer, Miramar and Le Trayas. In Le Trayas watch for the large Marina on the left. 5.7kms later cross a bridge with green railings which goes over the railway. Just past the bridge there is a bus sign on the right which says Cap Roux. Beyond are two parking areas on different sides of the road.

Directions:

(1) Walk back down the road for approximately 50m and take the road on the left with a barrier and sign Forêt Dominale de L'Estérel. *The views of the coastline are exceptional and get better the higher you go! There is a railway running along the coast between the road and the sea but it doesn't seem to detract from the beauty of the red coastal rocks, the jagged inlets and tiny beaches. On the headland opposite the start of this walk there is a fort with four gun emplacements, a relic of the Second World War.* Start up this wide smooth road where no cars are allowed to go up from the coast although they do arrive in the other direction. As you walk up you can appreciate the towering reddish rocks of the Pic du Cap Roux, which is in fact a number of jagged peaks, and in front is the Rocher de St. Barthélemy, alt. 203m. Getting nearer you can see the railings put up to help people reach the viewpoint on the summit, perhaps worth a climb as these enormous rocks give the impression of falling right into the sea despite the intervening railway and road.

After 5mins you go through another barrier. *Amongst the myriad vegetation on this walk are Mediterranean pines, green and cork oaks, mimosa trees, French lavender (the French call it lavende anglaise!), tall white flowering tree heather, blue flowering rosemary, white laburnum, box bushes, giant hellebore, various species of cistus, the beautiful Asphodel lily and the strawberry tree (see 'Introduction: Flora and Fauna').*

Keep on this wide road which steadily heads west. You pass a small fountain on your right next to a cluster of mimosa trees (25mins). *In mid February we saw a yellow Cleopatra butterfly which is a member of the brimstone family with an orange flush on its top wings.* There is an impressive crater-like gorge in front of the cliffs of St. Barthélemy before the road curls south by a big conifer tree (obviously planted) with a seat underneath. Beside the road to the right is a sign Promenade de Cap Roux durée 2hrs, and just beyond on the left is the start of the walk up St. Barthélemy. As you continue there is a good view of the coast ahead and the St. Tropez peninsula with the Maures mountain region behind. *The slopes of the Pic de Cap Roux mountains have lots of reddish scree which almost glows between the bright green of the Mediterranean vegetation.*

The road twists round and levels out through another barrier, reaching a flat area called the Plateau d'Antéor, where there is also a car park.

(2) Opposite the car park go up to the right ignoring the first two narrower turnings (55mins). This is a defined path (initially going northwest) but there are no markings. Shortly after at a T-junction bear up right. There is a yellow circle on a rock but these markings are few and far between. Below you can see the road you walked along as the path heads northeast.

(3) When you come to a cairn on a shoulder turn up right (1hr 15mins) following intermittent orange circles. This is a medium steep climb which still affords magnificent coastal views.

(4) At the Col du St. Pilon (1hr 30mins) where there is a large cairn, cross the ridge and take the path down the other side behind the cairn. This narrow track curls northeast round the back of the mountain going slightly down at first and now you get sweeping views of the Estérel. *On the horizon is Mont Vinaigre (Walk No. 8) and up left is the imposing television tower of the Pic de L'Ours.* Five minutes later ignore a path to the right and a large sign saying Pic de Cap Roux (a more direct way to the summit). You are now following blue circles, heading down left over patches of scree to a small open area which is a good spot to stop and admire the surrounding scenery (1hr 40mins) *(you can see the widening of the Grenouillet River as it leaves the ravine, near the Col de Belle Barbe, and the various peaks walked around on the Lake Ecureuil Walk No. 9).* The path continues becoming bushier as it loses height (eastwards).

(5) At a T-junction bear up right (1hr 45mins) to the Source de La Ste. Baume which is a series of terraces with a fountain on the top. Go straight on through a high wooden trellis to a grotto with a white cross in front. Retrace your steps to the Source and follow the sign to Chapelle St. Honorat which is the upper path left (1hr 50mins). Climb two terraces to the fountain (source) and bear left again.

(6) Take the first turning sharp back right by a small built-up wall. The path goes up medium steep with intermittent roughly hewn steps and a support bar over a rocky and steepish section. Follow the intermittent blue circles. *When you get to a small overhang you can just see the sea back on the left with the Pic de L'Ours up on the right.* The path goes round a gully (southwest) and under a ruined wall (all that is left of the original chapel); there is a tiny plastic statue of the Virgin in the wall! It continues down a number of rocky steps to the Grotto of St. Honorat (2hrs 10mins). *This is a large grotto underneath the rock, primitively decorated with a number of plaques to St. Honorat on the rock walls, artificial flowers and small statues. A notice (difficult to read) says that St. Honorat founded the monastery of the island of Lérins. According to popular tradition St. Baume sheltered Honorat while the monastery was being built. He was born around 380 AD into a pagan family. A monk lived here for more than 40 years (it could have been St. Honorat) and said of the Estérel: "When I think of my refuge I think of my place of paradise. It takes long to learn something and life is short". (This is a translation and not all was legible.) It is a lovely secluded spot and if you clamber up the rocks near the caves you have the perfect lookout!*

Retrace the steps to where you took the sharp right turn (No. 6 - it takes about 30mins there and back). Go right and upwards round the back of the mountain (northeast then east). Ignore a path going down left towards the Col de Cardinal, a rather lovely curved dip between the Pic du Cap Roux and the jagged Pic d'Aurelle.

The path becomes fairly steep over patches of scree and doubles back on itself. *You get a wonderful view of the coastline over on the left, with the two small flat Lerin Islands shimmering in the sea, and Cannes behind the wooded Peak de Théoule (looks like a small Christmas pudding from some angles!).* When you get back round to the front of the mountain you can see the road you started on and the parking area. Ignore a sign to Plateau d'Antheor and Grotte St. Baume and bear up to the observation point at 453m (3hrs). *Here there is a rather old plan and it is difficult to pick out the surrounding peaks from it. Nevertheless the view is extensive - the whole of the coastal area in front and the Estérel region behind - it is so beautiful that you can only catch your breathe and marvel!*

(7) Go back the way you came up and follow direction Plateau d'Anthéor etc. (although you will not be returning there). The path goes along the front of the mountain and then over patches of scree, following blue and orange circles. Keep straight, ignoring a left branch (3hr 15mins) but make your way towards some towering rocks (south).

(8) At an intersection with a sign indicating Pic de Cap Roux for those coming up, turn down left (right would take you back to the St-Baume). The path twists and turns down becoming bushier. You can again see the Rocher de St-Barthélemy. At a T-junction go right underneath a big rock (left is a longer way back) - 3hrs 30mins. There are now orange and red markings. The path becomes like a tunnel with high bushes each side and is flattish, with periodic patches of scree and open spaces.

(9) Just before you come to the cairn at the Col du St-Pilon, turn down left (there is a faded orange mark) - 3hrs 40mins. Careful - take the second turning left and not the first one which also has an orange marking and is steeper.

This path goes back across the slope at a lower level continuing to lose altitude, crossing big patches of scree. It then levels out before going down again fairly steeply to join the road opposite St-Barthélemy on a corner where there is the Pic de Cap Roux sign passed on the outward journey (4hrs).

(10) Turn left on the delightful last stretch down the road to the parking area (4hrs 30mins).

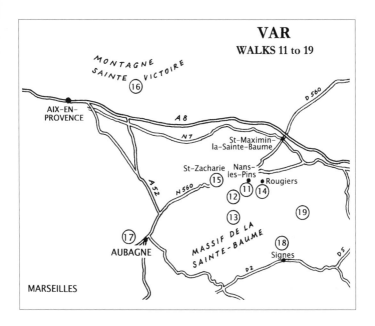

Var

Walk Nos. 11 - 19

Less glamorous than its neighbour Alpes Maritimes, the Var is nevertheless just as beautiful and its coastline has escaped the urban development which has taken over so much of the Riviera.

The coastal region stretches from the Estérel mountains in the east (which for practical reasons have here been included in the Alpes Maritimes area) to the town of Aubagne situated not far from Marseille. A varied jagged coastline of rocky inlets, creeks and sandy beaches, it includes the chic resort of St. Tropez, situated on one of the loveliest bays of the whole southern coastline. Only discovered in the 1950s, this once quaint fishing village is now the haunt of film stars, writers and artists.

Further east along the coast and now almost a suburb of Toulon, Hyères was the first place discovered and visited by the élite as a winter resort but was subsequently overshadowed by Nice and Cannes. 6kms off the coast are the three unspoilt Isles d'Hyères.

Toulon is the Var's largest town and port and France's second largest naval base. Because of this it was badly bombed in the Second World War. Renowned in Roman times for the manufacture of a purple dye which was the popular colour reserved for emperors and other leaders, it is still a bustling commercial centre, despite a ten per cent decline in its population since 1985 due to the transfer of naval personnel to Brest in the north. Toulon is ringed with hills from where there are good views of the town and the Mediterranean beyond

Behind the coastline, from east to west, are the Estérel (see Alpes Maritimes) and the Maures ranges, the latter a huge unspoilt forested area where there is little habitation. Further north is the long ridge of the Massif de Sainte Baume (see Walk No. 13) and northeast the white looming mass of the Sainte Victoire near Aix-en-Provence, beloved of the celebrated painter Cézanne (see Walk No. 16). A busy motorway cuts across the region north of these ranges but the Var extends right up to the famous Verdon Gorge (see Walk No. 40) and the large artificial Lac de Ste. Croix.

Between is a land of rocky hills, rolling countryside, forests and vineyards. Northeast start the limestone plateaux which spill into the Alpes Maritimes. There are hundreds of pretty little villages, some of them perched on rocky outcrops, others hidden in the folds of the hills and the only town of note is Draguignan. It is a tranquil and thinly populated area except in summer when it is swelled by tourists and second home owners whose village houses remain shuttered much of the rest of the year.

Because of its extensive forest ranges the Var is the region most ravaged by fires (mainly in the Estérel and Maures). These are caused mainly by the mistral, which fans the flames rapidly, burning up the rich forests of cork and chestnut, with their abundant animal and plant life turning large areas into bushland. Enormous sums of money are needed to create fire breaks and install water cisterns. Efforts are now being made to introduce flocks of sheep to stop the bush growing and create pastureland.

Agriculture consists of vineyards, horticulture and sheep rearing. The Var was the first Provençal area to produce wine, going back to the Greeks and the Romans. It produces 90 per cent of the Côtes de Provence but is known particularly for its Bandol red wines; Bandol being a small town on the coast east of Toulon which has been exporting its wine from the area since the 15th century. As in the Alpes Maritimes, the growing of spring flowers to send to the markets up north has long been a number one industry. The 1960s saw the construction of hundreds of greenhouses when numbers of French Algerians were repatriated to the area.

Sheep rearing continues but is less important than in the neighbouring Bouches du Rhône. The flocks leave the coastal plains in June and are taken to the higher regions north near the Verdon Gorge to remain there till October/November. This is called the transhumance (see Northern Provence).

Where to base yourself when walking in Var:

All the walks are within an hour's drive of the small town of St-Maximin la Ste. Baume (population 9594) on the N7 and just off the motorway to Cannes. It sits on a small plain but is surrounded by wooded hills and to the south is the impressive long ridge of the Ste-Baume. Its claim to fame is the basilica where according to legend Mary Magdalene, who lived for years as a hermit in a cave on the Ste-Baume, and St. Maximinus are buried in the crypt. The monastery and basilica were built by Charles of Anjou, who discovered the relics in 1279, and in 1295 they were acknowledged as authentic by Pope Bibufacio VIII. The Dominican order responsible for the relics lived in the monastery and the basilica became a place of pilgrimage. During the Revolution the monastery was taken over by Lucien Bonaparte, Napoleon's youngest brother, who turned it into a food depot. The Dominicans returned and only finally left in 1957 when the site was bought by private benefactors and turned into a cultural centre. The basilica attached to the monastery is conserved as it was when finally finished in 1532 and makes an interesting visit.

Brignols, further east on the N7, is bigger than St-Maximin and stands on a hill overlooking countryside stained red by the Bauxite mines from which over a million tons of metal are mined annually. This has not spoilt the quaint medieval aspect of Brignoles which makes a good centre.

The author stayed in Nans-les-Pins, a small village on the D80 south of St-Maximin which has a golf course on its outskirts. It is a surprisingly sophisticated village attractively set round a tree-lined square where there is a small lively market on Wednesday mornings. There are a number of new houses in the pine woods surrounding the village and this is obviously a popular retirement spot. On the hill behind are the ruins of the medieval village and feudal castle built in the 12th century (see Walk No. 11). It has only two small hotels and one 4-star near the golf course. There is a charming campsite in the woods. Otherwise there are few hotels in the little villages around the Ste-Baume and not many chambres d'hôtes, though there are plenty of campsites.

Walk No. 11
CASTLE RUINS AND SAINTE CROIX, NANS-LES-PINS

Difficulty:	Easy walk although be careful around the castle ruins.
Time:	2hrs.
Height gain:	270m.
Maps:	Cartes IGN 3345 OT Top 25 Signes.Tourves 1:25,000.
	Cartes IGN L'Arrière Pays Toulonnais 1:50,000.
Depart from:	Chapelle de la Miséricorde, Nans-les-Pins.
Signposting:	Good new signs - yellow, red and blue splashes.

Observations:
A delightful short walk above Nans-les-Pins with maximum views, especially of the nearby Sainte Baume mountain. It is especially recommended for people who are interested in the Mediterranean trees and bushes which flourish in the area. Please note that the walk around the castle ruins is done at your own risk.

How to get there:
From St-Maximin-la-Ste-Baume take the N560 and then the D80 to Nans-les-Pins. As you come into the village, go straight at a crossroads where there are traffic lights. In the centre of the village, passing the village square on your left, continue up the narrow street called Grand Rue (there are two fountains) to the quaint little chapel at the top (Chapelle de la Miséricorde). Turn left and park in a small parking spot on the right (there is a P sign so you can't miss it).

Directions:
(1) Go out of the car park and turn left passing in front of the chapel. *The Chapelle de la Miséricorde was built by the White Penitents in 1623 (see Walk No. 1).* Beyond there is a noticeboard indicating the start of several walks. Follow signs to the Circulaire du Vieux Nans et Ste-Croix and the Sentier Botanique which is also part of the walk. Walk up the Chemin de la Bouaou on a wide paved path at the side of the chapel till you reach a T-junction.

(2) Go left following the sign Sentier Botanique, Ruines du Château on a wide stony path with initially a hedge on one side and a fence on the other. There is a yellow arrow followed by yellow and blue flashes. You quickly leave suburbia behind as you contour the side of a hill bearing south and rising gently through open bush country. There is a lovely view to the left of the

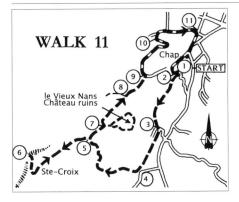

dominating ridge of the Ste-Baume.

After 10mins there are ruins on both sides of the path which are probably part of the old château higher up. There is a sign on the right, *Ruines des maisons du Vieux Nans deserted in the 15th century and reoccupied by "pest-ières" (people fleeing from the plague) in the 17th century.* The path then goes down to a T-junction (15mins).

(3) Turn right uphill for about 20m and then branch down left (there is a yellow splash on a telephone pole) on a narrow path. There is a house through the trees on the left and an old stone wall on the right. Follow this path till it reaches a paved road and more signposts.

(4) Turn up right following the sign Sentier Botanique/Ruines du Château (20mins) and through a barrier. There is a notice here saying that this path was constructed with the help of pupils from the Nans-les-Pins primary school. All along this path there are wooden signs in front of trees, bushes and plants native to the Mediterranean region, including Aleppo pine, wild asparagus, vibernum, honeysuckle, amelanchier, cistus and pistachio.

At a fork go right (there is a large blue cross on the left). The wide path goes up medium steep and there are blue splashes. Shortly after a sign on the left indicating Ancien Cabane de Charbonnier (old charcoal burner's hut) there is a signpost left to Sainte Croix (40mins).

(5) Take this narrow path left, which goes to the cross and back, following red splashes. The bushy path goes up and under wires. There are beautiful views of the Sainte Baume ridge on the left and behind over the extensive ruins of the old village and château. The path winds upwards and then bears left. On the right is a large heap of rocks and then a second one which you cross following red splashes. At the summit there is a cross in a concrete base.

(6) When you scramble to the top the view is glorious (1hr). *South is the Sainte Baume ridge ringed by an extensive forest. West and north are rolling hills and wild looking country unspoilt by signs of habitation though there is evidence of extensive forest fires. In the foreground is the Montagne de Regagnas with the St-Jean de Puy straight ahead and the projecting "Baou"*

Playing boules in Nans-les-Pins

of Mt. Olympe to the right. On the horizon is the white ridge of Mont Ste, Victoire. To the east you can see the village of Nans-les-Pins.

Retrace your steps to the signpost (1hr 15mins) and turn up left passing a pretty picnic area where the path bears slightly to the left and the end of the Sentier Botanique.

(7) At a narrow crossroads there are blue splashes on the stones indicating Nans left, but if you follow the splashes ahead they lead to the ruins of the château on the top of the hill. Watch for a blue left fork sign and an arrow on the way up. **Careful here** - there is a worn red danger sign and you go up at your own risk. Keep to the indicated path and do not wander off to explore the ruins further as they are crumbling. *The castle and fortified village were built in the 12th century when all habitation was on the top of elevated land so that the villagers could see the enemy approaching. They were inhabited until the 15th century and then again in 1720 when distraught peasants were fleeing from the plague.*

The views are extensive in all directions and you can see the rock summit and the Sainte Croix clearly behind. Down below in front is Nans-les-Pins. Retrace your steps and turn right to Nans (1hr 25mins) which is a pleasant path but steep and rocky for a while so you have to watch your feet. At a fork go down right (blue cross on left).

(8) The path goes down through dense wood and tall bushes to a T-junction where there are signs. Turn right and continue to a barrier and another T-junction at a paved road. Here is a sign saying "interdiction de pénétrer à l'intérieur des ruines et de circuler aux alentours" (do not go into the castle ruins) (1hr 40mins).

(9) Turn left (right is *privé*) and after a few minutes you reach a paved road and the village cemetery behind a wall with attractive clipped rosemary bushes (rosemary for remembrance) in front. This is a typical village cemetery; most of the crosses and stones are identical, presumably the work of the local craftsman. Passing a dead orchard on the right the road reaches the outskirts of the village.

(10) Where the road divides keep round to the right towards the church spire (do not go straight by the old washhouse where there is a GR sign). This takes you into the village proper on the Chemin de la Font Vieille.

(11) Turn up right in the Place du 18 Juin 1940 and continue to the chapel at the top (this is the same street you drove up) (1hr 50mins).

Walk No. 12
CHAPEL OF NOTRE DAME D'ORGNON

Difficulty:	Medium but fairly long circular walk.
Time:	5hrs.
Height gain:	No appreciable height gain.
Maps:	Cartes IGN 3345 OT Top 25 Signes.Tourves 1:25,000* (see below).
	Cartes IGN L'Arrière Pays Toulonnais 1:50,000.
Depart from:	From the Chapelle de la Miséricorde, Nans-les-Pins.
Signposting:	Good - follow the red/white GR splashes and also the yellow splashes. Note: For the last half hour to the chapel there are faded red splashes or none at all. You are on private property and the owners would not let the way be repainted.

Observations:
A long full day walk with no great height gain in an area where you will meet very few people - this is the real Provence! The signposting is good except for the last part to the chapel which is on private property. We actually met the owner of the property who turned out to be a charming Israeli gentleman who laughingly said that he was going to turn the chapel into a synagogue! He does not mind people coming through his newly acquired land as long as

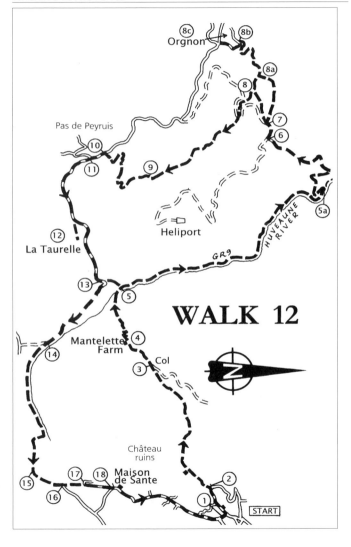

Orgnon

Pas de Peyruis

Heliport

La Taurelle

GR9

HUVEAUNE RIVER

WALK 12

Mantelette Farm

Col

N

Château ruins

Maison de Sante

START

there are no markings.

> *On the 1:25,000 Signes. Tourves No. 3345 map the last part up to the chapel is missing. It is also not shown on the adjoining No. 3344 St-Maximin-la-Ste-Baume which is unusual. The whole walk is clearer on the L'Arrière Pays Toulonnais 1:50,000 edition.*

How to get there:
From St-Maximin-la-Ste-Baume take the N560 and then the D80 to Nans-les-Pins. As you enter the village, go straight at a crossroads where there are traffic lights. In the centre of the village, passing the village square on your left, continue up the narrow street called Grand Rue (there are two fountains), to the quaint little chapel at the top (Chapelle de la Miséricorde). Turn left here, which is your only option, and park in a small parking spot on the right (there is a P sign so you can't miss it).

Directions:
(1) Go out of the car park and turn left passing in front of the chapel. *The Chapelle de la Miséricorde was built by the White Penitents in 1623 (see Walk No. 1).* Beyond there is a noticeboard indicating the start of several walks. Follow the sign to Sentier circulaire de Notre Dame d'Orgnon 5hrs. Walk up the Chemin de Bouaou which is a wide paved path at the side of the chapel to a T-junction.

(2) Turn right following Notre Dame d'Orgnon par la Vallée de l'Huveaune (there is also a sign left to the chapel so you could return this way). You are now on a path with yellow splashes (attempts have been made to obliterate the older red and blue ones). The path goes above the cemetery down to the right.

Five minutes later (yellow cross ahead) turn left through a barrier and take the main path, not the narrow one going up sharp left. There is a sign which says interdiction d'entrer dans les ruines (do not go inside the ruins). Continue through cool scented woodland with lots of bushes and small oaks. Ignore the path to the left indicating Ruines du Château.

Following yellow splashes continue on the main path which goes to the Col de Mantelette. The path bears round to the left (20mins) and you can now see the ruins of the castle and the cross on the peak. This area was ravaged by a forest fire in 1980. It is dotted with bare tree stumps and dead branches but the vegetation has grown up covering the worst aspect of the charred remains. As you continue there is a good view ahead of the edge of the western edge of the Sainte Baume with its TV aerials and observatory.

(3) The path goes down gently to a sandy intersection at the Col de Mantelette (33mins) where you go straight on (crosses on stones indicate where not to go) and descend into a valley. Go past a fig tree by a ruin and then an old water cistern on the right through the bushes to a T-junction (40mins).

(4) Take the more obvious way to the left (no signs here) and after a few minutes you reach the Mantelette farm on the left situated in an idyllic glade with a lone tall cypress near it. It has been recently renovated and there is a sign on it saying Association Privée de Phari. The path continues down into a delightful open valley with not a house in sight - you can see a jeep track running right through it. Ignore a path off to the left and bear right at a T-junction (yellow splashes). You can now hear the Huveaune river flowing through bushes on the left.

(5) When you arrive at a junction (50mins) go right following indications St-Zacharie Chapelle d'Orgnon. Do not cross the river left by a wooden bridge (signs to Sainte Baume, Nans-les-Pins par les Aumèdes) nor over a concrete ford immediately after. You are now on the GR9 so follow the red/white splashes. The jeep track turns into a narrower valley with the Huveaune river on the left; the slopes are attractively scattered with woodland including oaks, pine and broom.

The track crosses the river (55mins) by a little concrete ford (there was not much water when we did the walk but you may have to remove your shoes after heavy rainfall). The river is now on the right as you continue through the valley and the Bois (woods) des Fauvouillères as indicated on the map. Cross another ford a few minutes later by a minuscule waterfall - the river comes and goes, sometimes down on the left in a miniature gorge, at other times level with the jeep track. There are tall rocks on the right as the path continues level and then reaches a green barrier with a "one way only" sign on it which seems to guard the entrance to the valley. Up to the right is another barrier with a cross (1hr 15mins). Go on straight crossing another ford 5mins later - the slopes each side are less high here and the river is now down on the right.

(5A) At an intersection (1hr 25mins) leave the GR9 which goes straight on, and turn left, signposted Notre Dame d'Orgnon. The wide track swings back left and upwards - now follow the yellow splashes again. Go up medium steep, direction southwest, for approximately 10mins and then round the side of the hill through scattered pines. Turn left at a T-junction (yellow cross on right) - 1hr 35mins. The terrain has now levelled out and there are stunted oaks and bushes.

(6) Ignoring all branches off, keep on the main path which bears left and comes to another intersection. Right is a barrier which says Bellevue S.47, half right is a cross. Continue straight past a big green tank and branch right 100m later at a T-junction (it says Heliport here). Keep on the main track to a pass in a clearing with tall pines (1hr 50mins). There may be a number of horses in a corral to the right and hidden in the trees behind some sort of habitation. There is a sign saying La Mouère. The jeep track continues down.

(7) Careful here: Just past the corral there is a narrow path to the right with yellow splashes. This goes down into the valley where there are signposts. If you miss it go straight down the jeep track round a lefthand bend and into a righthand hairpin. You can see the valley on the right and the chapel of Notre Dame d'Orgnon perched on top of a bushy crag (how on earth did they manage to build it there!). It looks quite a distance away.

(8) On the hairpin there is a crossroads with yellow signs on both sides - go right and descend into the valley to the signposts. You will come back across here on the return journey. The path into the valley passes newly planted oak trees inside protection cylinders.

(8A) Follow the sign to Notre Dame d'Orgnon along the narrow bushy valley which seems to go lower and lower while the chapel on its crag appears higher and higher! The path comes to a green barrier (2hrs 10mins) and crosses a low concrete bridge over the stream. Here you see a yellow splash but from now till the chapel there are no more splashes (though you can see the occasional faded red markings). **You are entering private property, and although you are allowed to continue the owner does not want signs of any kind (see above).** Respect these wishes and do not stray off the main path which winds up medium steep.

(8B) When you reach a T-junction turn right (2hrs 20mins). There is a fascinating old well on the left where you can peer through a grill to the water far below. Just after the well is another metal gate, at an entrance to a property. Careful here: Just before the gate turn up right, but keep to the top field with bushes on your right rather than going straight across the field as otherwise you will get on the wrong path. Enter the woods between two laburnum trees (in bloom when we did the walk in May).

(8C) Turn left on to a narrow rocky path which goes behind an old house on the left and starts to climb past a rusty iron cross on the left. This is the first of the stations of the cross (Chemins de la Croix) which go up to the chapel - the path winds up with an old stone wall on one side passing all the crosses till it reaches the chapel (2hrs 20mins) perched on the top of a bushy crag. *It is normally shut, but looking through the keyhole you can see that it has an altar and benches etc. In fact mass is celebrated here every Easter Monday followed by a Fête Champêtre (a local celebration, there is no real translation for this word). Otherwise the chapel is kept locked.*

Just beyond the chapel is a large crucifix (altitude 420m) which was erected in 1919 in memory of the Second World War. This is an ideal spot for a picnic as the view is magnificent - you can see right down to the village of St-Zacharie with the Raganas mountain behind and the St-Jean de Puy mountain to the right (Walk No. 15). The Mont Sainte Victoire is visible on the skyline on a clear day.

The Chapelle Notre Dame d'Orgnon is situated on an ancient Roman temple which was the site of the original village of St. Zacharie. Reconstructed in 1832 there is an inscription written inside the chapel: "The inhabitants of the region, even before 1033, dedicated a sanctuary here to the Virgin Mary. It fell into ruins in 1428 but was restored in 1609".

Retrace your steps to the ford (2hrs 40mins) and 5mins later you are back at the signposts in the bottom of the valley. Follow the signpost indicating Nans-les-Pins par le Pas de Peyrius, straight up the jeep track. At the jeep track (8) go straight across following yellow splashes (2hrs 50mins). This wide path undulates gently upwards into the pretty Chambeyron valley which has sporadic woodland and a tree planting scheme with lots of plastic cylinders dotting the hillside.

Keep to the main path bearing right and following the yellow splashes. There is now a steady climb up the hillside in wide bends to a plateau (3hrs 15mins) where you have a good view of the surrounding mountains including the eastern end of the Sainte Baume with its TV aerials and observatory. It is quite bare up here with only low shrubs including cistus and numerous herbs, the classical Provençal garrigue.

(9) Go straight on, not round to the left where there is an obvious path with a cross. There is a ruin of a charcoal burner's hut on the right. From here you can see down to the Peyruis river valley on the right with a tarmac road and other jeep tracks. The path winds down fairly steeply southwards into the valley, passing a long ridge of rock with pines on top. There is a rock escarpment coming down from the other side and the road goes through where they meet - this is the Pas de Peyruis.

(10) The path reaches the narrow tarmac road at an attractive glade (3hrs 30mins) where it is clearly indicated to go left through the Pas de Peyruis (yellow markings). The Peyruis River runs far down on the right amongst rocks and the whole area is extremely pretty. Continue down past the ruins of the old village of Peyruis (not really visible) till you see a bridge over the river on the right (3hrs 35mins).

(11) Do not cross the river but continue straight on a wide jeep track through a barrier at a sign La Taurelle. The river is still on the right and beyond you can see the road going up. This leads through a wide shallow valley where there are cultivated fields on the right - we saw hay being collected when we did the walk.

(12) You can see the building of Taurelle farm which it is worth going off the road to visit - the farm itself is of no interest but the site is idyllic and you can walk over the foundations of an ancient Roman villa!

Regain the road (3hrs 50mins) and continue down the wide valley - lots of new trees were planted here in 1992. *There is a large sign here indicating that the firm Guigoz (baby milk manufacturers) were responsible for replanting the 1660 new trees. On the right are small cultivated fields and mown hay. There is also an enchanting small lake which looks even more beautiful with a small conical hill behind it. It looks a delightful spot to stop for a quick dip but there is a sign at the end of the lake saying fishing and swimming prohibited!*

(13) Continue on the main jeep track which bends left to more signposts (4hrs). You have now met the GR9 again. Follow the sign Nans-les-Pins par Les Aumèdes (there is also Nans-les-Pins par la Mantelette which is a shorter way back and taken on the early part of the walk). Follow the GR9 splashes along the wide jeep track which has rejoined the Huveaune River flowing on the left.

(14) Cross a cement bridge which has a GR splash and signpost Source de L'Huveaune par le Vallon de Castelette (do not go up right). The track climbs gently via spaced out woodland through a green barrier (4hrs 15mins) where there is a sign Forêt Dominale de la Sainte Baume. As you climb up through sparse pine forest look for a sign indicating Nans-les- Pins straight ahead (4hrs 20mins). Here the GR9 goes off to the right to the Sainte Baume.

(15) From now on follow yellow and orange splashes along an attractive undulating path through intermittent woodland and clearings. The path then bears downwards around to the left - there is a wall on the righthand side. Soon there are one or two houses visible through the trees on the left. The track goes through a further fire barrier where it says S.35 La Taurelle and there are more signposts 200m later (4hrs 30mins).

Go left following the sign Nans-les-Pins and you are now on the GR9A and the well-known Chemin des Rois - to the right is indicated La Grotte de Ste-Marie Magdalene (see Walk No. 13). The track continues to Les Aumèdes where there is a large factory on the left which looks deserted. At the factory the road becomes concrete.

(16) Watch for a sign to the left which indicates Nans-les-Pins/Sentier Botanique and GR markings. The narrower track goes through tall pine forest with an occasional house visible through the trees.

(17) At a tarmac road turn right (4hrs 40mins) through open cultivated country. Continue to follow the red/white signs through Le Centre de Cure et de Rééducation Respiratoire (a centre for respiratory problems).

(18) The narrow paved road goes gently up and then down. Follow a signpost straight on to Nans-les-Pins direct, where the Sentier Botanique is off to the right. This takes you into the village faster, along the road where you parked the car. Turn left into the car park (5hrs).

Walk No. 13
TOUR OF THE SAINTE BAUME - Alt. 1148m

Difficulty:	Strenuous but no difficult scrambling.
Time:	5hrs 15mins (includes walking time there and back to the shrine without extra time for looking around).
	Note - in summer 1998 the shrine was closed for renovations.
Height gain:	475m.
Maps:	Cartes IGN 3345 OT Top 25 Signes.Tourves 1:25,000.
	Cartes IGN L'Arrière Pays Toulonnais 1:50,000.
Depart from:	Hôtellerie de la Sainte Baume on the D80.
Signposting:	Good in parts - follow yellow splashes carefully at the start through the wood. Along the top are the red/white splashes of the GR9.

Observations:
A delightful and dramatic walk with magnificent views. The path through the forest at the bottom of the mountain is quite long (2hrs) but very beautiful. If you feel you may not manage the whole walk just walk up to the shrine and back, or up to the Col du St- Pilon.

Information on the Sainte Baume:
The Sainte Baume, 30km long and 12km wide, is a long craggy limestone mountain, not far from Marseille, Toulon and Aix-en-Provence. Since the 12th century the impressive grotto hewn out of the rock face on the southern side has been a place of pilgrimage linked to the cult of St. Mary Magdalene. According to Provençal legend Mary Magdalene passed the last years of her life preaching and converting in Provence; she died and was buried in the Basilica of St-Maximin-la-Ste-Baume.

Since the 5th century the shrine has been inhabited by different religious denominations: the Cassianites (415 - 1079), the Benedictines (1079-1295) and the Dominicans Prêcheur (prêcheur means preaching) from 1295 until the present day.

The Hôtellerie, where the walk starts, is run and lived in by the Dominicans. It is a place of worship and retreat as well as a place where people can stay.

There is an interesting museum opposite the Hôtellerie, the Ecomusée de

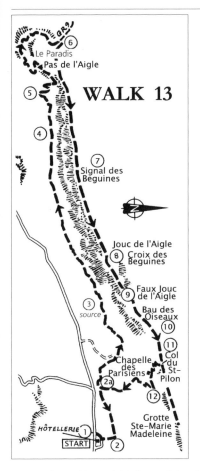

La Sainte Baume, with fascinating exhibits about the mountain and the region. It also gives an insight as to how people lived and worked in the area before it was opened up to tourism. Open every day except Thursdays from 15 April to 30th October, 9.00 to 12.00 and 14.00 to 18.00 (out of season 14.00 to 18.00 only). Entrance fee - children free.

Last but not least the Sainte Baume is one of the major stopping places for the famous Tour de France cycle race!

How to get there:
From St-Maximin-la-Ste-Baume take the N560 towards Marseille for 9kms. Then take the D80 to Nans-les-Pins and Plan d'Aups. L'Hôtellerie is 8kms from Nans-les-Pins and there is plenty of parking.

Directions:
(1) Take the path to the east of the Hôtellerie, just after the La Terrasse café. There is a sign saying Grotte de la Sainte Marie Madeleine - haut lieu de prière et de pélerinage (Grotto of Saint Mary Magdalene - a renowned place of prayer and pilgrimage) - see above for further details. You are starting off on the GR9.

Go along this straight flat path bordered to the right with hawthorn bushes. A few minutes later you enter the Fôret Domaniale de la Sainte Baume which is a réserve biologique.

(2) Turn left onto the indicated *Chemin des Roys/Grotte Ste-Baume. The Chemin des Roys, or path of kings, commemorates all the kings who have walked that way to worship at the grotto. It was also the road from Nans-les-Pins to the Sainte Baume until the construction of the D80 in 1897.* The

89

well trodden wide flat path goes straight through a mature forest of pine, beech and oak. Follow the yellow splashes.

(2A)   At a picnic area, ignore the path up to the right signposted to the Grotto (this is where you will return). Continue straight through a barrier (yellow splash on an electricity pole) with the picnic area to the left (15mins).

   Be careful: About 5mins after the parking area, watch for a yellow arrow on two stones showing a path bearing up to the right (it is easy to miss). This is a slightly narrower path going up through woodland towards the rock face of the Sainte Baume; follow the yellow markings carefully as there are quite a number of alternative branches. Be careful again at a rather confusing intersection where three paths join - do not take the main one going left, nor the one right, but the one in the middle which is the narrowest and has the yellow markings (25mins). Five minutes later you reach the Source de Ravel (spring), which is an ugly basin with a pipe coming out.

(3) Cross over the larger track and continue upwards following the yellow splashes towards the towering cliffs which you catch glimpses of through the trees. Be careful to branch off right where the flashes indicate (35mins) and ignore all other paths. You pass a high white bank as you continue east and veer to the left with the cliffs on your right. The path meanders through dark, rather menacing woods with lots of tall trees and little undergrowth. At a fork go right (marking on stone on left) which leads to a large standing rock on the left of the path (45mins). On it is a memorial plaque to Dr. Joseph Poucel (1878-1971) recalling that he loved this magnificent forest and made many botanical discoveries in the region. This is the start of what is called *Le sentier merveilleux*.

   The path goes on through this wood for what seems like a long time - keep following the yellow splashes as you undulate along the bottom of the cliffs which can be glimpsed from time to time through the tall trees to the right. There are some majestic ancient trees in this forest that have grown untouched for centuries; formerly belonging to the church, the whole of this vast woodland area is now a nature reserve. The path climbs steadily and you think you are going to emerge from the trees but you don't.

   At a jumble of rocks follow the yellow splashes left (1hr), then right immediately after at a T-junction (left drops down to the jeep track you can see from time to time through the trees). Continue through the forest. Keep right at the next fork following yellow splashes and a few minutes later there is an enormous gnarled yew tree on the right surrounded by big boulders.

(4) The path comes out on to a larger track where you turn right (1hr 30mins) - remember to keep the cliffs on the righthand side! This is a wide track with lovely beech trees either side which finally reaches a gigantic beech tree (1hr 50mins) in a delightful glade.

Walking the rocky ridge of Sainte Baume

(5) At the beech tree take the little path to the right (still yellow flashes) which heads upwards towards the cliffs. You are now leaving the forest behind you as bear up right at a small T-junction. There are magnificient views down across the valley and village of Nans-les-Pins with the mountains beyond - the Montagne de Regagnas left, Mt. Olympe above St. Zacharie (see Walk No. 15) with in front the plum pudding shape of Mont Piveau and right Mt. Aurélien. In the distance is the dramatic grey ridge of the Mont-Ste-Victoire. The path enters a charming grassy ravine with cliffs either side, like a wide cleft. There are huge cliffs to the right. This is the Gorge de St-Cassien.

Careful: At a lefthand corner the yellow splashes turn up right on a steep but easily negotiable path to the top of the Ste-Baume ridge at the Pas l'Ai which takes 5mins. This will save 20mins if you are tired or in a hurry but you miss walking through a dramatically beautiful area called Le Paradis - and it really is paradise!

Continue down the ravine which in springtime is like walking through a rock garden - *the slopes are ablaze with a kaleidoscope of flowering rock plants such as thyme, rosemary, potentilla, heavenly blue, creamy rock roses: it is quite overwhelming. The grass is an intense green, there are delightfully flowering bushes and the weirdly shaped white rocks frame this idyllic small patch of intense beauty.* At the end is a jumble of rocks which looks impenetrable at first glance but there is a way through! Immediately on the other side fork back hard right and clamber up to the ridge with the ravine down on the right. There is a path but it is not always very clear.

(6) On the ridge (2hrs 25mins) - turn right (southwest) following yellow markings, newly painted in 1998, which soon join the more defined path of the GR9 coming up left from the village of Signes to the south. The red/white GR splashes go across the summit (west) from now to the end of the walk. It is not easy to follow although if you look back you can see the path more clearly. The summit of the Sainte Baume is rather featureless and rocky as it is a limestone mountain. *In springtime it is colourful with flowering rock plants and herbs. There are also orchids, the majestic lily like asphodels and wild narcissus amongst many others. There are no big trees and few bushes except at the eastern end.*

There are of course fantastic views in all directions and to the south you can see along the coast as far as the Cap de l'Estérel with the ocean shimmering beyond. Keep to the GR as there are other paths which take you under the cliffs and you may find you are gradually descending the northern slope before you should!

(7) The GR continues across the ridge to a cairn at the Signal des Beguines (2hrs 55mins).

(8) Further on watch carefully for a GR sign bearing left on a short scramble round the back of the rocky cliff and up to the summit of the Jouc de l'Aigle, 1148m; the direct way up would be too difficult. At the top there is a cross marked on the map as the Croix des Beguines (3hrs 20mins).

Pick your way over the rocks of the Jouc de l'Aigle and turn right (clear GR red/white splashes here) down a narrow cleft in the rocks. It can be slippery so take care. The path bears left round the bottom of the cliff and then up again to the summit and several cairns called the Faux Jouc de l'Aigle (faux meaning false!) (3hrs 40mins).

(9) Continue down past cairns and follow the red/white splashes. Go left (3hrs 45mins) avoiding the way ahead marked by a cross even though it looks as if it is going in the right direction.

(10) The path goes down and left round the Bau des Oiseaux - in springtime the rocks here are bright with clumps of heavenly blue flowers. You feel you will not get back up to the summit but you do!

(11) At the Col du St-Pilon (4hrs) follow the GR9 which turns off right down the north side of the Sainte Baume to the Hôtellerie. (The GR98 continues along the crest to the tall TV aerial and other installations you can see on the skyline. There is a path all the way down to the village of Gemenos, a suburb of Aubagne.)

The GR9 is a well-defined jeep track, initially a series of wide stony steps. There is a shrine on the right near the top and soon the track enters tall beech forest where the cliff edge is littered with huge ivy-covered boulders. It reaches a tumbledown chapel on the right called Chapelle des Parisiens (4hrs 10mins). For much of the way there is a low fence made of intertwined branches on the left.

(12) Five minutes later there is a junction by another shrine. Right goes directly down to the Hôtellerie but first go up left and climb the 150 steps to see the famous shrine of St. Mary Magdalene (the 150 steps representing the 150 Ave Marias of the rosary and the 150 psalms of David) - this is what thousands of pilgrims come every year to see and venerate. The shrine is an impressive though not particularly attractive building right in the cliff face - from the path below it towers above so it is quite a stiff climb; the Beatitudes are inscribed on plaques on the way up to encourage you!

When you arrive at the top of the steps look back at the bronze statues of the crucifixion in a cleft in the rock face, erected in 1914. *The grotto or church itself is hewn out of the rock and is dark with huge statues lit up by hundreds of candles (a statue of Mary Magdalene surrounded by stone plaques giving thanks for wishes granted etc.) and has some lovely stained glass windows in the front. It is interesting to read the names of the famous people who have visited the shrine over the centuries, including Henry II in the 14th century on his return from the Holy Land and Louis XIV.*

There is a somewhat eerie feel to the place but it is amazing to think that a shrine could exist here for hundreds of years in such a remote spot - interestingly the grotto remains at the same temperature winter and summer ie. 12° centigrade. (For further details see above.)

Retrace your steps back to the intersection (4hrs 45mins). It takes approximately 30mins to get to the shrine and back not counting the time you take to visit. Continue downwards on the wide jeep track, passing another spring on the right, Source de Nans (a concrete fountain). The path gets smoother lower down and reaches the intersection by the picnic area and car park passed on the outward journey (5hrs). Turn left and retrace your steps to the Hôtellerie - watch carefully for the GR splashes and the Chemin des Roys signpost where the path turns right out of the forest (5hrs 15mins).

Walk No. 14
WALK TO THE OLD VILLAGE AND CHÂTEAU OF ROUGIERS

Difficulty:	Medium with some scrambling over rocks on the way down from the Piégu. Alternative walk there and back to the Château is medium steep but short.
Time:	lhr 10mins (short walk) 3hrs 30mins (longer walk).
Height gain:	250m.
Maps:	Cartes IGN 3345 OT Top 25 Signes.Tourves 1:25,000.
	Cartes IGN L'Arrière Pays Toulonnais 1:50,000.
Depart from:	Centre of Rougiers.
Signposting:	Follow green splashes carefully all the way.

Observations:
A very pleasant walk in a relatively undiscovered area, so if you want to get away from it all this is the place! The way down from the Piégu is rather a scramble but well worth it. I have looked in vain for information on the delightful little village of Rougiers - happily I can find nothing so let us hope it remains "undiscovered"!

How to get there:
From St-Maximin-la-Ste-Baume take the N560 direction St-Zacharie (Marseilles). At the crossroads with the D80 to Nans-les-Pins turn left towards Brignoles. A few kilometres later on you will see the sign to Rougiers on the right. Drive into the village and park in the central square.

Directions:
(1) Walk out of the square following the sign *site médiévale* direction south. This goes in front of the village school down the Rue des Ecoles and then up right on the Chemin St. Anne. On the hill you can see the ruins of the old village with the ruined château above and the church which appears intact. Continue gently upwards on a paved road till you come to a large cruxifix at a crossroads (5mins). Go straight over here and continue for a short distance but, where the road curls round to the left at a sign Les Glacières CD95, go straight again.

(2) *Careful here* - almost at the start of this road, where there is a sign saying *Gîte d'étape* and just before a stone building with a fence round the top, look for green arrows and the number E41 indicating a narrow path up the side of the building. Go up this narrow path which winds fairly steeply through

94

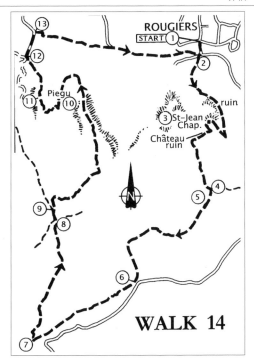

woodland all the way to the medieval village (35mins). At two initial forks keep left following green splashes - the path is evident all the way up and there are some obvious short cuts.

Higher up it gets stonier and looks as if it has been used for hundreds of years! There is a branch off to the right to further ruins. Keep going, past a grotto with a rock holding it up which looks exactly like a tree trunk, till you reach the church of St-Jean (40mins).

This is an old chapel in a lovely setting but in need of further restoration. It has a small refuge on the side which must originally have been used by pilgrims. On a rock in front there is a statue of the Virgin and child. From this rocky promontory there is a magnificent view of the ruins just below, the green mountains beyond and the village of Rougiers - centrepiece in the valley. **If you don't want to do the long walk** *- look around the church and château and then retrace your steps.*

(3) Otherwise: make your way to the ruins of the old château behind and, still following green splashes, go straight down past a picnic area on a defined wide stony track passing a green water tank on the left. Continue down with woods either side until you reach a track off to the right (55mins).

(4) Go right here - there is a green arrow on a rock with E41, also yellow splashes and a sign Gambord S23.

(5) *Careful* - almost immediately look for a green splash to the left in a small clearing and take this path (southwest). After merging about 5mins later with a path from the left, you should then follow green and blue splashes. This is a pleasant path meandering through woods, glades and some small fields of grain planted for the wild animals to feed on before they are shot during the hunting season. The path bears to the left - do not go right (there is a cross on a tree). Continue to ignore all branches off and be careful to follow green/blue splashes.

(6) The path almost reaches a paved road D95 at a large pile of stones which is all that remains of an old sheepfold (*bergerie*) (1hr 15mins). Keep going with the road on the left, through an open clearing where a path goes off to the left. Continue straight following green/blue splashes, going under the wires of a pylon (1hr 35mins) and crossing a wider track.

(7) After a few minutes you can see the road on the left again and 5mins later the path reaches a wide jeep track where you turn sharp right (north) following green splashes and a sign ET41. This is where you leave the blue splashes. The jeep track goes down gently under high tension wires again past two fire signs. On the right is Cambon S23 and the track is entering Fumeou S25.

(8) After the jeep track flattens out go straight at a crossroads (1hr 55mins).

(9) Immediately after go right at a fork (there is a very faint green sign on a rock saying Piégu) and then straight away right again. The path passes another grain field with a small ruin behind. The wide track heads gently upwards towards the Piégu ridge, but since you cannot see it you feel you are wandering around in woodland without getting anywhere! Just keep to the path with the green splashes and ignore a yellow marked path off to the right. Finally, when the woods open out, you can see the ruined village and the church over on the right.

The track narrows and becomes stony and bushier as you approach the top of the Piégu. Without warning you reach a huge pile of stones which the path crosses to the summit (2hrs 15mins).

(10) From this ridge of stone there is an extensive view facing south. Straight ahead is the rocky eastern edge of the Ste-Baume called the Paradis - on the extreme left is the Mourre d'Agnis ridge and on the near left the medieval village and château of Rougiers. Down on the right is Nans-les-Pins.

Continue following green splashes - the path circles round the end of this bushy rock spur to a lookout and borne (marker). From here there is an extensive view north over St-Maximin-la-Ste-Baume with the Mont Aurélien ridge to the left of the town and other mountains beyond - it is amazing how wooded the region looks from on high! The path starts to descend and there are two further lookout areas. You are going down a steep and narrow, rocky bushy path, so watch your footing here. There are four tricky places where you have to scramble over rocks but there are green splashes all the way.

After about 20mins of scrambling, the path becomes flatter and goes through a long delightful leafy tunnel where the branches of the trees meet overhead. There is a high rock on the left at one point (2hrs 40mins) - if the sun happens to be filtering through the leaves it is even more idyllic!

(11) At a fork (3hrs) keep straight following green splashes past a ruin in a glade (you can see the jeep track already on the left).

(12) Turn down right when the path joins the jeep track 5mins later.

(13) *Careful here.* After passing a house on the left, look for a narrow path on the right on a slight corner. There are no green splashes but a green cross on a tree. (If you have missed the path you will reach the D1 road from Rougiers to Tourves at the official end of the green E41 path.) This raised wooded path takes you towards the village. Go straight, ignoring other branches. Down on the left are cultivated fields and vineyards. The path merges with a wider path coming in parallel from below.

(14) At a T-junction turn right on to a jeep track. It goes behind the outskirts of the village with gardens and new houses on the left and reaches a road where you turn down left passing the Gîte d'étape and green E41 signs at the start of the walk. Retrace your steps into the village (3hrs 30mins).

Walk No. 15
ST-JEAN DE PUY AND MONT OLYMPE - Alt. 819m

Difficulty:	Medium. Strenuous if including climb to the top of Mont Olympe.
Time:	4hrs 35mins - 5hrs 45mins including Mont Olympe.
Height gain:	569m.
Maps:	Cartes IGN 3344 Ot Top 25 St Maximin-La-Ste-Baume 1:25,000.
	Cartes IGN L'Arrière Pays Toulonnais 1:50,000.
Depart from:	Parking in St-Zacharie
Signposting:	Good - for much of the way you are on the GR9. Part of this walk is on private property so please keep to the paths.

Observations:

A long and rewarding walk with glorious views of Mont Sainte Victoire to the north, the Sainte Baume ridge to the south and rolling wooded hills in all directions. The climb up Mont Olympe is an added challenge for the extra hardy!

Situated at the foot of the Sainte Baume hills, St-Zacharie is a large village with a long main street, and strangely enough, lots of traffic! Its attractions include a number of old fountains, a church founded in the 12th century but restored many times since, containing two 17th-century altars, and an altar in the Mairie dedicated to Jupiter. In the 1920s St-Zacharie was the capital of the ceramic industry (tiles, pots etc.) and over 500 people worked in the factories until the Italian market finally took over the production of ceramics.

How to get there:

Go to the village of St-Zacharie on the N560. If you come in from the direction of Nans-les-Pins (north of the village), turn right off the N560 at a T-junction onto the D85 signposted Trets (left is signposted Aubagne Marseilles). This is the Cour Louis Blanc, an avenue of trees where you can park your car in the middle.

Directions:

(1) From the parking spot, walk along the D85 which goes out of the village. There is a red/white GR slash on a telephone pole as you are on the GR9 which you will follow all the way to l'ermitage du St-Jean du Puy. Near the start you pass a sign on the right indicating a *sentier botanique* (nature walk). These are now very popular in France.

(2) After 10mins the main road bends left after a large unfinished loading bay, but go straight following a wooden sign *sentier botanique* (there is a GR notice on the left 30m further along). This is a narrow paved road, soon turning into a jeep track in an attractive shallow valley.

(3) At the first fork bear left on the GR9 (signposted Cantossier). Follow the red/white splashes ignoring all turnings to right and left. The path rises gently as it continues along the side of the valley with several large attractive houses on the left. *In springtime the bushes along this path are especially lovely with wild honeysuckle, yellow flowering broom, elderberry and lots of white may.*

(4) As you round a corner (30 mins), go right by GR splashes into the rocky narrow valley of the Fenouilloux. The path is clear and there is a smell of herbs (thyme and rosemary) in the air as you press along between tall yellow broom bushes, prickly gorse and the purple flowering cistus. You cross twice over the stream bed of the Fenouilloux (which can be dry or flowing depending on the season) and as you go higher the vegetation becomes sparser and the

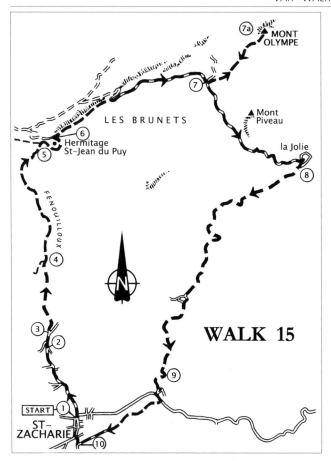

path rockier. The path crosses the valley at an attractive waterfall which is a refreshing respite (if the water is flowing) where there is an old stone wall (45mins). Turn right (sign on rock) and continue on the other side of the valley - there is an overhanging rock at one point. Five minutes later, just after recrossing the stream bed, be careful not to miss the GR sign on the path up left. Continue up gently with the stream bed initially nearby on the left and then later on to the right. *There is a ruin on the other side of the valley with some old terracing; it looks romantic but is a reminder of the hard times the mountain farmers had trying to scratch a precarious living in the most unlikely and inhospitable places.*

It is quite a lengthy climb up this valley. Keep carefully to the main path and freshly painted GR signs. When you finally reach the top (1hr 20mins) there is a brown signpost indicating you are on the GR9 which goes from the Jura to the Cote d'Azur - a long way indeed!

(5) Go right in the direction L'Ermitage de St-Jean de Puy 10mins/Trets 1hr 5mins (left indicates Peynier par la Regagnas 4hrs). There is a magnificent view right down to St-Zacharie in the valley below with the long silhouette of the Sainte Baume on the horizon. The path loops round l'Ermitage (1hr 30mins) which consists of two large low buildings, gardens and an extensive picnic area with attractive stone tables and shady areas - there is a stone tower from which you get an extensive view to the north of the wide plain, the nearby town of Trets in the valley and on the horizon the white craggy walls of the dramatic Sainte Victoire mountain. To the west you can see as far as the Carmague with the sea beyond. There is an observation table indicating all the peaks.

L'Ermitage de St-Jean du Puy existed since the 5th century but the tower was not built until the beginning of the 18th century. On the side of old stone walls there are some interesting memorials in Provençal which are difficult to understand. There is also a small plaque saying that the French "maquis" operated from here during the World War II. It is an interesting area to wander around and have lunch.

(6) Follow the GR path which goes below the buildings, through an archway with a small cross on top and down towards a parking area, but do not follow it left down to the town of Trets in the valley below. Instead continue down to the parking area which is a wide expanse with several signposts. There is a signpost back on the right to Mont Olympe and Rocher de Onze Heure (Peynier left 30kms). There is also an interesting map here showing the local landmarks. *If you go over to the edge of the ridge and look right you will see Mont Olympe which is a high jagged rock jutting out over the valley below (like the Baous above the town of Vence in the Alpes Maritimes).*

Take the jeep track right towards Mont Olympe through a barrier (to stop cars going into the car park when necessary) and keep on this wide track, undulating gently just beneath the top of the ridge (south side). *To the right is St-Zacharie in the valley below and all around are extensive vistas of rolling hills with no signs of habitation; the Sainte Baume is a blue smudge on the near horizon. Straight ahead is the rock of Mont Olympe.*

Ignore the first two crossroads, continuing straight passing a 155 digit sign on the left which indicates a water cistern. You are now crossing the area on the map called Les Brunets (2hrs). The track goes by a field of vines and there is a *chemin privé* sign to the right. *(Note: On one occasion when the author did this walk there was a chain across the path saying "Chemin Privée Domaine Jolie", presumably intended to exclude motor vehicles since this is an established walking trail.)* Continue downwards till you come to a large crossroads in an open sandy area where there are some splendid pine trees (2hrs 15mins).

(7) Here there is a choice: You can either go right and continue down to a large farm called La Jolie or go straight on the path towards Mont Olympe (the climb to the top is medium/strenuous and should not be attempted in wet weather). It takes about 40mins up and slightly less to return.

Mont Olympe extension:
The path is marked all the way with blue splashes which should be followed carefully. It goes up two high mounds, like shoulders, before the final stretch which is quite steep and rocky; watch your feet carefully as you scramble to the top over scree and boulders (2hrs 50mins).

(7A) At the top there is a squat concrete block and extensive views in all directions. *The smell of wild thyme, rosemary and other herbs on the top of this mountain, which is rocky but bushy, is quite overwhelming. It is worth taking a stroll along the flattish bush-covered summit after the effort you have taken to get there! To the south the tree-covered hills roll into infinity and just in front right is a pretty conical mountain called Mont Piveau, 703m.* You can see that there is a path both sides of this mountain so you can choose which one you take as both go to the farm of La Jolie.

Retrace your steps down from Mont Olympe carefully following the blue splashes. **Careful here** - the scree and rocks can be slippery if it has been raining.

At the original crossroads (7) with the pine trees (3hrs 25mins), take the jeep track left which goes round Mont Piveau. This is a very attractive path through open country dotted with fir trees, stunted oak and numerous different bushes and herbs - the conical rocky summit of Mont Piveau is always on the left. The path goes down through a small valley (lots of fallen trees on the slopes) and seems slightly elevated so that the views of forest-covered hills are breathtaking. It continues to wind round Mont Piveau and then bears southeast. There is a barrier indicating Domaine de la Jolie and later, on a paved section, you pass a water cistern No. 307 with the buildings of the farm just behind on the right. Continue down to where the Domaine is snugly situated in the middle of the valley floor with fields around it (4hrs 5mins). It looks curiously isolated as there are no other buildings anywhere in the vicinity. As you go down you can see the jeep track continuing on the other side of the valley.

(8) Continue to a T-junction and go right (or take the obvious short cut) down the bottom of another attractive narrow valley which is quite rocky to the right. The bushes and trees become denser as the valley narrows into a winding ravine with high rocky cliffs each side - the colours of the rocks and bushes on the slopes are spectacular in springtime. Continue down ignoring any branches. Pass a sign La Galtesse S74 to the right with a clearing and observation hut on the left.

The ravine opens up and narrows again before widening where there are a number of beehives on the right. There are old stone walls each side and signs of recent cultivation. The track passes a few shacks (4hrs 45mins) on the left with what looks like a swimming pool and some lovely cherry trees before widening out into a cultivated area with a number of scattered houses and smallholdings. After an open barrier with signs Proprieté Privé La Jolie it goes through an area where the slopes are covered with felled tree trunks (this is the Bois de St-Clair, or used to be!).

The track meets the GR9 again (5hrs 5mins) at Chemin Cerisier (Cherry Road). Continue till you see a conglomeration of buildings ahead with the name Zone Artisanale (5hrs 15mins) where you reach the N560.

(9) Following GR splashes cross the road left to the Auberge de la Foux. Opposite the Auberge bear right over the River Huveaune and continue on a defined path. Where there is an intersection of four ways, be careful to look for the GR sign on a narrow path to the right of a track marked Proprieté privé. Continue through bushy vegetation, open areas and houses till you reach a T-junction on the outskirts of the village (you are on the Chemin Jean Moulin). Turn right and over a bridge across the river to the Place 4 Septembre. Turn up right on the rather noisy main street back to the Cour Louis Blanc (5hrs 45mins).

Walk No. 16
MONTAGNE DE SAINTE VICTOIRE - Alt. 1011m

Difficulty:	Strenuous (long walk) - there is nothing technically difficult but you need stamina as there is plenty of walking over broken terrain.
	Medium/strenuous (short walk). YOU MUST TAKE PLENTY OF WATER. There is a notice at the start that this walk should not be done from July to mid September because of fire hazard. Also avoid if it is very windy.
Time:	3hrs 30mins short (up and down).
	5hrs 30mins long walk (circular).

102

Height gain:	585m.
Maps:	Cartes IGN série bleu 3244E Trets Montagne Ste-Victoire 1:25,000.
	Editions Didier Richard No.14 Du Luberon à La Ste-Victoire 1:50,000.
Depart from:	Village of Vauvenargues - 425m.
Signposting:	Good - follow the red/white splashes of the GR9 up and across the summit. Green splashes on the descent. **Careful** - although these splashes were newly painted in 1997 they are sometimes difficult to see.

Observations:

A really challenging walk - a classic of this region. Try to avoid weekends and choose a clear day when it is neither too hot nor too windy.

Orientated west to east, the white limestone ridge of the Montagne Ste-Victoire can be seen for miles around as it towers east of Aix-en-Provence. The precipitous white cliffs of its southern edge contrast sharply with the reddish soil at the foot of the mountain, while the northern side is gentler, covered in thick forest. The mountain was the subject of many of Cézanne's paintings as he was born and lived in nearby Aix.

The chapel itself is quite austere - it was constructed in 1654-1661 on the ruins of a monastery which existed since the 5th century. The monastery was inhabited by the Carmelites and then the Benedictines, who only lived up here a short time because of the climatic conditions. The site was abandoned in 1879 and consequently the buildings fell into ruins and for a while were used as a sheepfold.

In 1955 Henri Imoucha from Marseilles founded an association called the Friends of Ste. Victoire and it is thanks to his enthusiasm and the work of volunteers that restoration has slowly taken place over the last forty years. There is a plaque to the memory of Henri Imoucha 1901-1990 on the wall of the church. Mass is once again celebrated here from time to time. Restoration has meant that rainwater can be collected off the building roofs, thereby supplying the only source of water on the mountain. After the terrible fires in 1989 many new flowers and shrubs were planted round the church giving it a verdant look amongst its austere rocky surroundings.

How to get there (from Aix-en-Provence):

Take the D10 to the village of Vauvenargues (12kms). In the village there are numerous parking spots including a large car park at the bottom of the village. However, the walk starts near the Mairie at the top of the village so the choice is yours!

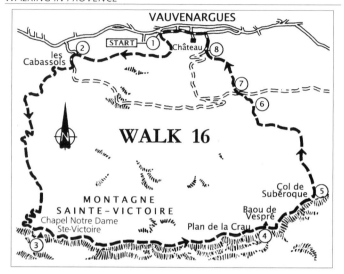

VAUVENARGUES

WALK 16

MONTAGNE
SAINTE-VICTOIRE
Chapel Notre Dame
Ste-Victoire

Col de
Subéroque

Baou de
Vespré

Plan de la Crau

les
Cabassols

START

Château

Directions (from top of village):

(1) Walk out of the village at the top end and turn down left just after the
Mairie and the Pompiers (fire station). There are no signs here. As you walk
down a medium steep jeep track you can see a large château on the left, the
church and parts of the village. You reach the stream (Ruisseau de la Cause)
and a lovely little leafy valley. With the stream on the left keep to the level
path going westwards towards the GR9 in and out of leafy clearings. Keep
to the main track, passing a deserted building on the right, to a T-junction in
the hamlet of Cabassols, although you see few houses (30mins). At the T-
junction the path joins the GR9 although this is not immediately evident.

(2) Turn down left (the right turning goes to the main road). Soon you see
the red/white splashes of the GR which you will follow all the way to the
summit. Cross the stream at a concrete bridge and shortly after there is a
large map for walkers showing the paths and the Ste-Victoire area. *There are
warnings in four languages, including English, that there is no water on the
mountain and all rubbish should be taken away. You are also told that the
walk should not be done between July and September nor when very windy-
all slightly off-putting but good common sense!*

Go down past two houses and through a fire barrier by GR splashes (do
not go up left here) to an open sandy area with pines. The track (called

Chemin des Venturiers on the map) is wide and defined, mostly red and cindery but with some parts paved in concrete. Soon it starts to become fairly steep, going mainly through tall pines, holm oak and yellow flowering broom. Initially there are a number of evident short cuts. *The altitude gain up this track is 475m and it is quite a tiring climb. Ahead you can see the tall cross on the summit of the Ste-Victoire with the priory church just underneath-at first glance it looks a long way up!*

The woods finally thin out and the views extend in all directions. To the north (behind) is the long ridge of Le Gros Baou above the village of Vauvenargues. The wide track comes to a small clearing which is the end of the line for any four-wheeled vehicle. There are a number of paths out of this clearing but take the one in the middle, with the red/white GR markings, before a bench (1hr 30mins). This is now the last spurt to the summit on a narrow rocky path winding upwards in large zigzags through low shrubs. *As you go higher you can see the intense blue of what look like three lakes down in the valley to the right. It is in fact one stretch of water, the Lac de Bimont, which has a vaulted dam at one end called the Barrage de Bimont across the Infernat river. It supplies water to Aix-en-Provence and the surrounding villages.*

The path finally reaches the 17th-century church of Notre Dame Ste-Victoire at 900m (2hrs). *It is quite a large church with a sort of courtyard which used to be cloisters, a big well, and a building behind, the former monastery, which is now used as a primitive refuge for travellers. The church is currently being restored. There are normally lots of people milling around here, especially at weekends, although they tend to go no further than the cross above before retracing their steps downwards. Take time to go into the chapel and look around.*

(3) It takes approximately 10mins from the chapel to the cross above. The GR path goes underneath the chapel and up the side, climbing fairly steeply for 45m. *At the top the wind whistles and there is a bunker-type building and an 11m high cement plinth with a 17m iron cross (Croix de Provence) above it. The view from here is magnificent with the whole of the Var region of Provence at your feet including the nearby Sainte Baume massif and to the left (east) the town of Aix-en-Provence.*

NOTE: For those who do not wish to continue the circuit along the mountain and down, which is fairly strenuous, just retrace your steps to the village. (This is what the majority of walkers do.)

Longer walk:
Walk down from the cross and pick up the GR red/white splashes just below. These go east all the way along the summit of the mountain - watch for them carefully as at times they are few and far between and the path tends to come

Cliffs, Montagne de Sainte Victoire

and go. Shortly after starting off you will see green writing on a rock which says Vauvenargues par Sentier des Plaideurs - passage difficile, and a GR9 sign.

If your conception of "passage difficile" means hanging from vertical rocks by your fingertips or clutching chains across vertiginous drops, then be reassured - all it means is that there is some picking your way across rocks as you go down, with no horrid steep slopes. (The notice may be intended simply to dissuade people from swarming across the mountain and getting lost!)

Thread your way across the summit, looking very carefully for the red/white splashes. The signs are mostly near the summit so if you find you are dropping below make for the top and you will pick them up. (There are massive drops to the right where the huge cliffs drop hundreds of metres to a desolate heathland.) Take note where the splashes indicate a detour to the left around thin fissures in the rock face. You reach a mini summit with a cairn.

At the top there are numerous interesting rock plants and herbs, such as thyme, rosemary and lavender, though not the abundance of flowers you see on the Sainte Baume and few shrubs. Ignore a green arrow to the right as this indicates a path down to the front of the mountain and you certainly don't want to go there! The path meanders along the top over the Plan de la Crau and then up to the highest point of the walk, namely Baou de Vespré, Alt. 1010m.

The GR signs were repainted in 1997 however they can deteriorate rapidly in the exposed conditions.

(4) At the Baou de Vespré (3hrs 30mins) there is a small cairn on the headland and another one further round the slope. From here you get a good view of the continuing ridge and the Pic des Mouches which is the highest point at Alt. 1011m. From here the path goes down to the Col de Subéroque where there is a cairn just below the crest and clear green arrows on a rock indicating left to Vauvenargues (3hrs 45mins).

(5) The path is clearly marked with green splashes all the way down and is rather steep, bordered by shrubs, mainly boxwood and juniper. The slope is rather relentless and you feel you are descending for hours! The winding path makes for a hill with a jumble of rocks on top. When you actually arrive there you find that the path goes to the left of the rocky summit and there is not too much of a scramble.

After negotiating the hill there is a magnificent view of the wide green valley below (called the Delubre) and the roofs of Vauvenargues beyond. The path continues steeply down over endless small rocks - at one point you go through masses of juniper bushes. Eventually you come into scattered oak woodland and then, as you get lower, the trees become denser and taller.

(6) At the bottom of the valley (4hrs 40mins) there is a clear green arrow pointing left and upwards - a slight shock as you feel you have done all the climbing you want to for one day! However the path soon goes around and down the side of a hill. It then widens and becomes almost sandy through tall pines before narrowing and descending again into another valley bottom over the (normally) dry bed of the Infernat stream.

Continuing westward you now see the long summit of the mountain on the left and the tremendous drop you have come down - it is very impressive! The path climbs gently out of the valley and meets a jeep track coming in from the right (5hrs 30mins). Here there is another green sign indicating Sentier des Plaideurs and ahead on the ridge is the silhouette of the iron cross.

(7) Go left on the jeep track and, about 20m later turn right on to a wide path (green splashes) going through shaded woodland. It soon becomes narrower and stony as it drops down to a clearing with a stream (could be dry some parts of the year) which you cross. Continue up through continuing woodland and then down again, with a view ahead of an imposing square-shaped château. *This 17th-century building overlooks the valley and was lived in by the painter Pablo Picasso during the last years of his life (1881-1973); he is buried in the park in front. It is still privately owned by his family and no visitors are allowed in the grounds.* Continue down with the river below on the right and follow the green splashes till you meet a jeep track in a clearing with a map (the same one you saw at the start).

(8) Turn right on the jeep track which crosses the river on a concrete bridge and meets the road. Bear up left through a car park and walk up the hill through the quaint old village, which seems to go on for ever! If you parked your car at the top you may wish it was at the bottom(!) but there are some attractive cafés on the way and this walk deserves to be celebrated (5hrs 30mins).

Walk No. 17
MARCEL PAGNOL COUNTRY

Difficulty:	Strenuous - vigilance is needed to follow the different coloured splashes but the views are worth it.
	The shorter walk is much easier though there is some uphill climb. NOTE: Because of fire hazard no walks can be done here between 1st July and the second week in September when the hunting season starts.
Time:	Long walk: 5hrs (add 20mins if you wish to climb the Garlaban and 10mins for the Grotte de Grosibou).
	Short walk: 2hrs 15mins.
Height gain:	508m (to Garlaban).
Maps:	Cartes IGN Série Bleu 3245E Aubagne/La Ciotat 1:25,000.
Depart from:	Entrance to the village of La Treille.
Signposting:	We should call this the walk of many colours! At the start follow red splashes, then yellow, blue, red again and finally green. The short walk is red/yellow/green.

Observations:

A classic walk which will attract all lovers of **Marcel Pagnol** and his wonderful books and films, such as *La Gloire de Mon Père (My Father's Glory)*, *Le Château de Ma Mère (My Mother's Castle)* and *Manon des Sources*. Here is the countryside he loved, preserved for posterity and now yours to explore!

When we first did the walk, armed with a map showing the different walks from the Marcel Pagnol Information Centre, we thought we would have no trouble finding our way. At the start, we encountered hundreds of schoolchildren with their teachers. But they were doing just a short sightseeing tour and hurrying on we quickly left them behind. The small map showing all the different coloured walks was very confusing and before long we were

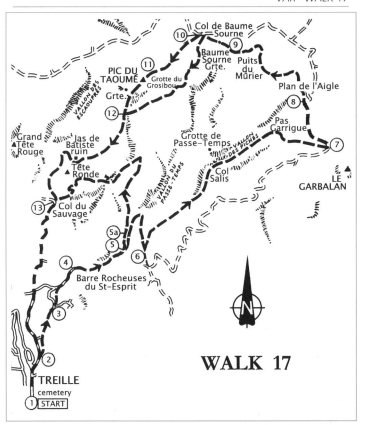

WALK 17

lost. Eight hours later and practically dropping with tiredness we found our way back to the car - the path marked on the map had become private property and you could no longer get through - what's new! When I complained to the Marcel Pagnol centre in town (as distinct from the Tourist Office) they kindly offered me a guide for the day who showed us the right way round beginning from the village of La Treille. He was also a wonderful source of information on the region. So the moral of the story is to follow directions carefully and not the little map handed out at the information centre!

Aubagne, which is just over the Var border in the Bouches du Rhône, was the birthplace of Marcel Pagnol in 1895. It might have been a peaceful country town in those days but it is now bustling with life and industry! It has expanded so much that it has almost become an outer suburb of Marseilles. However, it has preserved some of its ramparts and old town centre. There is a huge market on Tuesdays which is worth browsing around for Provençal specialities.

How to get there:
Come off the motorway at Aubagne Centre (A50 or A52) and make for the centre of town. Watch out for signs saying Sentier Marcel Pagnol at a roundabout. This takes you onto the D44 (signposted Ecoures). Continue for 7.5kms through the villages of Ecoures and Camions Les Bains following all signs to La Treille. Look carefully for a right turn off the D44 to the village. Go past the Etablissement Thermal and the clinic St. Bruno on the right and park further up on the left side of the road just before the bus station where it says Fin de stationnement.

Directions:
(1) Walk up the road past the cemetery where Marcel Pagnol is buried and into the village. Make for the square in front of the church where there is an attractive fountain which was used in the original film of *Manon des Sources* made by Marcel Pagnol in the 1950s. Turn right in front of the fountain down a narrow street which meets the main street (Chemin des Bellons) where you turn up left. Continue up fairly steeply till you come to a large house on the left where there is a plaque indicating that it was here that Marcel Pagnol 1895-1974 wrote the first pages of his book *Souvenirs de l'Enfance*.

(2) Just before this house turn down the narrow street on the right called Chemin de Passe Temps (ignore the sign in the other direction to the Vallon de Passe Temps). **Note: from here on follow faded red splashes.** This road goes down through tall pine woods before narrowing into a small valley and then on to a smaller path at a house up on the right marked No. 64. *This now built-up area was the route taken by Marcel Pagnol's father and uncle when they went to the "Chasse" (hunting) and was recorded in the book and film* La Gloire de mon Père.

(3) You reach a paved road again (20mins) and shortly afterwards an intersection. Continue straight following red splashes and a sign Relais de Passe Temps. Just before the road ends at the Relais look for a track right where there is a red splash and a chain across to stop cars going up (30mins).

(4) This is a wide stony track along a pleasant bushy valley and through small clearings (some pylons and wires around). Keep to the main track. It becomes sunken as it passes through a rocky gorge before opening up again.

(5) Continue along this delightful path. Soon after a small hut on the left, which is a hunter's lookout post, look carefully for yellow markers going up a long slab of stone to the right (the red markers continue straight) - 45mins. *From now on you walk mostly through "garrigue"- see 'Introduction: Flora and Fauna'.*

ALTERNATIVE SHORT WALK

(5A) For the shorter route - continue past the yellow markers on the right and almost immediately you come to a sandy clearing with a lone pine tree. On the trunk is a clear yellow marking indicating a path straight up - there are also yellow splashes on the stones at the start of the path so you can't miss it (the path with red splashes goes off right and up the centre of the valley).

This yellow route takes you up the lefthand side of the valley. Up right on the other side of the valley is the long overhanging rock face of the Grotte de Manon. The path is narrow and stony going through low bushes and climbing medium steep. At a rocky ruin take the yellow arrow to the right and continue up before levelling out and going down into a dry rocky gully. Follow yellow splashes, carefully avoiding all paths with yellow crosses at the start.

The path makes a large pointed curve and then doubles back down the valley in front of the Tête Ronde. Ahead are the Grottes des Pestiférés (see long walk) and further right the pink slopes of the Grande Tête Rouge, known as the "Redhead" because of its bauxite - to the immediate right is the Tête Ronde. The path becomes red and there are pieces of bauxite underfoot- it reaches a disused mine, all that is left of the mining done by the Germans during World War II, when they were also looking for uranium.

Continue on the yellow path which joins the green one from the longer walk at the Col de Sauvage where there is a no entry sign on the right (1hr 40mins). Turn left and ignore yellow splashes which continue for a few metres to a sandy clearing and then go off in another direction.

FROM NOW ON FOLLOW GREEN SPLASHES AND THE DIRECTIONS OF THE LONG WALK FROM POINT 13.

Much of this area was ravaged by fire in 1979 and again in 1997. All the bushes were burnt and have not yet reproduced.

CONTINUATION OF LONG WALK
Note: From now on follow yellow splashes.

(5) For a few minutes the path crosses the long stone slab of rock and becomes narrow and stony going up medium steep (northeast). Behind is a good view of the Passe Temps valley you have just come up. Continuing along the side of the valley, there is a first glimpse of the outskirts of Marseilles. Straight ahead is the rock outcrop of Les Barres de St. Esprit with a cross on the summit. On the other side of this rock is the Vallon de Marcellin which was bought by Marcel Pagnol in 1930 in order to construct a Cité du Cinema where he could make his films, but the project never got off the ground. The land still belongs to his descendants.

(6) *Be careful here:* Just before ruins on the right, which are not easy to see, bear up left at a small crossroads following blue markings (there is a yellow cross here) (1hr). **Note: From now on follow blue markings.**

The path continues fairly steeply upwards, direction north/east, with good views of the surrounding hills. To the left in the distance are the Grottes des Pestiférés, the Tête Rond and the Tête Rouge and to the right of them the Pic de Taoumé. Straight ahead is the Grotte de Manon. This is not really a cave but a long overhanging rock face which can be reached by a detour to the right. (It takes about 10mins to go up and down.) Otherwise keep going up, direction north, to the Col Salis (1hr 30mins).

Continue on following blue splashes into the Valley des Piches. Down below to the left is the large Grotto de Passe Temps. The path initially loses height and then becomes stonier through a small gorge as it rises steadily to the end of the valley. As the surrounding bushes become more pronounced, watch carefully for a right turn where there is a blue sign further up but no sign on the actual turn (1hr 55mins). The path becomes steeper and rockier as you scramble out of the valley and over the Pas de Garrique. At the top you can see Aubagne over on the right and straight ahead the rock outcrop of the Le Garlaban, Alt. 712m with a cross on top. The path crosses the plateau and continues towards the Garlaban to a sandy intersection where it meets the wider orange road coming up from the alternative parking area (2hrs 15mins). There are signposts here including one to the Garlaban, 10mins there and back - which is very optimistic! It takes at least 20mins but is well worth the effort for the spectacular view and detailed orientation table. **Note: From here follow red splashes carefully** (there are also orange squares on wooden posts).

(7) Shortly after the point where you arrived on the blue path, turn hard left on a wide track towards the Plan d'Aigle, Alt. 729m which is the highest point but disappointingly covered with TV aerials. The track goes through a barrier to a corner where it continues off right to the Plan d'Aigle. Turn left here (there is a red marker and a wooden post with an orange square) - 2hrs 30mins.

This rocky path curls round the end of a valley on the left and over the top towards the southwest with a clear view of the Galaban hill left. There are two tiny fields to the left as the path bears left in a clearing. The red markings are not clear here so be sure to keep the Plan d'Aigle behind you.

(8) On the horizon to the right is the impressive range of the Massif de l'Etoile with the extraordinary square hump of the Pilon du Roi sticking out. There is also a wonderful view of the whole of Marseilles. The path becomes red and cindery and starts to descend into a wide dip reaching a beautiful little field of wheat - there are some lovely pine trees which makes a change from the endless shrubs (2hrs 50mins). This is an ideal picnic stop called the Puits du Murier. The *puits* (well) is behind a small green door in the rock and was the only well in this mountain area which provided water all the year round.

(9) Go to the left of the field, passing the well, and 50m later take a narrow turning between bushes to the right (yellow marks on small tree). **Note: From now on follow yellow splashes.**

This path (bearing west) climbs medium steep towards the Col de Baume Sourne. As it goes round the edge of the Le Jardinier valley there is an extensive view of the nearby Taoumé, Les Barres de St. Esprit and on the horizon the Cirque de Carpiagne. Keep going round, ignoring a track down to the valley floor on the left. The path reaches a large impressive cave called La Baume Sourne (3hrs) which is worth a look inside. *Obviously an ancient dwelling place, it has been excavated by archaeologists where they have found bones and ancient tools but the excavations have been abandoned due to lack of funds. In 1997 bulldozers were making the entrance to the cave smaller, probably to preserve the contents from prying eyes.*

After the cave climb up steeply to the Col de Baume Sourne (3hrs 10mins), a wide sandy area with pines. From here you can see the white slopes of the Sainte Victoire to the north and the Sainte Baume to the east. There is a large map with details of the various trails and mountains.

(10)   Note: From this Col follow the blue splashes which go off to the left over the Pic de Taoumé.

Alternative path: You can continue to follow the yellow splashes on a path which goes round the south side of the Pic de Taoumé; this is easier but misses the Grotte de Grosibou.

Take the blue path to the left and follow the blue (and orange) splashes carefully as you clamber over the rocks on the top of this rocky range. You arrive at the summit of a first peak and then walk along a ridge on a wide path to the second rocky peak called the Pic de Taoumé (3hrs 30mins). *There are fantastic views in all directions, particularly of Marseilles in front with the Mediterranean and three small islands beyond.*

The path continues up and down over the rocky crags (south/west) - *down to the right is the barren valley of the Escaouprés which was particularly hit by the 1979 forest fires which swept through these mountains for five days when the mistral wind was blowing.*

(11) The rocky narrow path reaches the Grotte de Grosibou (clearly marked) 5mins later. *This is a dramatic narrow cleft in the rocks which has been immortalised in the story* La Gloire de Mon Père *by Marcel Pagnol when he and his friend Lili sheltered in it during a storm and were frightened by a huge owl.* You can squeeze through this narrow passage if you are thin (leave your rucksacks outside), walk through and go round the rock to the start again - it takes roughly 10mins. It is a scramble but is rather fun!

Note: After the Grotte de Grosibou the blue markings disappear - now you follow red splashes!

(12) The path starts to go down fairly steeply over rocks and then becomes smoother and flatter before meeting the alternative yellow path from the Col de Baume Sourne, coming up from the left and crossing to the right (3hrs 45mins).

Following the red splashes go steadily down ignoring all branches off. There is a good view of the Vallée de Passe Temps on the left and ahead is the Tête Ronde which the path skirts right round - to the right is the Grande Tête Rouge ("large redhead" so called because bauxite gives the slopes a pinkish tinge). Later on you can see a purplish pile which is all that remains of mining by the Germans during the World War II. They were also looking for uranium. You will see pieces of bauxite as you go round the Tête Ronde.

The path reaches the Jas de Batiste where there are ruins of a large sheepfold (*bergerie*) - all that remain are old walls and rocks. There is a large fig tree which indicates that water is nearby. The path circles right round the Tête Ronde (south/west) on a stony path. On the right is a good view of the Grotte des Pestiférés, a big cave in the rock face where people took refuge in the 17th century when the plague was raging through Marseilles. They may have been safe from the plague but they were killed by bandits instead! You come to a long green fence (around a water cistern) and a barrier. On the slope to the left is some small wind-catching apparatus and solar panels. **Note: From here follow green splashes!** Go down alongside the fence to the Col du Sauvage, Alt. 321m (4hrs 20mins).

THIS IS WHERE THE SHORT AND LONG WALKS MERGE AGAIN.

(13) When the path comes to a large open area surrounded by bushes, keep straight following the green splashes. ***Careful*** - do not follow the yellow splashes to the right here.

On the slope to the right are a number of beehives and an abandoned bauxite mine to the left with lots of red deposits. The path later swings round to the left but go straight following the green splashes (actually this is just a short cut) continuing south, losing height rapidly, with the hamlet of Les Bellons visible ahead. At the entrance to the village (4hrs 30mins) there is another map.

Les Bellons is where the Pagnol family rented a house for the summer during 1904-1910 until the mother Augustine died at the age of 38. Marcel was 15 at the time. The house, called La Bastide Neuve and privately owned, is indicated on the right. It is rather unassuming with a large fig tree in the garden. Immediately after is a buvette (open air café).

Continue downwards through private houses (there is no actual village here) with an attractive olive grove to the right which is still part of the estate of the Magnan family - *David Magnan was the real name of 'Lili' the childhood friend of Marcel Pagnol who was killed in World War I; this part of the road is called Chemin de Colonal Magnan in his memory. It is interesting to note that the olive trees are deliberately planted in small groups so that nets can be spread around them and the olives collected more easily.*

At the entrance to the village at a small crossroads (Quatre Chemins des Bellons) there is a little road off to the left which connects the road taken on the outward journey through the earlier part of the Passe Temps valley. Continue straight down the Chemin des Bellons above this narrow valley. There are occasional houses as you continue down towards Treille past the villa where Marcel Pagnol wrote the first part of *Souvenirs de l'Enfance* (4hrs 50mins).

Continue down the main village street and past the cemetery on the left. *Here Marcel Pagnol was buried in 1974 in the same tomb as his three year old daughter Ester and his mother Augustine (other members of his family are in a nearby tomb). His tomb is made from marble extracted from the famous quarries near Cassis.* Continue till you reach the parking area (5hrs).

Walk No. 18
CIRCUIT DU LATAY

Difficulty:	Medium but you have to follow the instructions carefully.
Time:	4hrs 35mins (includes visit to chapel). Add 15mins if you take route 6B.
Height gain:	220m.
Maps:	Cartes IGN 3345 OT Top 25 Signes.Tourves 1:25,000.
	Cartes IGN L'Arrière Pays Toulonnais 1:50,000.
Depart from:	Signes - 350m.
Signposting:	No signs or splashes till beyond the Colonie de Vacances. Then follow intermittent green splashes before meeting up with the red/white splashes of the GR9.

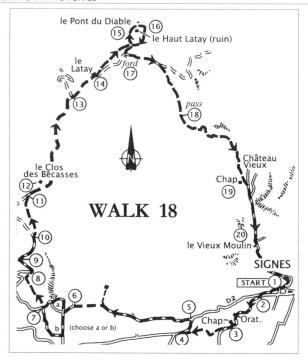

Observations:

This is a very pretty walk, best done on a hot day as there is lots of cool shade! Don't be put off by the somewhat complicated instructions. The irrigation channel of the **Latay** stream is particularly idyllic and somewhat unusual. The channel was originally built to irrigate the fields in the region, rather like the famous water channels in the Valais region of Switzerland.

The author has done this walk five times. The first time we got lost. The second time we found the right path but started off on an old GR way which the Tourist Office said was still possible despite the sale of the land to a private person! The third time we met the owner of the property who told us we were not allowed to go through his land. The fourth time we found a way through the Colonie de Vacances which we then verified twice! Nevertheless it may be easier to take the longer way round if there are lots of children about.

Signes is an old Provençal village of around 1600 inhabitants situated to the south of the Sainte Baume mountain, 35kms from Toulon and 45kms from Marseilles. It has quaint narrow streets and ancient houses. The church of St-Pierre was built in 1096, restored in 1656 and again in 1857.

How to get there:
On the motorway from Marseilles to Aix-en-Provence, exit at Aubagne and take the N8 direction Toulon as far as the crossroads at Le Camp du Castellet (19kms). Turn left here on the D2. After 10kms you reach the village of Signes. Park in the large car park on the main road (Square Marcel Pagnol) opposite the Ecole Primaire Jean Moulin.

Directions:
(1) Walk out of the car park and turn right along the D2 (direction west). On the left are tennis courts and a football ground belonging to the school, then the Maison de Tourisme on the right.

(2) After a few minutes turn left at a roundabout, leaving the D2, onto a narrower road called Chemin St. Clair where there are houses right and a large farm on the left. Soon there is a tiny chapel on the left with an interesting plaque on the wall stating that in 1707, 200 inhabitants of the village (Signeois) were massacred at this spot by 1000 Austro-Sards brigands who came rampaging through the countryside. *(That's what I love about Provence - you never know what fascinating snippet of history you are going to discover round every corner!)*

The road bears right over an old stone bridge and starts to go up past a dilapidated shrine and through holm oak forest till it comes to a small chapel on the right in a sandy area with scattered pines (15mins). There is an iron grille in front and you can see from a plaque inside that it was renovated in 1973. It is obviously used for services as there are benches and an altar.

(3) Take the jeep track to the right of the chapel which goes up a low hill past tumbled rocks on the right, and then levels off before dropping down to meet the road (there is a house right).

(4) At the road (D2) turn right (30mins) and walk along for a few minutes.

(5) At a righthand corner take the narrow road to the left, signposted Chemin de Chivron along a shallow valley. There are fields to the right with scattered houses and trees beyond; left is woodland, a stream (Rau du Latay) and then the D2.

Ignoring entrances to private houses, take a track to the left (no signs) before the road goes round right (40mins). The dried out river bed is still on the left (fields with ribbon fencing and some houses on the right). Continue through open fields and past a majestic cedar tree before reaching a road

(50mins) where you get your first sighting of the narrow irrigation channel of the Latay stream which you will be following for a large part of the walk.

(6) This road is the entrance to the Colonie de Vacances de Chibron which is technically private *(see 'Observations')*.

Here there is a choice:

(A) Continue straight on a narrow path (a mass of blue tents with concrete bases to the left). This takes you on to another road leading to the buildings of the Colonie but do not continue down to the left. Go up to the buildings and keeping the swimming pool to your right go through on a path which crosses a dry river bed and arrives at a sandy parking area in the scattered pines and woodland (1hr).

(B) Note: adds about 15mins to the timings. Go left on the road through a barrier and walk down with tents on the right (Latay water channel to the left) to the main entrance to the Colonie de Vacances. Continue down past ponds to the right and across a bridge. Down on the left is an enormous quarry. Cross another barrier - there are artificial ponds on the left and then on the right and further on a round pond in the quarry which the Latay channel spills into - what an ignominious end to a beautiful stretch of water!! Shortly after turn right at a sign Le Latay - if you go much further you hit the D2 again. *This is the road that cars take to reach the parking area at the start of the traditional Latay walk (there and back only).* The jeep track now follows green splashes with a good view ahead of the rocky Sainte Baume ridge. It goes by an attractive looking Auberge on the left and arrives at the sandy parking area.

(7) Look for a path going straight up from the parking area (a red splash at the start) and later E14 on a tree followed by intermittent green splashes. It is a wide and rocky path going straight up through stunted bushes and scattered oak and pine trees. At a fork go right - the path to the left leads to the nearby road (1hr 10mins).

(8) Shortly after you join the road anyway just before a lefthand hairpin.

(9) Go up the road to a T-junction (1hr 15mins) - *all sorts of signs here warning you not to pick mushrooms and that "sangliers" wild boar are being killed in the region!* Go right signposted Latay ET41 (1hr 20mins). You can now hear the rushing water of the Latay channel which goes under the road. ***Careful*** - just after this look for a little path (green splash) up to the left. It goes beside the water for a few minutes before reaching the road again.

(10) Cross the road and continue following the water on the other side along another narrow path (1hr 25mins) - there is a red splash at the start and then a green one. **From now on keep to the narrow path beside the water channel.** This is a very pretty walk beside the water, through tall grass and undergrowth, with a tree-covered gully down on the right. The path crosses

118

tree trunks and parts of the water course have been shored up with cement (it is obviously well looked after).

The gully dwindles into a dried up river bed (1hr 25mins). The path becomes overgrown though still clearly defined. At one point the river goes across a tiny stone aqueduct while the path goes down and up across the dry stream bed.

(11) Cross the jeep track again (1hr 40mins) and continue beside the water - for quite a while you can see the jeep track on your right. The green splashes disappear.

(12) The path crosses a jeep track leading to a house up on the left (lots of yappy dogs here).

(13) Keep going over another crossroads and then onto the road which you cross again. Stay on the path around a water tank with a green door and a pipe running into it; there is a sign right saying "Propriété Privée" to the right. Soon a stream appears on the right and is visible from time to time. After another stone aqueduct and a precipitous rubbish dump on the right (2hrs), the channel continues with an old high stone wall on the left partially covered with ivy. It feels rather cosy with thick woods, path, narrow irrigation canal and then the wall!

After a clearing on the right the wall ends and the path comes to a jeep track by a no-entry sign and a majestic sycamore tree (the canal continues on the other side in a culvert but you cannot walk along it).

(14) Follow the jeep track to the right past the tree to another wide track where you turn right at a T-junction. Over on the left there are two old houses which look rather run down - they are all that remain of the hamlet of Le Latay (2hrs 5mins).

Be careful - after a few metres on this wide track, shoot down right again to the narrow path beside the irrigation channel. You are now on a raised path with a clearing down on the right and the main jeep track on the left.

When you reach the road again (2hrs 15mins) the water channel goes underneath and emerges on the other side. ***Careful here*** - cross the road and continue on the narrow track alongside the water channel on your left (green splash). On the right is a wide ford and parking area. This path continues along the channel on a raised leafy path with the Latay stream down on the right and the main jeep track beyond. It passes a stagnant pool on the right. The channel becomes a rushing jet of water as it tumbles through narrow mossy banks on the left before calming again at an open area to the right with a path through it - this is obviously a popular spot for picnics and barbecues.

(15) After a tiny waterfall left the channel disappears into the ruins of the old mill (2hrs 30mins). Stay on the path for a few minutes (careful as it becomes steep and full of tree roots), with the river flowing down to the right and you reach a pretty mossy waterfall, *Le Pont de Diable* (*diable* meaning devil) cascading into the stream below.

Retrace your steps to just before the mill and jump over the narrow canal where you can see a path on the other side. This takes you behind the old mill which is part of the ruined hamlet of Le Haut Latay. Keep going upstream until you have the canal on the left and you can see where it descends to the stream creating the attractive waterfall. This is the last time you see the narrow Latay watercourse.

A few minutes later look for green and GR red/white splashes and cross the stream right by a tiny ford (you can continue straight for a few minutes to see the ruins of a church, but retrace your steps as this path will take you out of your way).

(16) After the ford the path climbs up the other side to a large jeep track. The green signs now disappear and you follow the GR9 red/white splashes until the end of the walk (2hrs 40mins). Turn down right with the river running attractively on the right (good picnic area in a meadow here) and after 10mins you reach a fire barrier just before the wide ford (*gué* in French).

(17) Turn up left east (GR signs on tree) and the track climbs up and through a barrier. You can see a large ruin over on the left with a modern building behind it. **Careful here** - after around 6mins watch for red/white splashes going up to the right and take this narrower path (the main jeep track is a no through road and there is a clear GR cross ahead).

This stony path goes up medium steep for about 15mins, curving southwards with a pylon over on the left. It arrives at a low pass in the woods, Alt. 727m, where the pylons appear straight ahead (3hrs 5mins).

(18) A few minutes after the pass the path starts to go down. Ignore a first left turn almost at the pass and take the second clearly marked with red/white GR splashes. The path descends quite steeply towards the south-east, passing under the pylon wires as it winds down into a valley.

Bear left just before a dilapidated wooden hut (3hrs 15mins). Go through the wooded valley bottom and steeply up the other side and along the slope still heading southeast. As the valley widens out you can see straight ahead a chapel on the top of a wooded hill which looks rather enticing. The path continues along the side of the valley and starts to descend again; down on the left is a farm called Château Vieux and a round reservoir.

(19) Continue downwards and, almost opposite a new house on the left, watch out for a narrow path on the right with a cross on a plinth (3hrs 50mins). This takes you to the little chapel of Notre Dame de la Nativité where there is also a small primitive refuge for travellers. Part of the chapel has collapsed, but there is a grille to the remaining part which looks badly in need of restoration though there is an altar and benches. If you take the little path behind the chapel there is a good view all round from this summit, especially to the north which looks especially wild with no houses in view (4hrs 5mins).

Retrace your steps to the main path and continue down right almost immediately there are further signs of habitation to the left. The path joins the ET30 at a T-junction and crosses over the Raby Rau stream at a small stone bridge before passing a shabby stone shrine to the right. The track becomes paved as it enters the lower part of this wide valley where there are some attractive houses and an olive grove on the right. On the other side of the valley are tall tree-covered rocks called Les Hautes Côtes and the road goes between tall rocks which appear to guard the entrance to the valley.

(20) The stream is still on the right as the road passes a small mill sunken in the undergrowth and being restored. Cross the river on a bridge and then go by some allotments on the left before the outskirts of the village where there is a large map of the region. The road enters the Rue de l'hôpital which continues into the Rue Louis Lumière and then into the pretty little village square (Place du Marché) - a delightful place to have a drink! At the bottom of the square turn right into the Rue St. Jean which goes into the Rue Marseillaise. Here take the steps down right (Rue Ferrayette) to the lower part of the village and the car park

Walk No. 19
LE MOURRE D'AGNIS - Alt. 905m

Difficulty:	Strenuous/medium - there is a long climb up at the start.
Time:	4hrs 30mins.
Height gain:	495m.
Maps:	Carte IGN 3345 OT Top 25 Signes.Tourves 1:25,000.
	Cartes IGN L'Arrière Pays Toulonnais 1:50,000.
Depart from:	Large municipal car park in Mazaugues.
Signposting:	GR red/white splashes up to the ridge, across and down. From then on intermittent green splashes.

Observations:
A dramatic walk along the Mourre d'Agnis ridge from a delightful typically Provençal village. The views from the summit are extensive and include the Sainte Baume and the southern Alps.

How to get there:
From St-Maximin-la-Ste-Baume, take the N7 to the entrance of Tourves and

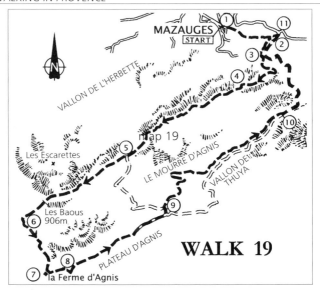

then the D1 direction St-Zacharie. Shortly after crossing the Provence Canal take the D64 on the left which joins the D95 just before reaching Mazaugues. Drive through the tiny village - the car park is on the D64 near the centre.

Directions:

(1) Walk out of the car park and turn into the Place Marx Dormoy with the church on the right, then up left on the Grand Rue. There is a red/white splash of the GR99 on the low pavement at the start (not obvious) and another further up on a pipe. Continue up this street which soon deteriorates into a narrow, bushy, stony path. It goes up fairly steeply to the east. A shallow wooded valley appears on the left and then another on the right with a jeep track running through it. Beyond is the long ridge of the Mourre d'Agnis.

(2) Turn left at a T-junction. The path flattens out and, where there is a large GR cross on a tree, take the narrower path up right - this is the right-angled turn you can see on the map (15mins) and is where you come in on the return journey.

The path goes up through broom bushes and then slackens off and becomes sandy as it goes down into a dip at the top of the valley - the wooded ridge of the Mourre d'Agnis looks close and high.

(3) At an intersection (20mins) go straight on (left goes to the jeep track), following the clear GR splashes. The path goes up the shoulder of the ridge bending to the right (30mins), then becomes rocky for a while. There are lovely views in all directions. After levelling off round the top of the valley, you can see the little village of Mazaugues through the trees to the right. Then the rocky path climbs again towards the west and goes on through stunted oak forest and clearings.

(4) You reach the top of the ridge at a large slab of rock (1hr). There are fantastic views in all directions. North is Mazaugues in a wide valley backed by tree-covered ridges. *Over to the left is the long southern ridge of the Sainte Baume. Behind is the rocky summit of the Montagne de la Loube with its TV mast.*

Walk along the wide rocky ridge top (direction southwest) with intermittent woodland and sweeping views. Over to the right is the Vallon de l'Herbette flanked on the left by an impressive cliff wall called Les Escorettes. Keep to the path with clear GR red/white splashes past a cairn with a pole sticking out of it. The ridge falls sharply down on the right and the long line of the Mourre d'Agnis ahead looks particularly striking.

(5) At a fork (1hr 30mins) take the narrower path right; there is a GR cross on a stone to the left. (The wider path off left is a quicker way down off the summit if you want to shorten the walk.) Later you pass a small cairn which marks a path coming up the side of the ridge.

Further on is an area on the left dotted with pretty stunted fir trees as though they have been planted amongst the rocks on purpose; further left the view is marred by pylons. The path undulates along the top crossing Les Baous at the highest part of the ridge, 905m - in this case a large flattish slab of rock. Continue along this dramatic rocky edge with tremendous drops to the right and a flat plateau to the left. After Les Baous the path starts to lose height gently with a pylon straight ahead on the ridge. Follow GR signs carefully and a few minutes after a *borne* (boundary stone, looks like a trig point) look for a clear GR sign on a rock indicating a left turn (2hrs 5mins).

(6) This takes you away from the edge of the ridge and across the top (south). At first the path is grassy and flat through scattered woodland, leading downwards towards a farm called the Ferme d'Agnis. As you wend your way down the view opens up on the other side of the ridge and you can see a delightfully unspoilt valley below. The path is irritatingly stony and the descent seems long. It passes a dramatic pine tree embedded in the rock behind it before flattening out and you see a building through the trees left which is part of the farm.

(7) You reach a grassy area and a T-junction (2hrs 30mins). The isolated farm is off to the right and looks as if it has been recently renovated. Go left at the

Walking Mourre d'Agnis

T-junction (the GR splashes have disappeared here). The path turns into a jeep track (now you know how they get to the farm!).

(8) Follow the jeep track (east) until a defined T-junction (2hrs 35mins). Go left here - again there are no markings though according to the map the GR goes off to the right.

The flat, wide sandy track follows blue markings for a while through the Plateau d'Agnis, an area of scattered tall pine trees and shrub. Go through a fire barrier. The pylons are still off to the right and left is the southern edge of the Mourre d'Agnis with attractive rocky shapes sticking out of the green forest. Continue straight where a large road goes off to the right and there is a yellow and green water tank (for helicopters to pinpoint perhaps?). The path continues level through an area where hundreds of fir trees have been planted by Guigoz, a French baby milk powder manufacturer.

To the left there is a battered wooden cross stuck into a millstone with four old cypress trees around it - one wonders what circumstances gave rise to such an isolated grave. Further over on the left is a squat building. There are a number of tiny cultivated fields round about sown with wheat for wild animals - the animals are later shot in the hunting season.

Keep on the main level jeep track and ignore any paths branching off. The blue signs go off to the right (2hrs 55mins) but continue straight.

(9) *Careful* - approximately 5mins later where the track starts a wide loop to the right take a narrow path to the left at a small cairn - this looks as if it was the original route. There are rare green splashes. A few minutes later go straight at a junction (this is where the short cut comes in according to the map). The jeep track can be seen on the right for most of the way down. The path meanders through heathland and then down in a series of wide bends to a valley below called the Vallon du Thuya.

Once at the bottom of the narrow valley (3hrs 15mins) the path meanders through delightful young oak and beech trees, passing a rocky cliff. As it descends deeper the trees almost meet overhead so you feel you are walking through a green tunnel. Shortly after ruins in the trees right the path meets the jeep track again (if you had stuck to it at the cairn you would have arrived here, but it would have taken you longer).

(10) At the jeep track turn left (3hrs 45mins) and continue gently upwards past the high rocks of the eastern end of the Mourre d'Agnis through an area where the conical shapes of the rocks are quite impressive. On the right is a densely wooded valley with a rocky ridge rearing up the other side. The jeep track turns right round towards the northwest, through a green fire barrier (3hrs 55mins) where there is a large water tank and a sign Forêt Domaniale de Mazaugues and continues round to the front of the Mourre d'Agnis ridge. *In May the mass of yellow flowering broom bushes along the side of the road hums with bees.* The GR path you took on the outward journey is just up on the left. The jeep track goes northeast away from the mountain through another fire barrier (Protection incendie Agnis 9) where it becomes concrete.

(11) Just before reaching another road (D64) turn hard left (no sign) on a large track going upwards. At a T-junction a few minutes later turn right (Number (2) on map p122). You are now on the GR99 where you came up on. Continue back to the village (4hrs 30mins).

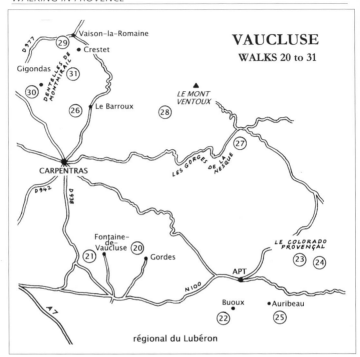

VAUCLUSE
WALKS 20 to 31

Vaison-la-Romaine
29
Crestet
Gigondas
31
30
26   Le Barroux

LE MONT
VENTOUX
28

DENTELLES DE MONTMIRAIL

LES GORGES DE LA NESQUE
27

CARPENTRAS
D 977
D 942
D 938

Fontaine-
de-
Vaucluse   20
21   Gordes

LE COLORADO
PROVENÇAL
23   24

APT
N 100

A 7

Buoux
22

Auribeau
25

régional du Lubéron

Vaucluse
Luberon and Mont Ventoux areas

WALK Nos. 20 - 31

The Vaucluse comes from the Latin name *Vallis Clausa* meaning closed valley,
though exactly which valley the name refers to is lost in the annals of history.
It is bordered to the West by the Rhône, to the south by the Durance and to
the northeast by the southern Alps.

It has a breathtaking scenic diversity. In the south is the brooding limestone range of the Luberon, dissected north to south by the wide Loumarin combe creating two separate mountain masses: the Petit Luberon which is a plateau carved by gorges and ravines and the Grand Luberon, which is higher and wilder. The whole area is now a national park, created in 1977 and consisting of 120,000 hectares. From Mourre Nègre (1125m), the summit of the Grand Luberon, only attainable by foot, offers a spectacular view of the surrounding countryside with the white slopes of Mont Ventoux and the Alps to the north. The area has been discovered and the little villages sprinkled along the lower slopes and on hilltops have been renovated and prettied up for the summer tourist season. Out of season they are peaceful and curiously dead.

These now "quaint little villages" were once the refuges of the Waldenses (Vaudois) religious sect who settled the area in the 15th century after it had been devastated by the plague. They were followers of a wealthy merchant from Lyon who embraced poverty and the preaching of the gospels in the vernacular. Forced to abandon Lyon he and his disciples fled in all directions. Living simply they escaped detection until the outbreak of the Reformation, when the French authorities started hunting down heretical sects. It was the Dominican Jean de Roma, the Inquisitor in Apt, who triggered the persecution and extermination of the sect. The villages were burnt and hundreds of people killed or sent to the galleys (Walk No. 22).

The Luberon also includes the Colorado Provençale (named after the Grand Canyon in America). Once a gigantic quarry, operated up to the beginning of this century for mining ochre, it is now a walker's paradise. A fascinating labyrinth of twisted peaks, cliffs and chimneys in a kaleidoscope of colours ranging from brilliant white to deep orange, the contrast with the deep green of the pines and gorse which often sit atop the sandy cliffs creates a breathtaking beauty. It is best visited out of season as it is very hot in mid-summer and abounds in snakes! (see Walk Nos. 23 and 24 for further information).

Further north between the Luberon range and the Mont Ventoux (1909m) is the Vaucluse Plateau - a sparsely populated arid area devoted to sheep and the cultivation of lavender. It is interspersed with limestone gorges (see Walk No. 27), canyons and a network of underground rivers, one of which, the Saorge, surfaces in the village of Fontaine-de-Vaucluse.

The whole area is dominated by Mont Ventoux which translates as "windy mountain", a deserving name as the wind here is constant and especially icy when the *mistral* is blowing. The name may derive from the Celtic *ven top* meaning white mountain. Snow-capped during the winter but permanently white all the year round due to its covering of shingle, Mont Ventoux is a landmark for the surrounding region. The lower slopes are covered by stately forests of Austrian pine, cedar and oak which were planted

Colorado Provençal - Chemin des Fées *(Walks 23 and 24)*
A typical Borie in the Luberon *(Walk 25)*

View of Gordes village

the traditional Provençal bread. At an altitude of 500-700m it is criss-crossed with oak truffle forests, wheat fields, lavender and cherry orchards.

Where to base yourself for walks in the Vaucluse

It is probably better to avoid the bigger towns such as Avignon, Orange, Carpentras or Apt, although they are certainly worth a visit on rest days. The author stayed in the little hilltop village of Saignon, above Apt, within an hour's drive of all walks. There are countless charming villages around the Luberon mountain, many with hotels, gîtes and campsites.

The villages on the other side of the Apt valley, on the edge of the Plateau de Vaucluse, would also be convenient centres. Rousillon is surrounded by ochre-coloured hills of all shades with a beautiful view northwards to the Mont Ventoux. There is a delightful short walk from the village itself into nearby ochre quarries. Gordes (see Walk No. 20), Rustrel, St. Saturnin-les-Apt and Venasque all have various types of accommodation.

It is better to base yourself further north for the Ventoux regions. Vaison-la-Romaine has a number of hotels, campsites and gîtes. If you prefer somewhere smaller, Le Barroux, a quaint hilltop village with its own castle on the D938 between Carpentras and Vaison-la-Romaine, has a good Logis de France hotel. The small villages around the Dentelles de Montmirail are in a beautiful location, surrounded by well-known vineyards and many of them with small hotels, campsites and gîtes.

Luberon region walks
Walk No. 20
ABBAYE DE SÉNANQUE, GORDES

Difficulty:	Easy walk with no great ups and downs.
Time:	3hrs (visit to the Abbey not included - leave at least 30mins. For opening times see below).
Height gain:	300m.
Maps:	Cartes IGN 3142 OT Top 25 Cavaillon 1:25,000.
	Editions Didier Richard No. 27 Ventoux 1:50,000.
Depart from:	Parking in Gordes.
Signposting:	Easy to follow - no signposts but blue and then red/white GR splashes. Note: the blue splashes do have a tendency to be dark and then light - lack of paint in the tin perhaps!

Observations:

A delightful walk with no long ups and downs and the bonus of a visit to a famous Abbey! There are marks all the way along so is not difficult to follow.

The **Abbaye de Sénanque** was founded in 1148 by a small group of Cistercian monks who had come from the Abbaye de Mazan in the Haut Vivarais. Due to numerous donations from the local aristocracy they were soon able to build an impressive abbey and acquire vast tracts of farmland. In the 14th century the monastery declined but managed to maintain its status as a monastery until 1544 when the Vaudois revolt erupted *(see 'Introduction: A Short History')*. Most of the monks were hanged and the buildings damaged. At the end of the 17th century only two monks remained and it was sold as state property in 1791. Luckily the new owner preserved the buildings and it was bought back by the church authorities in 1854. New buildings were built and once again the Cistercian order re-established itself. The monks were subsequently evicted twice during the anti-clerical movements which swept across France in 1880 and 1902. In 1927 a dozen monks returned to live in the abbey for forty years before moving to the Lerins Islands off Cannes and then returning in 1989. Since then the monastery has prospered and much of its present income comes from tourism.

The buildings, built in the local stone, have an austere beauty in keeping with the Benedictine rule of poverty and simplicity. There are no statues or stained glass windows but the rooms are big and vaulted. Only the parlour or warming room has a fireplace. The cloisters have discreet naturalistic motifs and the main rooms lead off this central area.

Abbey opening times:
From March to the end of October: 10.00-12.00 and 14.00-18.00hrs.
(closed Sunday morning).
From November to end February: 14.00-17.00hrs. Monday to Friday.
Saturday/Sunday 14.00-18.00rs. Entrance fee.

For further information concerning visits Tel. 04.90.72.05.72

The village of Gordes is perched on a hill at the edge of the Vaucluse
Plateau. Since Neolithic times the site has been occupied and fortified. In the
13th century Gordes refused to be linked with France and placed itself under
the flag of Beatrix de Savoie, wife of the Count of Forcalquier. It subsequently
suffered under the raids of robber bands and during the religious wars. In the
17th and 18th centuries it was known for its wool, shoe making and building
stone taken from the local quarries. In the 19th century the village declined
until it was almost entirely ruined by an earthquake in 1886.

Renovated and charming with its narrow cobbled streets, vaulted
passageways and tall stone houses Gordes is worth strolling around. It has
an austere Renaissance château which dominates the village and now
houses art exhibitions. Like many Provençal villages it is very popular during
the high season, though once you start walking you will meet no one!

The Borie village is worth a visit. From the map it looks as though you can
walk there from a turn-off just before you reach the road above the Abbey.
The author tried this but the path is overgrown and it was not possible to get
through. It is better to go by car after you have done the walk. Go back down
the village the way you walked in and follow the sign Village des Bories. There
is a large parking area by the side of the road and a second one much nearer.
There is an entrance fee to visit the village.

How to get there (from Apt):
Take the N100 direction Cavaillon for 12.5kms. Turn up right on the D903
which connects with the D2. Follow all signs to Gordes. Park in the centre of
the village - there are lots of paying parking areas. Gordes is a well-known
spot so be prepared for lots of visitors.

Directions:
**(Note: timings are from the parking at the château in the village
centre)**
(1) With the château on the right walk straight down towards La Poste (post
office). Keeping the post office on your right continue on this road through
a parking area which takes you along the ramparts of the village, past the
cemetery and here you see your first blue splash on the wall to the left. *There*

is a magnificent view to the right over the plain below with the long ridge of the Luberon mountain on the horizon. The path narrows going gently up between stone walls with some private houses on the right and extensive views beyond.

(2) Turn right uphill where the path meets a narrow road (15mins) following the blue splash. After 200m go left at a fork near a building on the right. The path continues between old stone walls until it meets the D15 (20mins).

(3) Turn right and continue up the road for about 450m passing a hotel on the right.

(4) Turn left shortly after at a sign saying Camping des Sources on the Chemin de Fontanille (there is a blue marking on a rock). The paved road goes up medium steep towards the campsite. Ignore the road to the right which is the entrance to a large private house called Fontanille.

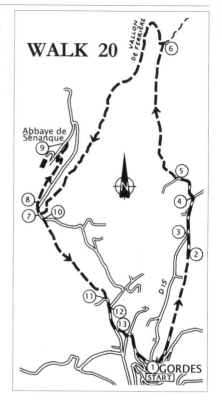

(5) At a fork just before the campsite, go up right by a red fire hydrant on a narrow road (blue splash here) which soon develops into a stony track. Keep straight with the wall on the right which degenerates into concrete posts before finally bearing off right. Follow blue splashes and ignore any paths branching off.

The track rises gently through bushy country and then descends into the Maillet Valley. When it reaches an open glade take the middle path straight (blue splash on a rock). The path narrows as it goes along the side of the attractive shallow Maillet Valley. Over on the right are open pastures and fields of lavender with low tree-covered hills beyond.

(6) At a T-junction by the end of a long field (55mins), turn down left still following blue splashes and shortly after take second right turn (blue mark on rock). Keep to the main path through an attractive pine forest before crossing some scree and climbing up the side of the hill. To the right is an impressive slab of grey volcanic rock at the start of a magnificent circle of cliffs which you look down on as you continue round - on the map the area is called Le Serre (this means claw or green-house in French but I think the first meaning is more appropriate!).

After the cliffs the landscape opens up into a valley (Vallon de Ferrière) through which there is a deep gorge. As the path continues round the side of the hill through bush and stunted woodland there are some sudden drops on the right to the gorge below. Down in the valley is the large building of the Bergerie de Sénaque and a number of lavender fields. Beyond, the D117 winds down from Venasque.

Soon you get your first glimpse of the huge Abbaye de Sénanque - *it nestles alone in the very bottom of the Sénanque Valley with a large field of lavender in front of it which, when it is in bloom in June, makes a magnificent purple panorama in front of the rather austere stone buildings.* The path gets bushier with more trees as it descends gently. It goes directly above the monastery and becomes rockier - follow the blue splashes carefully here (one path is blocked off by rocks). Later you can see right down into the courtyard of the monastery before the path gets so bushy that you feel you are walking through a tunnel. Go straight at the stoney crossroads just before meeting the road.

(7) At the road turn right (1hr 45mins) and descend to the Abbey by a sign Cote de Sénanque and a white/red splash of the GR6/97 straight ahead.

(8) Shortly after watch for a red/white splash on the next bend indicating left. This is the original mule track down to the monastery (cutting across the winding road) passing a stone water cistern on the right and underneath telephone wires. Keep straight and ignore a wide path going down left. Continue on the narrow path ignoring a further track left and an intersection till you reach the road 5mins later.

(9) Turn down left and follow the obvious way to the Abbey (2hrs 10mins). Afterwards retrace your steps up the road the way you came and take the little path right (*careful* - it is easier to miss on the way back but look for the red/white splash) back to the higher road where you came down from the ridge (2hrs 30mins). You are still on the GR6/97. Continue down the road towards Gordes.

(10) A few minutes later, where the road bears left, take the track straight by a barely visible red/white GR splash. Follow this bushy track avoiding any offshoots. Turn right when merging with another track and then immediately left (on the right are fallen pillars with a chain across). This is now an obvious mule track with old stone walls on both sides and wide flat stones underfoot (the original way from Gordes to the Abbey). You can see the village ahead.

(11) The mule track reaches a narrow road where you turn left (2hrs 45mins) (GR signs on wall).

(12) Shortly after it meets a wider road where you turn right into Gordes.

(13) At the start of the village turn left just before the sign Hotel Restaurant Domaine de l'Enclos and go down the narrow lane. At the end turn left on the road which goes up to the Château (3hrs).

Walk No. 21
FONTAINE-DE-VAUCLUSE AND WALL OF THE PLAGUE

Difficulty:	Medium - the way up the valley can seem long.
Time:	4hrs 30mins (this includes the walk to the Source).
Height gain:	520m.
Maps:	Carte IGN 3142 OT Top 25 Cavaillon/Fontaine-de-Vaucluse 1:25,000.
	Editions Didier Richard No. 27 Ventoux 1:50,000.
Depart from:	Fontaine-de-Vaucluse.
Signposting:	No actual signposts but red/white GR splashes and some green and blue splashes. Where there are no splashes the way is obvious.

Observations:

A delightful walk, somewhat long up the valley but amply rewarded with wonderful views on the return journey.

The village of **Fontaine-de-Vaucluse**, dominated by its 14th-century château on a high hill above the town, takes its name from *Vallis Clausa* meaning closed valley. It is charmingly dilapidated and near the central square there is a huge former printing mill. From the 15th century it was known for its prosperous paper mills but now tourism is the main revenue. Hundreds of people visit the famous spring which is the source of the Sorgue, the outlet of an underwater river fed by rainwater draining through the Vaucluse Plateau. Many explorations have been made of the deep chasm from which the water springs, the earliest in 1878 and the last as recently as 1985 when a remote-controlled submarine with cameras was used. It went down 315m and found that the water gushes from an imposing limestone labyrinth of caves and crevices fed by rainwater at the rate of around 900mm per year.

François Pétrarque (1304-74) was a famous Provençal writer and poet who lived in Fontaine-de-Vaucluse; there is a museum and library dedicated to his works which was founded in 1927. In 1760 Giacomo Casanova paid a visit to render hommage to Pétrarque as he was curious to see the place where the famous writer had fallen in love with the beautiful Laura de Sade.

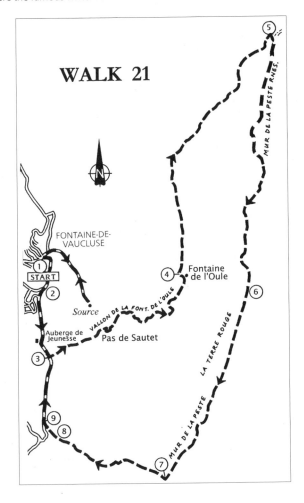

How to get there (from Apt):
Take the N100 direction Cavaillon for 26kms and then turn right on the D186, signposted Lagnes and Fontaine-de-Vaucluse. The village is 9km up this road. In the centre of the village, at the roundabout by the tall pillar, follow signs for parking areas.

Directions:
(1) At the memorial pillar which is dedicated to François Pétrarque (see above) and surrounded by enormous plane trees, look for green place indicators and follow directions to La Source (spring).

The road* goes along the River Sorgue which rushes along on the right with high cliffs ahead. The water is very clear and green, tumbling over huge rocks. The water wells up from a pool further up under precipitous rocky cliffs. This is the famous Fontaine-de-Vaucluse. *Note: After a long dry spell the rocks may be dry and the pool stagnant.*

Retrace your steps to the pillar (25mins).

(2) Turn left across the bridge over the River Sorgue and walk out of the village, passing a large parking area on the right. Shortly after turn left at a sign Auberge de Jeunesse - the road goes up and then bears left past the high wall of a cemetery to the left with flats over to the right (40mins).

(3) After the Auberge de Jeunesse on the right (indicated on the map as on the left!) and an end-of-the-village sign, turn left where there is a noticeboard saying La Fôret and a GR red/white marking (this is the GR6/97 which joins from the right).

The wide jeep track bears east past a plantation of young olive trees and enters a wild valley called the Vallon de la Font de l'Oule with dramatic rock formations each side. Keep straight and ignore a turning to the right. At a subsequent fork go right, and higher up pass through a fire barrier with a no-entry sign. The track goes up steadily up past high rock walls with some some dank looking caves to the left. It continues round a hairpin bend, where there is a man made wall, to the Pas de Sautet. There is a good view back down the valley and it looks as if you have come a long way!

After the pass the track continues up, passing a small cave - much of the area around has been damaged by fire. Further up the valley becomes more wooded as it widens and flattens out.

(4) At a beautiful old oak tree there is a huge cave up on the right with water in it and a concrete wall in front (1hr 20mins) - this is the Fontaine de l'Oule. Continue on bearing left past a water cistern No. 130. The track goes through

*On this road, apart from cafés and souvenir shops, there are two museums which can be visited - the Museum of the Liberation after the 1939-45 war, and the Vallis Clausa Paper Mill (you can see the old millwheel turning).

bushes, still rising gently, and the valley narrows again with shale on the slopes before becoming more woody. This is a long straight path which seems to be endless, but take courage, the view at the end is worth it!

(5) The track finally reaches a crossroads (2hrs 15mins). Turn right to the south (the GR6 goes off left towards Gordes), reaching a wide jeep track almost immediately where you turn right again (green splash here which later turns into blue). There is now a magnificent view ahead of the valley and the long ridge of the Luberon.

As you walk along the track you get your first glimpse of the renowned Mur de la Peste which follows this walk on the lefthand side for much of the way. *Le Mur de la Peste (Wall of the Plague) is a crumbling wall of stones about 20kms long. It was constructed in 1721 to stop the population fleeing from the plague which had broken out in Marseilles. It was punctuated by watchtowers and garrisons, little evidence of which remains today, and guarded by hundreds of soldiers. Despite all these precautions the plague continued to spread.*

The wide track is fairly flat along the top of a wide crest with open views (look back for a magnificent view of Mont Ventoux). Ignore a path down to the left with red arrows. There is a wooden lookout post on the left (2hrs 30mins) which is a great place to climb up on for lunch with an even more extensive view including the track ahead and the low crumbling wall of the Mur de la Peste! *It is interesting to note that the map indicates that you should be walking through forest but in fact this area has been swept clean by forest fires and all that grows here now is the Provençal "garrigue" (see 'Introduction: Flora and Fauna').*

The open track starts to go down with continuing views and little vegetation. It flattens out and then descends again veering left towards the south. You can see it snaking along in front across the top of the wide ridge and after a while you feel you should have turned off somewhere! There are glorious open views in all directions to compensate. The track becomes sandy and there are scattered pines and bushes. Down to the right is a valley.

(6) The track narrows - keep straight and avoid all offshoots (some may be short cuts but this is not obvious). On the right is the Terre Rouge hill (reddish soil here so hence the name!) with ruins on both sides - these could be ancient garrisons attached to the wall which you can see clearly (3hrs 20mins). To the right on the horizon you can now see Gordes with Rousillon to the right of it. Where the wall looks as if it has been restored for a short stretch, watch for a stone on the right with Mur de la Peste on it and the drawing of a man with a hood!

The track reaches a wide area where there is a water cistern and a large wooden board showing a map of the walks in the area (3hrs 35mins). *The other side of the board tells about the fire which swept the region in 1989 and relates that in 1991 replanting started of 4000 trees. These included species such as pines, oaks, cedars, and olives. Help was given by the children from listed local schools.*

(7) Turn right here over a slab of concrete where there are the red/white splashes of the GR6/97 which you follow till the end of the walk. At the start of the descent along the side of a narrow valley, there is a certain confusion of paths. Keep downwards over a slab of rock and follow the GR markings. As you drop down into this delightful valley there are a number of majestic tall cedar trees which must have escaped the fire.

There is a sign saying that this is the Sentier de l'Ecole de la Forêt so they are obviously going to make this a botanical walk as there are posts with numbers on them as you go down the path but no visible trees planted as yet.

The path descends gently into the rocky valley bottom - there are interestingly shaped rocky crags on the other side and a solitary pine tree which stands against a rock face and makes a striking photograph.

(8) After walking some distance go right at a fork (GR markings on a tree) just before the bottom of the valley where the path crosses a dry river bed and goes up on the righthand side of the valley.

(9) A few minutes later you meet the road (4hrs). Turn right and continue past the turning taken on the outward journey. Retrace your steps to the central square (4hrs 30mins).

Walk No. 22
FORT DE BUOUX AND AIGUEBRUN

Difficulty:	Medium.
Time:	3hrs 15mins (plus about an hour to visit the fort).
Height gain:	300m.
Maps:	Cartes IGN 3243 OT Top 25 Pertuis Lourmarin 1:25,000.
	Editions Didier Richard No. 14 Du Luberon à La Sainte Victoire 1:50,000.
Depart from:	Second car park for the Fort de Buoux.
Signposting:	Spasmodic - blue signs and some GR red/white splashes. On this walk many of the blue splashes seem to be crosses but take the path anyway.

Observations:

A really delightful walk with lots of historical interest. It is worth visiting the

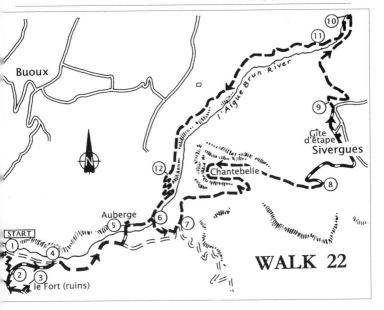

little village of **Buoux** itself which is just off the D113 and near the ruins of the original village of Saint Germain which is now completely covered with vegetation. The church of Sainte Marie, which dates from the 13th century, is 20mins by foot (take the road to the right of the Mairie) at the bottom of the village.

The site of the Buoux fort, perched on a promontory over the Aiguebrun gorge, was originally inhabited by neolithic tribes, before becoming an oppidum and later on a medieval fort with ramparts and a reservoir containing 60,000 litres of water. It was demolished under the reign of Louis XIV who feared that it would be used as a refuge by the Huguenots.

Sivergues was one of the villages where the Waldensian sect (*vaudois* in French - see Var chapter) sought refuge from 1490 to 1520. They were subsequently persecuted by the Baron of Oppède who ransacked the villages in the Luberon area where many of the sect had settled. Like many villages it was a huddle of ruins in the 19th century but has since been tastefully renovated. The little church of Saint Pierre et Sainte Marie built in the 16th century testifies to the small Catholic population of the village (2 out of 20 families), the remaining resting faithful to the Protestantism brought by the sect. A project to turn it into a holiday resort with flats, bungalows and a hotel by a German industrialist in the 1970s was happily turned down by the Luberon National Park Association. The village has been immortalised by the Provençal writer Henri Bosco (1888 to 1976) in his book *L'Habitant de Sivergues.*

How to get there (from Apt):

From Apt take the D943 direction Loumarin, then the D113 direction Buoux. When you arrive at Buoux (9kms) continue on the D113 past the Auberge de Loube till you reach a hairpin bend and a sign Fort de Buoux and Seguin. Turn left here and continue to the second car park which is on the right.

Directions:

(1) From the car park (there is a map of the region here) take the narrow track up where there is a sign, rather hidden, saying Fort de Buoux. Keep on the main track.

(2) This takes you up to the road where you turn right. *As you walk up the road you can see on the left a number of jumbled rocks covered with vegetation. These are the ancient tombs of the inhabitants of Saint Germain, a village which was razed to the ground in the 9th century by the invading Saracens.* The road goes underneath an enormous overhanging rock which is the largest Baume in Provence. *This sheltered early gatherings of primitive man. Take time to inspect the sculptured indents in the rock face where they attached the beams of their roofs, and also the vestiges of water channels.*

(3) Continue on the road and at a T-junction bear left following the sign to the Fort. *There is a house with a pretty garden where you pay an entrance fee to enter into the fort which is fascinating to wander around and one of the most important historical areas in Provence. You will be given a map (in English) with the names and numbers of all the different sites - there are 36 in all, including the fortifications, the guard houses, the ancient village with its fascinating water reservoirs, huge silos carved into the rock, and the walls of a 13th-century church. The site is magnificent, on the flat top of a rock massif, and the views of the surrounding area, particularly of the gorge in the Aiguebrun Valley, are really breathtaking.*

It is possible to go down the old staircase out of the fort at the sign Postern (No. 36). These steps (rather precipitous in some places) take you back to the house at the entrance to the fort (add about 15mins for this). **OTHERWISE** go back down the road passing the little path you came up on (on the left).

(4) The road goes out through iron gates to a junction where you turn hard right (30mins not including the visit to the fort) following the signpost Auberge de Seguins. *In front of you at the crossroads is a sheer rock face* *which is very popular with climbers and you can also see the caves used by hermits in the 5th century when Christianity was starting to flourish in Provence.* Keep going on this road which bears left to reach the Auberge (40mins), a very popular hotel/restaurant, especially at weekends.

(5) In front of the Auberge turn right where there is a sign Vallon d'Aiguebrun. *There is a buvette here - a good place to have a drink overlooking the green swimming pool. (I am told the green colour is due to the water which comes from a spring and that it is a delightful place to swim in!)*

The path is narrow, going round the back of the *buvette* and and then right, just above the floor of the valley with the Aiguebrun stream which you can hear down on the right. *The Aiguebrun River takes its name from the Provençal dialect "Aigo-broun" and means murmuring water - it is the only permanently running river in the Luberon area and has created a valley between the large and small Luberon ridges which extends to the Durance River in the south.*

(6) After a few minutes keep right at a fork where there are blue splashes and also red/white ones of the GR9 which joins from the left. Shortly after cross the river on a bridge which is so overgrown you are scarcely aware of it! The path gains height to a T-junction (50mins) where you turn up left. Go up right at the next fork, following GR splashes and then left onto a jeep track. Immediately after, at a hairpin bend and a clearing (55mins), leave the GR which goes around to the right.

(7) Take the path straight on where there is a sign saying Sivergues (blue splashes) - you are now on the Chemin de Chantebelle which dominates the Aiguebrun valley. *This was the famous* chemin de sel (*salt route*) *running from L'Etang de Berre near Marseilles through Sivergues to the town of Apt during the Middle Ages. It was wiser to take this track rather than the more frequented roads to avoid the numerous bandits who robbed travellers in the region.* This mule track continues high along the righthand side of the valley which is now more of a wide tree-covered gorge lined with impressive cliffs with caves in them. Shortly after the path passes a tall cairn and further on crosses huge slopes of grey boldery stones (1hr) where there is a ruin in the valley below.

On the other side of the gorge you can now see what was once the Bastide of Chantebelle (11th century) of which all that remains is a house built into the rock which until recently had a herd of goats and was well known for the production of goat's cheese. This site was in a privileged position during the Middle Ages as the cultivated ground was on the plain behind, with the woods below and a system of capturing water to rear the animals.

Keep on the main path with blue splashes, ignoring any branches down to the valley. There are old mossy walls along part of the path and if you look into the valley there are a number of crumbling walls which are all that remain of the once cultivated terraces. Ignore a branch off to the right (1hr 10mins) and follow the main path which goes right round the end of the gorge and gains height again. A few minutes later, at a hairpin bend, do not go off to the left where there are blue/yellow signs.

The path reaches Chantebelle (1hr 20mins) and the impressive rock with the house built into it. Continue on, following blue splashes - there are old *stone terraces to the left and some olive trees, signs of former cultivation. You are now on the other side of the gorge but much higher up. There are rocks to the right which hide the plateau above and across the gorge you can see the wide stony slopes previously crossed - if you look down left you can see a path running through the gorge itself. On the plateau to the left are the substantial farm buildings of Matrenon and La Bremonde.* The path climbs around another small valley. At an oblique T-junction bear left on the main track keeping to blue splashes.

(8) At a T-junction go left following the sign Sivergues 1km (1hr 40mins) - you are now on a wide unsurfaced road, rising gently. *If you look left you would hardly know there was a gorge as the flat plateau beyond looks so near.* The track reaches the first house in Sivergues which is built entirely into the rock (1hr 50mins). *The hamlet itself is worth a visit with its ancient houses, small chapel and also a borie. The old fort has been transformed into an attractive gîte d'étape called Le Fort d'Archidiacre.* In front of the gîte there is a sign indicating Aiguebrun/Seguin but do not take this.

(9) Continue on the same road following blue splashes and a few minutes later take the second turning to the left (not the first with a blue cross on it) where the road turns round to the right (1hr 55mins). There is a smart signpost here which says Aiguebrun. This wooded path goes down medium steep into the Aiguebrun valley - continue following blue splashes ignoring any offshoots. Straight ahead is a huge farmhouse (La Brémonde). Further down the path becomes a mule track with smooth stones and goes under a large overhanging rock. As you go lower the vegetation becomes denser.

(10) Turn left at a T-junction when you reach the valley bottom (2hrs 15mins): there is a blue arrow pointing back to Sivergues and the river is over on the right. *This valley is exceptionally fresh and humid with the vegetation of more temperate and colder regions such as holly and hart's tongue fern - there are huge oaks, black poplar, ash, maple, willows and lime trees.*

This is a wide clear path down the middle of the valley with the river on your right and tall white cliffs beyond - cool and refreshing on a hot day. *It feels as though you are walking through a tropical jungle as the vegetation is so luxuriant - there are lovely open green glades and big moss covered rocks. If you look down into the rocky pools, the water is clear and limpid. This is a paradise for picnics and barbecues and also a popular spot for riders so watch out for approaching horses!* Go straight across two glades ignoring a path to the right to an enticing meadow on the other side of the river in the second glade (2hrs 25mins). Soon after at a T-junction go right and then at a fork ignore another path towards the river on the right.

(11) A few minutes later at a further fork keep right crossing a rivulet and then the river (2hrs 30mins). You are now walking close to the water on the left where it is very mossy with dense vegetation; there are high cliffs on the right. After about 15mins beside the stream the path gains height and for a short while you walk along under overhanging cliffs before descending again. *The inaccessible caves which line this gorge have yielded tools hewn out of stone flint, attesting to a human presence here since early man.* Over on the left you can now see the path taken on the outward journey and the slopes of boulders.

(12) Keep straight at a fork (not up right) where the GR9 joins for a while and then branches off left just before you reach the the Auberge de Seguin. The track comes out at the Auberge (2hrs 55mins) - time for another drink before retracing your steps by the road to the car park (3hrs 15mins).

Walk No. 23
SHORT WALK AROUND THE COLORADO PROVENÇAL
(ancient ochre quarries)

Difficulty:	Easy but keep to the paths as the area is very eroded.
Time:	Walk A - (Sahara) 1hr.
	Walk B - (Cirque des Barriès) 1hr 30mins.
	Add more time for looking and taking photographs.
Height gain:	Negligible.
Maps:	Colorado Provencal (*site privé*) - ask in Tourist Office.
	(The above is a leaflet and outlines the colours of the walks).
	Carte IGN 3242 OT Top 25 APT (Parc Naturel Régional du Luberon) 1:25,000.
Depart from:	Parking area on the D22 (see below).
Signposting:	Walk A: GR splashes - green splashes.
	Walk B: GR splashes - green splashes.
	(the splashes have been erased in the Cheminées des Fées and Sahara regions).

Observations:

Important information - due to disputes between private owners and the French local authorities, a large area of the Colorado Provençal is officially out of bounds (since 1997) and there are no concise maps. The owners of the Chemin des Fées and Sahara areas claim they are becoming very eroded and dangerous due to the number of tourists. Waymark splashes on the trees have been blotted out (for example the green splashes on the way up to the Chemin des Fées have gone and there is a large notice at the start of the Sahara walk saying it is *Proprieté Privée*). The author has been told that negotiations are under way so things could change completely ie. the whole area could be turned into a National Park with official walks.

Meanwhile there are no actual fences and many tourists are still passing through - but walking there is at your own risk. For other information concerning the Colorado Provençal see Walk No. 24.

How to get there (from Apt):

Take the D22 direction Rustrel and just before the village where it indicates left D112 Rustrel 0.6km/St. Christophe 19kms (this is the second turning to the village), take a turning right. Note: there is no sign apart from a no-entry notice for buses. Continue for approximately 1km till you see a car park right and a sign giving information about Rustrel. At the entrance is a small wooden hut where there is an attendant in season. On the maps this is indicated as the Parking Municipal. Park here.

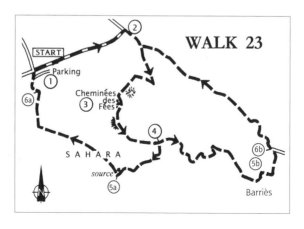

Directions:

(1) From the car park turn right along the road (you are on the GR 6/97) for a few minutes and turn down right when you reach a house on the left at a T-junction. There is a sign indicating Les Barriès 1.5kms.

(2) Go down the track and turn right crossing over the stream and continuing to the right - there is a big green arrow at the start only and then some white splashes. Otherwise the green has been obliterated (see above). The path is wide and stony going up medium steep through woodland.

(3) At the top it flattens out and you get your first view of the magnificent Cheminée des Fées (fairy chimneys). *These are huge pillars of ochre-coloured sandstone which rise up out of the quarry below. The surrounding cliffs are a kaleidoscope of orange, ochre, cream, yellow and white, the colours set off by the brilliant green of the trees and bushes growing out of the sand itself (for more information see p148).* Take your time to admire the view and take photographs - it is magnificent and unusual scenery.

The path goes round the left side of the quarry and then bears left away from it through bushes of tall heather (look for a dramatic white wall ahead right on the horizon), until it reaches a junction (30mins).

****End of instructions (1) to (3) for long walk 24.**

Here you have two options:

(Walk A) Turn right into the Sahara part of the Colorado Provençal and from there back to the car park (see note below concerning the Sahara).

(Walk B) Turn left and go round the Cirque de Barriès back to the start.

Walk A - Sahara

(4) Bear round to the right following the sign Sahara/Cascade (waterfall), following green splashes. The path takes you down steps in the ochre-coloured rock (a bit of a scramble) through a miniature canyon before getting back again on the forest track. *Note: Most of the paths in the Colorado Provençal are sandy - this is an area where there are lots of snakes so keep an eye out for them - in general they are harmless!*

The path goes deep into the sandy quarry area past gnarled trees and bushes. Keep carefully to the green splashes till you reach a sunken sandy clearing with pine trees. Go right - there is a green splash on a tree. The path starts to go down and crosses a rivulet of ochre-coloured sand to the right. There are tall sandstone cliffs visible through the trees. Bear round to the left and back over the rivulet - there are paths going in all directions so it is very important to follow the green splashes carefully.

(5A) In a clearing with trees and paths diverging, follow the sign on a tree indicating Sahara (40mins). Bear left (there is a long iron pipe to the right). Walk down over white sandstone mounds into a breathtaking area of weird sandy outcrops. *The colours of the towering sandy crags range from deep to pale orange and varying shades of cream, grey and white, offset by the green foliage of the trees growing with a precarious holding in the sandy soil. Some cliffs are cream with summits of glowing orange topped by vivid green trees - the blue sky behind combines a variety of colour almost overwhelming to the human eye.*

Follow an obvious path left through the shaped sandstone mounds and continue left down a short narrow path between red rocks. There are more rusty pipes, presumably left over from the quarrying, as you bear left by a tall pine tree with a sign saying Sahara/Cirque de Bouvène.

(6A) Bear right at the T-junction just beyond the tree - to the left is a very impressive sheer red sandstone cliff. Go slightly downwards on a wide sandy path and keep straight where the path narrows (field to left). Then turn left, cross the river and bear left again to a long stone aqueduct. Turn right in front of the aqueduct and cross over a wider river bed (could be dried up). Cross a clearing, go by a café (*buvette*) and straight on to the car park (1hr).

Walk B - Cirque de Barriès

(4) Turn left at the T-junction following the sign Cirque de Barriès and green splashes. At the next junction keep left and follow the green splashes ignoring all other splashes and offshoots.

(5B) As the path starts down a dry river bed **watch carefully** for a path to the right which is not evident. There is a green splash on a tree at the turning and further on left a torn-off sign and a green marking but nothing to indicate the turn right! A few metres later turn left where there is a green arrow on a stone.

The path reaches an attractive sandy area and continues up between two sandy columns to a bushy ridge where the slope falls abruptly to the left as it goes round the Cirque de Barriès. *There are lovely open views of the quarry below with the rolling hills of Provence in the background.* Continue through woodland and giant heather as the path gets wider and flatter. Go left at a T-junction (cross on tree).

(6B) The path meets a wide jeep track (1hr). Still following green splashes turn left and shortly the red/white splashes of the GR join from the right and continue till the end of the walk. *Look down left for a magnificent view of the ochre-coloured slopes and weirdly shaped mounds of the Cirque de Barriès - the cliff sides fall away very abruptly so be careful.* Continue along the jeep track going steadily downwards at first before flattening out past lavender fields and a ruin on the left and then through more open country between lavender fields. The path dips and crosses the Doua stream at a ford before meeting the road (point (2) on the map on page146). Turn left and walk back to the car park (1hr 30mins).

Walk No. 24
LONG WALK AROUND THE COLORADO PROVENÇAL
(ancient ochre quarries)
First read important comments under
'Observations' in Walk No. 23 on page143

Difficulty:	Medium (the walk across the actual quarries is strenuous).
	Do not stray from the defined paths as this is dangerous.
	Take lots of water as none available and it can get very hot.
Time:	3hrs + lhr for looking for signs, admiring the view and taking photos! Also add on about 1hr if you take the yellow path across the quarries.
Height gain:	Negligible.
Maps:	Cartes IGN 3242 OT Top 25 APT (Parc Naturel Régional du Luberon) - 1:25,000 though the path is not easy to see.
	Map out of booklet Découverte du Colorado Provençal by F.et C. Morenas - this shows it more clearly.
Depart from:	Parking area on the D22 (see below).
Signposting:	Green, blue and yellow splashes - you have to be vigilant to follow them - the place is like a labyrinth!

Observations:
It feels like a long walk because of constant stopping to admire the view and take photos so add at least an hour. There is apparently no up-to-date map or guide which shows a less complicated way around. It seems that different organisations have made their own walks with their own splashes. There is also the problem that the some of the area is private property and the people concerned want to close it and charge an entrance fee. Avoid this walk in July or August as it is too hot.

The name Colorado Provençal was invented in 1935 by a Provençal called Gabriel Jean (what other claim to fame he has is unknown!). During the French Revolution Jean-Etienne Astier discovered the quality of ochre in the region and decided to quarry it. The industry reached its height between 1920-1950 when 2000 people worked in the quarries extracting around 35,000 tons annually for use as a colouring material for building and painting. When synthetic colouring was discovered the industry declined dramatically. A very small amount is still quarried but most of the area has now been turned over to tourism, attracting crowds of people to admire the varied colours of the sandy rocks ranging from glistening white to deep orange.

The ochre is made up of marine sediments deposited 100,000-200,000 years ago, consisting of clay, sand and iron oxide. In order to obtain the ochre, the sand is washed away from the ore by strong jets of water - this is done twice between the months of September and May. The residue is transported to drying basins where the water evaporates leaving a 5cm covering of porous ochre. During the month of August it is cut into bricks and left to continue drying before being ground into powder. The ochre deposits cause a layer of silicon to form over the limestone which enables naturalists to study a vegetation peculiar to the region consisting of different species of ferns, laurels, heathers and herbs. Maritime pines and chestnuts also flourish in the soil. For further information read observations Walk No. 23.

How to get there (from Apt):
Take the D22 direction Rustrel and just before the village where it indicates left D112 Rustrel 0.6km/St. Christophe 19kms (this is the second turning to the village) take a turning right. Note: There is no sign apart from a no-entry notice for buses. Continue for approximately 1km until you see a car park right and a sign giving information about Rustrel. At the entrance is a small wooden hut where there is an attendant in season. On the maps this is indicated as the Parking Municipal.

Directions:
(1) (2) and **(3)** as for Walk 23 p145.

(4) Bear round to the right, not left which goes to the Cirque de Barriès. There is a sign on a tree saying Sahara/Cascade (waterfall). Green splashes start here. The path goes down steps in the ochre-coloured rock (a bit of a scramble) through a miniature canyon before getting back again on the forest track. *Note: Most of the paths in the Colorado Provençal are sandy - this is an area where there are lots of snakes so keep an eye out for them. In general they are harmless!*

The path goes deep into the sandy quarry area past gnarled trees and bushes. Keep carefully to the green splashes till you reach a sunken sandy clearing with pine trees. Go right - there is a green splash on a tree. The path starts to go down and crosses a tiny rivulet of ochre-coloured sand to the right. There are tall sandstone cliffs visible through the trees. Bear round to the left and back over the rivulet - there are paths in all directions so it is very important to follow the green splashes carefully.

(5) In a clearing with trees and diverging paths go up the lefthand side of the rivulet (there is a green splash on a tree).

Note: You can walk into the Sahara area and look around - then retrace your steps (add on around 15mins).

Keep up the steep narrow path (ignore branch to left) and circle round the top of the waterfall crossing over an iron pipe. Continue round underneath red cliffs with the waterfall, a mere trickle of water, on the right. Yellow splashes start (40mins). Leave the waterfall behind and the path bears left and up a sandy slope. At the top you can see down on the righthand side to the Sahara which has some lovely white cliffs - beyond is the Cheminées des Fées and ahead the Luberon ridge. Walk along the top of these white cliffs, which are somewhat vertiginous, keeping the drop always on the right. Follow the yellow splashes as the path turns away from the edge through woodland to reach the side of an enormous gorge at a T-junction.

(6) Bear sharp left and continue up the side of the gorge through lovely pine forest. *Across the gorge are huge cliffs of different coloured sandstones pitted with swallows' nests.*

At a further T-junction turn right on to a path with blue splashes up a wooded spur with dramatic views through the trees on either side. Continue to walk up the shoulder to the top of the mini canyon. At a fork keep left (right leads to a viewpoint at the cliff edge). The path dips and then goes steeply upward - look for blue markings on a stone at the top and bear left - straight on there is a big drop! Stay on the left track here if you don't want to walk near the edge, passing an old stone wall.

Continue upwards medium steep past a rock with blue markings and the name Regain (1hr 15mins). Regain is the site of a popular youth hostel near Apt and the owners were responsible for mapping the original walks in the area, hence the name at various points.

(7) At a fork turn right - end of blue splashes! (1hr 25mins). Change to yellow splashes which continue to the end of the walk. This path along the top of the canyon is called Sentier des Crêtes. It goes through bushes and stunted trees, reaching a long wheat field (1hr 35mins). Keep along the field side direction southwest (for some of the way there is a smaller parallel path in the woods if you want some shade) for around 15mins. The field ends but there is another smaller one almost immediately which you have to go into the woods to skirt.

(8) Ignore a path going down right with blue markings but take the next one down (1hr 50mins) where there is a yellow splash at the start and a signpost La Croix de Christol. This is the original track between Rustrel and Casaneuve-you can see Casaneuve on the horizon to the left before you turn down.

The path is narrow and stony descending fairly steeply down a dry river bed at the top - it would be a torrent in wet weather! It goes through cool pine woods and there are good views down onto the quarry cliffs. There is a wooden sign saying Rustrel and indicating you are on private property. At a T-junction keep right (left goes to the edge of a canyon) and ignore any branches off. The path widens and becomes sandy.

(9) You reach signposts at a junction of paths called Croix de Muset. Go straight to Istrane (2hrs) - left goes to Notre Dame des Anges and a campsite. Further on there is a rock to the left with Regain painted on it in yellow near a terrific viewpoint over the top of white cliffs which descend to brilliant yellow**.

Possible alternative:
It is possible to turn right here but the previous yellow splashes at the start have been erased and there is a yellow cross on a tree. This is perhaps because they no longer want people to take this path into the heart of the quarries which are very eroded. Although the author has done it without incident, go this way AT YOUR OWN RISK!

The path is tricky in that it twists and turns up right into the heart of the quarries; call it quarry hopping! Follow the yellow splashes extremely carefully as they are not always easy to see. There are places where some scrambling is necessary but there is nothing technically difficult. Avoid any path with a yellow cross.

(9A) One hour later after going up and down and round about you come to a T-junction where you turn down left. Careful this is an important intersection and there are yellow markings on both left and right hand turnings as this is one of the main paths into the Colorado Provençal. If you turn right you reach another quarry. As you go down the track you can see the hamlet of Bouvène ahead. The track bears to the right over grey rocks and down right across the River Doua into the hamlet. Walk through the village and turn right on the road at the top which takes you back to the parking (4hrs). End of alternative route.

(9)** Continue downwards on the same path following yellow splashes (there is a gully down on the right), past another rock to the right with Regain 97. Cross a small area of white sandstone mounds to a junction (2hrs 20mins) and following yellow splashes which go right then left, the path crosses the river Doua.

(10) After crossing the river you come to the road (water purifying plant to the left) with a wooden notice and map of the area. Walk up the road passing a smart house on the right and another on the left (marked Istrane on the map).

(11) Go right at a sign Parking Municipal 1.5km. (2hrs 45mins) on a narrow paved road (The Colorado is on the right), past the village of Bouvène down to the right and then the T-junction taken by car, till you reach the car park (3hrs).

Walk No. 25
THE NORTH SIDE OF THE LUBERON
Mourre Negre - Alt. 1125m

Difficulty:	Strenuous - there is quite a steep climb to the top.
	Take lots of water as there is none available all the way round.
Time:	4hrs 15mins.
Height gain:	530m.
Maps:	Cartes IGN 3243 OT Top 25 Pertuis Lourmarin 1:25,000.
	Editions Didier Richard No. 14 Du Luberon à La Sainte Victoire 1:50,000.
Depart from:	Village of Auribeau (no shop or café here).
Signposting:	No actual signposts - on some of the walk blue, yellow and red/white GR splashes.

Observations:

You cannot come to this area without climbing the well-known Luberon. Although the walk is steep the view at the top is excellent

The two small villages of Auribeau and Saignon are worth exploring - Auribeau, situated at the foot of the Mourre Negre, was developed in the 16th century after being abandoned for nearly two centuries. The present village is an attractive huddle of houses many of which are being restored.

Saignon, situated on a hill not far from Apt, is more sophisticated, even boasting a charming hotel in the tiny square opposite an attractive fountain which has two stone statues representing Agriculture and Abundance (these are copies dating from the thirties, the originals having been broken when a branch of the nearby elm tree fell on them). The ruins of the castle are atop an imposing rock which dominates the village and from which there are magnificent views over the surrounding countryside. The twisting narrow streets harbour houses dating from the 12th to the 18th centuries.

How to get there (from Apt):

Leave Apt in the direction of Digne-les-Bains (N100). At the first roundabout take the turning up right on the D48 direction Saignon. Keep on this narrow road which bypasses the hill village of Saignon, crosses the Plateau des Claparèdes *(see description of the Vaucluse above)* and reaches the hamlet of Auribeau (9.2km).

Directions:

Park at the entrance to the village on the Route Jean Moulin at the start of the road to the right signposted Parking Mourre Negre. If you cannot find space here then drive to the other car park which is nearer the start of the walk. The walk through the village will then be at the end.

Timings start from the entrance to the village.

(1) Ignore the road to the left signposted Castellet and walk up through this attractive Provençal hamlet. Take the first turning to the right, Rue St. Pierre, bear left to the Place de la Fontaine and then into Rue du Four and through the Place de l'Eglise where there is a lovely old church. *These are narrow short streets of ancient houses huddled together.*

Continue past the church down the road to the cemetery towards the main car park. Go down to the left of the cemetery wall. This leads onto a stony jeep track almost immediately with a cherry orchard on the left.

(2) At the bottom of this hill (the parking area is up on the right) go straight on where there is a "no entry" sign for cars and a shabby wooden sign saying Mourre Negre (10mins). **At first there are no markings but soon blue flashes appear!**

After passing two modern houses the road narrows to a track. There are

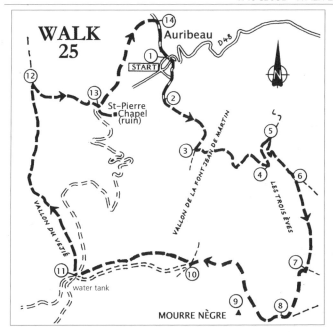

woods each side as it climbs fairly steeply and then opens up through tall bushes.

(3) *Careful* - as you climb up, look carefully for and take a narrow path off left (20mins). This path goes round the side of the hill and down into the valley of the Font Jean de Martin. It is a narrow bushy path but well defined with beautiful views 'down into the little valley and of Auribeau in the plain below.

Following the intermittent blue splashes the path starts to go up and then levels out before bearing down into the valley of the Font Jean de Martin which by now has narrowed into a gully. It goes along the bushy bottom past slopes of scree descending from both sides. Bear round to the left (clear blue arrow painted on a stone) and climb up across the scree and into woods again gaining height steadily.

(4) At a fork (40mins) go down left - blue splashes - instinct makes you want to turn the other way, upwards, but don't! The path curls round to the right and down steeply into another small valley or gully called Les Trois Eves. At

153

the bottom it is very bushy but goes up again quickly. At a sort of T-junction where there is a notice saying Regain 80, the path goes round to the left - it is still curling round the side of the hill with a good view of the hamlet of Castellet down below.

(5) Turn up right at the next defined T-junction (55mins) joining another path coming up from Castellet.

Further up the blue splashes give way to yellow ones.

The path goes up straight along the lefthand side of the same little valley Les Trois Eves - there are lovely views of the tree-covered mountain, and the aerials of the Mourre Negre peep over the trees on the right. There is a long climb up before bearing round to the left and onto a minor crest (1hr 10mins). At this crest, just after a yellow splash and dot, there is a little cairn and a narrower path up to the right.

(6) Turn up right - **there are no markings this way!**

The main path goes straight on down and into another valley so you will know if you have missed the turning. The path is defined and open at first with wide views to left and right - it goes through stunted woodland and bush with the occasional small clearing. There is a long climb up this slope before it levels off somewhat through tall pines trees.

(7) When the path reaches a rather overgrown T-junction (1hr 35mins) you may feel you have missed your way but turn right and it quickly becomes a wide rather disused jeep track. Veer left at a cairn and continue past another small cairn to meet the forest road at the top (1hr 40mins). There are no markings here so it would be tricky to do this walk the other way round.

(8) Turn right along the top on the forest road - the summit is wide and grassy with scattered pine trees.

Alternatively: (for an impressive open view), go straight across the road and up the grassy slope in front. At the top, amongst scattered pines, you will see the red/white splashes of the GR9 (this takes about 5mins). Turn right and go along the top of the crest until you meet a track - take the path up right to the Mourre Negre (2hrs)****.

(9) If you turned right on the summit forest road, you meet the GR at a round concrete water tank No. 26. From here you can take the obvious path up to the Mourre Negre, a huge and ugly transmission station (2hrs).

The view is extensive - north over the Calavon valley with hills beyond, including the white summit of Mont Ventoux and south, if it is clear, the Var hills and the unmistakable silhouette of Sainte Victoire above Aix-en-Provence.

Go back to the water tank and turn left down the forest road (direction northwest with the Mourre Negre on your left), where the view is quickly lost as you go down steadily beneath the north side of the summit (direction west) with stately pine woods either side. Pass a signpost (2hrs 25mins) describing the ravages caused by the *Chenil Processionnaire* in the pine trees (Latin *Thaunetapoea pityocampa shiff*) - see page 24.

(10) Just after the sign take an obvious path right underneath telephone wires. It runs parallel but higher than the road and there are extensive views each side, particularly of the Vallon de la Fayette and a forest road going all the way down the right flank. This parallel path reaches the road and then veers off it again - it is easy to see. Regain the road at water tank No. 28 at a multiple intersection (2hrs 45mins). The GR9 continues straight.

(11) Take a narrow path on the lefthand side of the water tank with blue splashes and the name Regain (do not take the more obvious unsurfaced road although this does go to Auribau). This is a stony narrow path with bushes each side which descends quite steeply into the narrow Vallon du Veiji. Initially you can see the road up on the right but it disappears behind tall slopes of scree as you go down deeper into the valley.

The stony descent winds its way among bushes of box and gorse and stunted oak trees. After half an hour the valley starts to open out and the path becomes flatter with taller trees each side.

Ignore the first narrow path to the right (3hrs 20mins) and continue past the rocky outcrop of the Baume de Peyrot through trees on the left. Ignore subsequent turnings left. The path becomes a jeep track and more open.

(12) Ignore the first track right at a clearing but take the next one where there is a blue sign on a slab of rock (not very clear) indicating Auribau (3hrs 35mins). Take this defined flat path (there is a lovely open view) and at a T-junction bear left. It goes through woodland which becomes quite dense as you pass a ruin on the right. It becomes wide and stony climbing fairly steeply.

(13) The path meets the unpaved road coming down from the summit (3hrs 45mins). Cross the road and go straight up a track towards the newly restored chapel of Saint Pierre & Saint Paul standing on a hillock with a sweeping view behind of the lower slopes of the Luberon and the village of Auribeau. There is a well-preserved Borie on the right and a number of ruins covered in creeper, of the medieval village of Auribeau.

The chapel has recently been restored and is kept locked. It dates originally from the 12th century but was first restored at the beginning of the 19th century (the date 1834 is on the facade).

Retrace your steps to the road (No. 13) and turn down right. There is a good view of the village as you walk down to meet the D48 at a clearing and a large sign saying Mourre Negre. There are usually a number of cars parked here as this is the main route to the summit.

(14) Turn right and walk towards the village by lavender fields and cherry orchards. What a feast of cherries you can have if you do the walk in early June (4hrs 15mins)!

Mont Ventoux walks

Walk No. 26
LE BARROUX TO LA ROQUE-ALRIC

Difficulty:	Easy pleasant walk with lovely views but read the directions carefully as there is a lot of twisting and turning!
Time:	3hrs 15mins (add 15mins if you walk to the summit of La Roque-Alric).
Height gain:	No appreciable height gain.
Maps:	Cartes IGN Top 25 3040 ET Carpentras 1:25,000.
	Editions Didier Richard No. 27 Ventoux 1:50,000.
Depart from:	Village of Le Barroux - in front of Hôtel Les Geraniums.
Signposting:	None but red/yellow splashes some of the way which were redone in 1998.

Observations:
A delightfully easy walk through woods and vineyards with some lovely views over the Venaisson Plain. Le Barroux is a typically picturesque hill village with sinuous narrow streets leading up to the castle at the top. Originally constructed in the 12th century and flanked by round towers, it dominates the surrounding countryside. It was the seat of a succession of Provençal lords until 1793 when it was destroyed by the Revolutionaries. The building remained in ruins until 1929 when it was acquired by M. Vayson de Pradennes. He took 10 years to restore it but during the 2nd World War it was burnt down by the Germans - the older villagers remember that it took 10 days to burn! It has since been restored again and now plays host to a series of art exhibitions.

Visiting times are weekends 10.00-20.00 (1 April to 1 June); June: 14.30-20.00; July/August/September: 10.00-20.00, and October 14.30-20.00. Entrance fee. Even if you do not go inside the castle it is worth wandering up there for the magnificent view.

The Sainte-Madeleine Abbey, on a wooded hill near Le Barroux, is also worth a visit if just to sit in peaceful silence in the magnificent austere church with its stained glass windows and unusual crucifix. If you come at the times of service you can hear the melodious Gregorian Latin chant of the Benedictine monks, (High Mass every day at 10.30. Sundays and Feast Days 11.00). Curiously, this is a very modern abbey which was only completed in 1981 but already houses a dedicated community of Benedictine monks. Their main source of revenue is from home grown produce, bread making, religious goods, books and records of their celebrated chant.

How to get there (from Carpentras):

Take the D938 signposted Vaison-la-Romaine for approximately 12kms until you see a sign left to the village of Le Barroux (you will already have noticed it from afar sitting on top of a hill). Drive up into the village and keep straight until you see a municipal parking area on the right. Then walk up the hill until you reach the Hôtel Les Geraniums.

Directions:

(1) With the front of the hotel on your left go straight along the Rue du Moulin to a T-junction. Turn left on to the Rue de la Fontaine Vielle. At another T-junction turn left again on the Chemin Carre - you can see the cemetery below straight ahead. Continue on the Chemin Carre for a couple of minutes and then turn hard right on the Avenue de Verdun which goes down between occasional private houses.

(2) When the road bends to the left with the cemetery down to the right, go straight up a wide track. At a fork bear up right to the chapel of St-Christophe with a large crucifix in front of it on the top of the hill. You can see the interior through an iron grille - it has been simply but tastefully renovated and is obviously in use. There is a good view of the village from here.

Retrace your steps to the road (15mins) and bear left. Almost immediately there is a wide gravel parking area to the left and a clear red/yellow splash indicating a narrow path to the left. Take this stony path (direction west), which goes round the hill with the chapel and descends into a small gully with a dirty rivulet. Cross the rivulet (red/yellow signs) (20mins) and go up the gully on the other side. Ignore all offshoots (red/yellow crosses on trees) and continue till you reach a small dam which looks rather like a large swimming pool with steps down into it (called L'Ecluse de Falque on the map).

(3) Turn right (note red/yellow cross warning not to go straight on), and walk along the side of the dam till you reach a plum orchard. Continue on, skirting the orchard through woods to a small vineyard and then left back to the orchard. At a T-junction go left (right is private property) which takes you back along the dam (35mins).

At a fork by the dam go up right following the red/yellow splashes. This is a wide track climbing gently into the pine forest with lovely views over the valley left. Continue straight where there is a clearing with a small stone hut on the right. The track descends for a couple of minutes and then branches right on a narrower path with some splashes. *It reaches a vineyard on the left where there is a a beautiful extended view over the plain and the village of Caromb with an impressive row of tall cypresses in the foreground and the long Luberon range on the horizon.*

The path bears round to the right at the vineyard and goes up gently again. Shortly after, where there is a red/yellow cross ahead, bear up to the right (45mins). Go up this path through stunted pines, ignoring two left branches, till you reach a T-junction at a jeep track, then go up right (blue markings have joined the red/yellow here). As you round the first bend there is an interesting craggy rock to the left (Le Graveyron) and another over on the right (Carabelle). The jeep track goes in wide zigzags round the bottom of the wooded slopes of the Carabelle - you can see a path winding up to the summit of the pine-covered Graveyron over on the left.

(4) The track reaches the D90A going from Le Barroux to the hamlet of La Roque-Alric at the Col de Vallade (1hr) where there is a good view of the rolling hills to the north. There are numerous markings at this low pass. Now there are three possibilities to the left - don't go down the road but take the middle tarmac jeep track up (yellow and blue splashes here) with a sign saying no entry for cars except for *riverains* (local residents) - on the extreme left is a narrower track.

The jeep track goes straight up with an apricot orchard and a hut to the right and pine trees on the left. Soon the view opens up on a low crest to a delightful vista of small vineyards on terraces. It then dips down again (there is a large house down on the right with a swimming pool) and arrives at a crossroads by vineyards called Col du Pontillard.

(5) Turn right onto a narrow road (1hr 10mins) and then left after 100m by a small red building (cross on telephone pole if you try to go straight on). Keep on the main wide track , turning right at a T-junction in the vineyard and then descending on a jeep track through pine woods. You are curving round the rocky crag of the Carabelle which you can glimpse through trees on the right.

   Just before moving out of the woods into vineyards at a T-junction do not take the path up the side of the hill to the right (red/yellow cross on tree) but carry on despite a blue cross on a tree - enigma! (1hr 30mins) and turn right still following the red/yellow splashes. Walk alongside the vines - there is a glorious view over vineyards to the plain below.

(6) *Be careful* - Before you go far along this track* and before it starts going gently down, watch for short wooden posts with red/yellow markings (these are difficult to see because of the undergrowth). These posts take you up right and along the bottom of a field of vines along the back of farm buildings.

   Cross a T-junction (avoid the farm to the left) on to another track and turn down left. *Otherwise you will arrive at another "no entry" to the farm - the owner does not appear to want you to walk through his property!*

Note the track ends at the farm of La Courjonne where there is a chain across and a notice saying "entrée enterdit" (no entry). Beware of barking dogs!

Village of la Roque-Alric

(7) Just past this entrance turn up to the right by the first pine tree and a post (1hr 40mins), direction north, towards some craggy rocks called Rocher des Trois Evèques (rock of the three bishops) - the higher rocky crag of the Carabelle is over on the right.

The path goes up medium steep through vineyards bearing round left (ignore a jeep track coming in from the right and further branches off) to reach an intersection at a jeep track with a large ploughed field left and a line of cypress trees. Here you get your first view of the jagged peaks of the Dentelles de Montmirail. Do not take the jeep track back hard left which returns to the farm entrance or go through the field to the left which is where the red/yellow GR splashes go down to the village of Beaumes-de-Venise. **From here follow the yellow markings plus occasional blue only.**

(8) Ignoring the red/yellow cross take the track up right towards the Rocher des Trois Evèques following yellow splashes. At a fork go right (yellow markings) to reach a low bushy pass (1hr 50mins). This is an excellent place to have a picnic and enjoy a panoramic view of the impressive teeth-like rocks of the Dentelles, the Crête de St-Armand with its television aerial and nearer, down in the valley, the hamlet of Lafare.

(9) At the pass there are numerous paths off but continue straight on following the yellow splashes. The track curls round and becomes wider as it descends towards the hamlet of la Roque-Alric which is attractively situated on a hill with a church at the top and a huge rock looming up behind - hence the name! A really idyllic spot.

(10) The path rejoins the D90A (2hrs 5mins). Turn right up the road and then left into the village - an attractive huddle of houses that are usually shuttered out of the season.

Detour: *It is possible to walk up to the church which you can see just underneath the rock. It has been recently renovated and is locked. From the church there is an obvious path to the top of the rock itself where there is a cross. It is a short, rather precipitous scramble but the view is worth the effort. It takes about 15mins there and back from the village.*

Walk up through the village bearing right on a hairpin. Ignore a first metal cross on the right and continue till you see a second one on a stone column (Jubilee 1875) ahead with the wall of the cemetery to the left. Turn left by a house (right meets the D90A).

(11) The road bears down left round a corner past an electricity pole on the right. Leave the road on the following corner, going right on a track (2hrs 20mins). **Careful here** - do not follow the yellow splashes which continue

The lower Verdon Gorge

Summit of Crémon *(Walk 43)*
Looking towards Lac de Castillan from Crémon *(Walk 43)*

down the road. **Note - there are no signs now from here to the end of the walk.**

This is a defined wide track initially above the road down left. It passes vineyards before entering a short narrow valley which looks curiously uncultivated. It then enters scattered pine woods as it goes up and over a rise. Keep on the main path until it reaches vineyards, ignoring any branches to the left.

(12) At a T-junction (2hrs 45mins) turn left (right leads back to the road). Continue to bear left through the vineyards, thus cutting off a long bend in the road. *The numerous vines are separated by hedges of broom which look especially attractive when they are in bloom in May and June.* The track joins the road (3hrs) by a sign saying Côtes du Rhône Villages/Beaumes-de-Venise, opposite an attractive clearing with pines and a small building called La Gaie.

(13) Turn left on the road with a magnificent view of the Mont Ventoux and the village of Le Barroux. Continue past the large winery of Domaine d'Ollone Champaga to the right. As you descend you can see the tower and roof of the Monastère Ste-Madeleine (details above) through the trees to the left. On the outskirts of le Barroux the V3 road joins on the left from Suzette. Enter the village on the Rue de la Peratoure (no through road) going upwards. Turn down right and then left on the Rue du Moulin back to the hotel (3hrs 15mins).

Walk No. 27
LES GORGES DE LA NESQUE

Difficulty:	Medium/strenuous - mildly vertiginous.
Time:	3hrs 30mins.
Height gain:	600m down!
Maps:	Cartes IGN 3140 ET Top 25 Mont Ventoux 1:25,000.
	Editions Didier Richard No. 27 Ventoux 1:50,000.
Depart from:	Parking in the village of Monieux.
Signposting:	Good - red/white splashes of the GR9 and brown splashes.

Observations:
An interesting walk though you should be reasonably fit to climb down into the gorge and then up again!

The Plateau de Sault is a complete contrast to the cosy vineyards around Carpentras. Sweeping fields of grain and purple lavender meet the eye and there are cows grazing in the fields. The landscape is wilder, the air is fresher- you feel you have entered another country!

Monieux, perched on the side of the Nesque valley, is dominated by a lookout tower on a rock above the village. Built in the 12th century it used to be part of a larger fortified system, similar towers being found in other villages in the region. Vestiges of the ramparts surround this idyllic unspoilt village. The narrow winding streets lead to a beautiful roman church dating from the 12th century. It has been renovated and enlarged over the centuries (there were 950 people in the village in 1851), but nevertheless retains its original dome. It is one of the few village churches open to the public.

The Gorges de Nesque is one of the most dramatic in the region. The high rocky cliffs continue for 4kms culminating in the Castellaras viewpoint on the D942, looking towards the Rocher du Cire (*cire* meaning wax or polish).

How to get there (from Carpentras):
Take the D942, direction Sault, through Ville sur Auzon and continue till it connects with the wider D1. Follow the D1 for about 21kms, and it is worth stopping at the Belvédère (beauty spot) for a magnificent view of the upland country of the Pays de Sault (see above for more information). Three kilometres before Sault turn right to Monieux on the D942, and continue for 3.5km to this small village which is the nearest place to the gorge. Park at the top of Monieux village in a well-indicated parking area.

On the return journey it is suggested that you stay on the narrower D942, which is the scenic route with views over the gorges and three tunnels.

Directions:
(1) Turn sharp right out of the car park by a wall with a red arrow and a GR sign. Walk down this narrow road through the village past a statue to the right of St. Anthony of Padua with Provençal writing beneath *(many commemorative plaques and statues have inscriptions in the old Provençal language which is now being revived)*.

The road goes through a wide terrace where there is an extensive view into the upper reaches of the Vaucluse plateau. *This wide upland valley is at a higher altitude than further south and more fertile with fields of grain and dairy cows - on the horizon is a low ridge of forest.* Go to the right (arrow on wall) and continue through the lovely old village houses under an archway where there is a cross on the wall. Many of the houses have been renovated and are obviously only used as holiday dwellings. The path narrows as it goes southwest out of the village by a strangely shaped old house with another cross and a GR9 arrow underneath. It goes along an attractive raised balcony track bordered by a stone wall, with the craggy peak of the La Côte Renard up on the right. Left are glorious views down into the valley.

(2) Go straight on at a sign towards Chapelle St-Michelle 1hr *(somewhat optimistic!)*. This is where the main GR9 path joins from the right (10mins).

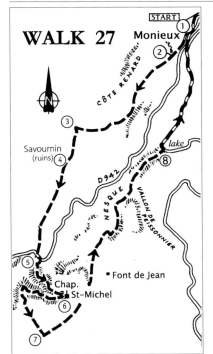

The path goes steadily upwards medium steep through scattered stunted woodland and bushes. An enticing small lake comes into view down in the valley before a dam where the Nesque River flows into the gorge. The path climbs higher above the valley for about 20mins, becoming rockier with some scree on the slopes right. There are occasional faded red/white GR signs. It levels out momentarily (look back for a good view of Monieux village with its tower on a rock above and the town of Sault in the distance), before climbing again and then undulating pleasantly along into stunted oak woods where the view disappears. Where there are open spaces you can see the D942 twisting and turning below.

(3) Look carefully for a red/white GR splash on a rock in the centre of the path indicating sharp down left (45mins). This narrow path goes down medium steep and then undulates through stunted woodland (south). It bears round right and ahead are the steep cliffs of the Nesque gorge. The D942, which winds high above the gorge, can be seen down on the left.

At an open area covered with small rocks, the path bears left and then right as it winds down over stones (GR signs). Turn left at a T-junction in a clearing by the ruins of the Savournin farm on the right (55mins). This is now a wider red, stony track which comes to a rockier area. At the bottom turn right at GR signs (1hr), and go gently down through oak woodland. **Be careful** - at a fork in a small clearing turn down left - there is only a faint red/white splash here. This wider path goes down to the D942 (1hr 15mins).

(4) Go straight over the road and down by writing on a rock indicating

Gorges de la Nesque

Chapelle St-Michelle (Michael) - there are GR signs and some steps at the start. Pick your way carefully down the steep path with some scrambling over rocks but nothing too demanding. You can see the densely tree-covered gorge below and a high, sinister looking wall of rock ahead with trees on the summit and black cave entrances. Now there are brown flashes alongside the red/white GR ones.

Pass in front of a large rock face and descend deeper into the gorge where there are taller oak trees and welcome cooler air. At a small promontory there are views into the gorge. The path continues down but not too steeply, going under another cliff and finally arriving at the bottom and the little roman chapel of St-Michelle which is built into an overhanging grotto of an imposing rock face (1hr 35mins). *Originally constructed in the 12th century the chapel has been restored many times, in particular in 1643, the date inscribed over the doorway; in 1954 the walls were partially cemented. There is a small altar with a statue of St. Michael, the archangel. He has lost his head, one of his wings and an arm but otherwise stands dustily above the tributes of wilted flowers presumably put there by walkers.*

Continue in front of the chapel through dense bushes following the GR red/white splashes across the bouldery bed of the river. *When the author did this walk there was hardly any water and it lay in a stagnant pool. After coming so far one expects a clear stream rushing delightfully over boulders as described in the Michelin Guide!*

(5) Do not follow the blue splashes which go along the river bank but take the path going steeply up underneath an overhanging rock, clearly marked with red/white GR splashes. Go up underneath another huge overhang. You can see clearly where you came down on the other side of the gorge with the road above. At a rocky lookout there is an extensive view into the gorge. The path climbs away from the lip of the gorge through woodland, curling round to the left and continues higher back towards the edge. The chapel is down on the left hidden in the trees.

Do not go left where there is a red/white cross, nor right where there are brown splashes. *If you do not suffer from vertigo take your picnic while the path is still hugging the edge of the gorge to appreciate the views.* Leaving the edge of the gorge bearing southeast, the bushy path reaches the top through grassy clearings, and piles of stones.

(6) At a fork bear left on the more major path (2hrs 5mins) which undulates along a sandy path through woodland to a T-junction. **Careful** - go left here despite a red/white cross on a tree (2hrs 15mins). The GR9 goes off to the right. Now follow brown splashes (there are also blue ones). The path undulates along to the northeast, meandering through woodland and then sparser vegetation. Up ahead on the other side of a narrow valley is the farm of Font de Jean in attractive open fields.

The path dips into the narrow valley through occasional grassy clearings. Ignore a left branch with a brown cross and a second one where the main path bears to the right. At the bottom there is an attractive clearing on the right. The path continues on towards the end of the gorge, with views down into it through the trees on the left. Keep on the main stony path (2hrs 35mins) gradually losing height along the lower reaches of the gorge through bushes and trees with views of the cliffs and grottos on the other side. There are remnants of terraces so there must have been some habitation in this region. Continue round a huge cliff coming to small clearings with waving rushes and grasses as the path levels along the Nesque River at the open end of the gorge. Here the narrow river flows sluggishly over stones and through rushes.

The D942 road can be seen again up on the left and the huge cliffs on the other side of the gorge loom nearer as it narrows. The wide path is delightfully shaded and bushy as it hugs the river, skirting another long cliff pitted with holes. Shortly after it reaches the lake by the dam at a paved road (3hrs 5mins).

(7) Turn left here passing a very welcome café (Gîte des colverts). *This is a delightful lake with a picnic area and children's playground, surrounded by rushes and alive with ducks and moorhens. It is a fishing area and hence not* *suitable for swimming.* The road goes along the lefthand side of the beautifully cultivated valley with the village ahead dominated by the tower on its rocky summit.

(8) Join the D942 at the entrance to the village. Cross the road and up through the houses to the parking area and the church (3hrs 30mins).

Walk No. 28
LES GORGES DE CURNIER - south side of Mont Ventoux

Difficulty:	Strenuous - through a narrow gorge and then some up and down climbs. Lots of walking over loose large stones. Don't do this walk if there has been recent heavy rain.
	There are no streams so take plenty of water on a hot day.
Time:	3hrs 30mins (shorter walk) 5hrs (longer walk).
Height gain:	640m.
Maps:	Cartes IGN 3140 ET Top 25 Mont Ventoux 1:25,000.
	Editions Didier Richard No. 27 Ventoux 1:50,000.
Depart from:	Parking behind Les Colombets farm near Bedoin.
Signposting:	None - infrequent yellow arrows with B on them in the gorge and after. GR red/white splashes on the top - yellow splashes on the downward slope on the shorter walk till the path joins the red/white splashes of the GR91. On the longer walk you are on the GR91B and then the GR91.

Observations:

Both long and short walks are challenging. The way down on the short walk is quite stony and the longer walk is more interesting. The gorge at the start is fun to walk through and gives you some idea of the terrain of the Mont Ventoux. The Tourist Office in Bedouin sells a booklet containing 7 walks in the area with maps and rather scanty text. The yellow arrow with B is one of the walks (timed at 6hrs, which seems ultra-conservative!). For further information on Mont Ventoux see Introduction to the Vaucluse region above.

Bedouin is an attractive little village perched on a hill at the foot of the mountain. It is dominated by an enormous Jesuit style church which was built in 1708 on the ruins of two former churches. It was renovated in 1821.

How to get there (from Carpentras):

Take the D974 towards Bedoin and again at a roundabout at the entrance to the village. Just before the Garage Les Lavandes on the left (white with

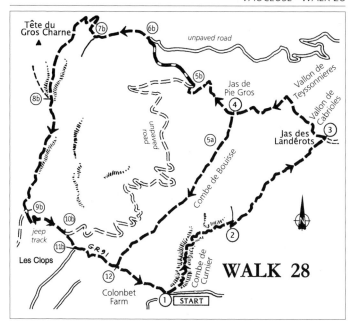

blue shutters) turn up left on a smaller road (no name) and continue past a sign saying Belezy Domaine Naturists (Nudist Centre) through vineyards and cherry orchards (do not go off on the Chemin des Clops). Continue on, keeping right at a fork, then left on the Chemin de Colombet just before the road bears round to the right (2kms from Bedoin). Keep going at a farm with a parking sign. The road deteriorates for about 500m till it arrives at a parking area surrounded by woodland (1km from the Chemin de Colombet turning).

Directions:
(1) The path through the gorge begins at the end of the car park where there is a chain between metal posts. There are no signs or splashes but the way is obvious. (Do not take the GR91 which goes across the start of the car park- you will come back this way.) **Follow rare yellow arrows with B but not at the start.**

The path is clear and stony, bearing right round a tall rock and entering the gorge almost immediately. On either side are tall grey pitted cliffs rising abruptly from the floor of the gorge which, when wide enough, has quite dense bushy vegetation such as juniper and broom with stunted oaks and pines. The gorge narrows and then widens into a small clearing before narrowing again. The path has obviously been strewn with stones (probably to avoid erosion) and there are some slopes of scree descending to the floor of the gorge. One expects a river to be running through these rocks but there is no sign of water although one can imagine flash floods developing after heavy rainfall.

Look high up to the left and there is an impressive hollow in the imposing cliff face (15mins). The stony path twists and turns and the gorge gets narrower and sometimes very bushy. The rocks tower above and look as though they will meet in the middle; in one place there is just enough width between the rocks for one person plus rucksack. It is dank, dark and cool with a quietness which is rather sinister. The gorge must be alive with bats in the evenings. Where it starts to widen again there is a sign 17 on a tree (25mins); continue on the main path and ignore a little turning left. You pass through a small area of bushes and small trees.

The path slowly gains height as it continues to wind between the rocky walls. There is a ruin on the right underneath a cliff (30mins) before it passes under a big overhanging rock and climbs over scree and boulders. Ignore a steep path up to the right over scree with no markings which is in fact a short cut (45mins). Continue up medium steep for about 5mins till you emerge from the gorge at a T-junction (50mins).

(2) Turn right on a wide balcony track with a stone wall to the left. **Careful** - soon after take a path up to the left with B and a yellow arrow pointing in the direction you have come from and a faded red splash. Take this narrow stony path up fairly steeply through bushes. After a few minutes there is a high rock wall to the right and the gorge is hidden down on the left.

The track widens with an impressive view of the summit of Mont Ventoux up on the right and the jagged peaks of the Dentelles de Montmirail on the horizon to the left. South is an extensive view of scattered villages in the plain before the long Luberon range. The track goes endlessly upwards through bushes of box, juniper and green oak. From time to time there is a yellow arrow with a B. Finally you come to a tall pine tree standing alone on the left (1hr 30mins). Down on the right is the wooded Vallon du Coste d'Antoni.

The track becomes less defined and rather churned up before reaching a T-junction where, on stones in the path, you see the red/white splashes of the GR91B which goes round the south side of the Ventoux mountain. Just beyond the junction but out of immediate sight are the ruins of a *bergerie* (sheepfold) called the Jas des Landerots (1hr 40mins) - you can see the roof of the Jas from further down the slope. Follow the red/white splashes of the Grande Randonnée GR91B.

(3) Turn left at the T-junction (direction west) and continue on a delightfully narrow path with stunted trees and bushes undulating round the contours of the mountain and down the top end of little valleys (Vallon de Cabrioles and the Vallon de Teyssonnieres), crossing areas of scree. You can see the long grey rock wall of the Combe de Bouisse down on the left. The Gorges de Curnier are hidden in the trees.

The attractive path goes past ruins in thick woodland (2hrs), over more patches of scree and through woods round the mountain; avoid a path down left over scree marked with cairns. At the ruins of another *bergerie* called the Jas de Pie Gros in a clearing (2hrs 20mins), you leave the GR which continues straight (see longer walk directions below).

SHORTER WALK A - follow yellow splashes
(4) Turn down to the left where there is a yellow marking on a rock. The narrow path goes down fairly steeply through thick bushes, at first overgrown as though infrequently used. It becomes irritatingly stony (these are again stones that have been put on the path to avoid erosion).

(5A) Ignore a branch down to the left into the Combe de Bouisse and back into the Curnier gorge (alternative way back but not done by author). At times the bushes are so dense you have to push your way through. Watch for a break in the bushes to the left (by a small cairn) which leads to an overhang with a lovely view of the Combe de Bouisse (2hrs 35mins). As the path continues down it opens up and there is a lovely view ahead with the village of Bedoin dominated by its church to the right and the smaller Baux to the left. To the immediate right is the tree covered Vallon de Bonnet de Capelan.

The path widens and becomes even stonier and more irritating, in spite of open views of the slopes and the plain below. The vegetation becomes sparse and arid. Lower down the going becomes easier through stunted bushes and pines, before meeting the wide defined track of the GR91 along the bottom of the mountain (3hrs 15mins). **Follow red/white splashes to end**.

Merge with Longer Walk B
(12) Turn left and walk along this wide flat sandy track through pine trees with little undergrowth, past the farm of Les Colombetes to the parking area (3hrs 30mins).

LONGER WALK B - follow red/white GR splashes
(4) Continue past the ruins of the Jas de Pie Gros bergerie where there is an interesting round stone building with a grille in front of it. If you look through the grille you will see a huge water cistern. This was obviously (and may still be) used to water the sheep and goats as there appears to be no water

outlets in this area.

Follow the clear red/white splashes (the yellow arrows with B continue here as well). The narrow bushy path continues round the mountain, crossing patches of scree and gaining height slowly. Shortly it opens out and there are spectacular views of the plain below and the village of Bedoin. It flattens somewhat as it circles round the top of another tree covered valley, the Vallon du Bonnet de Capelan.

(5B) At a fork go up to the right following the GR splashes and yellow arrow with B - there are yellow markings on both paths which is confusing (2hrs 35mins). Still gaining height gently the path continues until it hits a jeep track 5mins later. Turn right on the jeep track following the GR splashes (cross on tree left) and continue upwards.

(6B) At a hairpin bend go left where there is a clear GR splash on a rock (2hrs 55mins). (***Careful*** - do not take the path down left just before the bend). Continue along the side of the mountain on a lovely open path. Ahead is a rocky outcrop and you wonder if you are going to have to climb over it! Up on the right you can see the traffic on the D974 going up to the summit of the Mont Ventoux.

The rocky hump disappears when the path skirts it and starts to go down. The landscape is completely open as you descend quite rapidly through rocky bushy country. A large wide tree-covered ravine called the Combe de la Malaval gradually comes into view on your righthand side (3hrs 10mins).

(7B) Five minutes later do not go straight on (where the B yellow arrow goes) but continue down right following the GR splashes. *Note: the yellow path is a possible steeper short cut down to the GR at the foot of the mountain (not done by the author).* The rocky path winds down over patches of scree. It bears down right and then left twice, which from the map looks like a two-pronged fork, quite steeply over further patches of scree till it reaches the bottom of the ravine (3hrs 30mins).

Continue along the bed of the tree-covered ravine still descending but not so steeply. It is a very attractive path with the sunshine filtering through the oak trees. At times it is smooth and easy but there are still patches of scree and stones to be negotiated. The ravine narrows and rocks appear on the lefthand side.

(8B) At a fork (3hrs 35mins) continue down left following the GR splashes. A few metres later there is another path going up right with the name Rabayettes marked in red on a rock - this goes up to a Gîte Forestier with a telephone situated on the road up to the summit of the Ventoux.

Descend through delightful woodland alongside high cliffs on the right called the Tête de Gros Charne, going deeper and deeper into this attractive narrowing ravine. You reach what initially look like ruins under a high overhanging cliff (3hrs 50mins) but on inspection turn out to be the walls of primitive sheep pens - this must have been a herding route down from the upper slopes of the mountain.

Further on there is another huge overhanging rock to the left and more on the right with fascinating indentations like the openings of large caves. In one place there is another wall of a sheep pen in a larger indentation hollowed out of the rock; it can only be reached by a small clamber up a slope and the interior is so small it could only house the shepherd rather than the sheep! Just after this, the path goes right underneath an impressive rocky overhang (3hrs 55mins).

After these rocks the path continues on downward but the rocks each side are less impressive and the ravine opens out. Ten minutes later a trickle of water appears in the bushes on the right but no sign of a proper stream (this trickle probably dries up in high summer). More rocks appear on the right as the tree-lined path goes below some strange pitted brown cliffs, quite unlike the grey granite ones over on the left. The ravine widens again as the track crosses some scree and passes more sandstone rocks to left and right.

(9B) You reach a wide jeep track at a clearing (4hrs 15mins) where the GR91B meets the GR91 going along the foot of the mountain. Turn left still following GR splashes (brown ones also) ignoring the no entrance sign *(sauf riverains)*. Continue on the jeep track with green fields and vineyards to the right, so you have reached cultivated country at last. Go upwards bending left, right and then left again passing a building with a reservoir surrounded by a high fence. Shortly after a path comes down from the left (this is the yellow arrow B path) (4hrs 30mins). Ignore also a path going down right and keep straight on the wide jeep track.

(10B) Five minutes later look carefully for a path going down right with big GR splashes on a tree. Go down to meet another jeep track at a parking area called Les Clops (4hrs 40mins).

(11B) At Les Clops turn left (the GR also goes right) and continue past some attractive cedar trees to the left. Keep going over a crossroads. Shortly after, the path from **the Shorter Walk A comes in from the left** (4hrs 45mins).

(12) Continue straight until you reach the car park at the Colombet farm (5hrs).

Walk No. 29
VAISON-LA-ROMAINE TO CRESTET

Difficulty:	Easy with some walking along a road at the end.
Time:	2hrs 45mins (from the Roman Bridge) - add on 15mins if you visit the castle on the top of the hill.
Height gain:	Negligible.
Maps:	Cartes IGN 3040ET Top 25 Carpentras/Vaison-La-Romaine 1:25,000.
	Editions Didier Richard No. 27 Ventoux 1:50,000.
Depart from:	The Roman bridge in Vaison-La-Romaine.
Signposting:	None - some of the path has red/yellow splashes and later blue splashes.

Observations:
This is the walk I got lost on with my son, though once you know the way it is delightfully easy! A slight pity that there is some road walking at the end. Take time to explore the little village of Crestet and also to visit the castle and town of Vaison-La-Romaine (see Introduction to the Vaucluse region).

Perched on the top of a crest, Le Crestet merits its name (in English anyway) and is one of the loveliest Provençal hamlets - the sort of place one dreams of living in! Crestet castle was originally built around 850 and Roman and Gothic elements are a witness of its successive alterations. The construction was done in a rectangle 40m long 23m wide - the highest of the two towers is 21m high and the walls are 2.4m thick. It belonged to the bishops of Vaison-la-Romaine until the Revolution. A ruin in 1982 it was renovated in 1985 and is now in private hands.

How to get there (from Carpentras):
Take the D938 signposted Vaison-La-Romaine for 27.5kms and park your car in one of the main car parks in the town. Make for the Roman bridge at the bottom of the old town.

Directions:
(1) From the Roman bridge walk up into the old town and turn left at a telephone box which takes you under two arches. Turn right at a T-junction where the former Hôtel de Ville (town hall) is facing you with iron grille gates. The cobbled street goes by a hotel on the right and an old fountain before entering the quaint Place du Vieux Marché which has another fountain and a café (10mins).

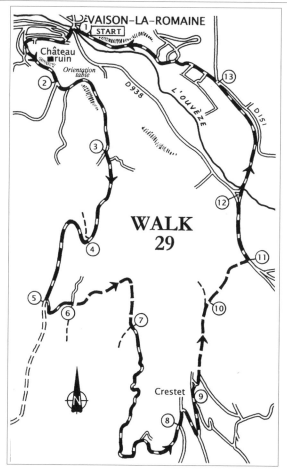

Deviation to the castle:

Go into the old town, turn left instead of right at the T-junction (see above), and follow signs indicating Château through the sinuous cobbled streets to the ruined castle on the top of the hill. Here there is an extensive view of the town and the valley. Retrace your steps to the Place du Vieux Marché.

Continue straight through the Place du Vieux Marché on to the Chemin des Remparts, which winds round the ramparts of the old town passing a restaurant on the left. After a few minutes turn up left on the Chemin des Fontaines and through a car park - the huge rock on which the castle stands towers above the partly ruined arched aqueduct on the left, then becomes a sheer face as the road continues round the back of the castle and past occasional houses.

(2) Turn left where it again says Chemin des Fontaines and Crestet (15mins). On the right is the Domaine des Roches Forts where there is free wine tasting. The road goes gently up (direction east) with a large quarry on the right. Left is an orientation table (20mins) - there is a good view of the castle on the extreme left with Vaison-la-Romaine and the Ouveze valley ahead.

The road is flat and continues in wide loops with quarries still on the right. On a corner bearing left at the start of a group of houses (higher part of the hamlet of Pierre Grosse), ignore a turning to the right.

(3) Keep going through vineyards. There is a sudden view of the medieval village of Crestet perched on a hill ahead left. The road bends again at the gates of a house on the left followed by a high hedge, with other houses dotted about, and enters pine woods.

(4) At a fork keep to the major road bearing left (30mins) - there is a yellow arrow here and another soon after but no more for a while after that. Continue past apricot orchards and then dense woodland, mainly holm, kermese and deciduous oak trees.

(5) At a fork on a bend bear down left (45mins), still on the Chemin des Fontaines! It swings round to the left by a building on the right. Down on the left is a shallow bushy depression interspersed with apricot orchards and up right are vineyards and a ridge of hills (50mins).

(6) When the road becomes an unsurfaced track, at a small crossroads, continue straight by a small building - (left is to a farm and right is a continuation of the yellow/red local GR path). Here begin the yellow/red splashes. This is a wide raised track passing through orchards and intermittent woodland, with lovely views of the plain below left and nearby farm. When it bears right (yellow arrow on concrete water cistern) there is another view of Crestet village with the two towers of the château.

(7) Keep straight as the going becomes sandy through pines and do not take the path up to the right with a yellow marking on a tree. The track is wide and flat curving through woodland past small concrete water cisterns - there is the very occasional yellow/red splash.

Ignore a turning to the left by a little concrete hut and subsequent Chemin Privé signs (this is nevertheless an official walk).

The track subsequently curls left and does a large loop round the edge of a bushy shallow valley, going over a stream (culvert) and crossing four drywater gullies. Ignore any deviations as the track starts to climb to the village.

(8) At the entrance to the village by a stone wall (1hr 40mins) turn left. Ignore the road going out of the village to the right at the sign Chemin de Verrières and go straight past a cross towards the tiny square to take a look at the old 12th-century castle which is now a private house. There is an orientation table so visitors can enjoy the extensive view over the village and spire of the church down towards the plain - the white summit of Mont Ventoux is straight ahead. *The same view can be contemplated over a drink or meal from a nearby small café/restaurant which has a lovely balcony.*

Make your way to the bottom of this delightful little hill village through the minute square with an old fountain in front of the 14th-century church- it has an iron grille over the entrance so that visitors can see the interior. Through an archway by the church is the village washing trough which has a glorious outlook and one can picture the village ladies gathered around gossiping while scrubbing their clothes. Go down the steps at the side of the washhouse and at the bottom, in front of another shire with an iron grill, turn left on the Rue des Calvaries. The narrow road passes an iron cross and goes down out of the village round two hairpin bends with little walls. There are blue splashes here. ***Careful*** - Do not go out of the village on the bigger D76 road.

(9) At the second right hairpin bend go straight on instead of round the hairpin (1hr 55mins). On the left is the wall of a driveway coming down from a private house and then a turning area for cars. Continue straight on to a wide track (blue and brown splashes). There are lots of broom bushes to the right and a little house followed by vineyards.

(10) ***Careful*** - just after the vineyards look for blue splashes going down to the right on a very narrow path (2hrs) which is difficult to see as the splashes are covered in ivy (there is a blue cross on a tree straight ahead). This is a rather unused raised path going steeply down between overgrown terraces through woods and thick undergrowth, part of it on a dry stream bed which could be slippery in wet weather - this could be part of the original track linking the village of Crestet to Vaison-la-Romaine. Near the start there is an iron cross on the side of the path. Go steeply down the wooded hill to reach the busy D938 by a fruit warehouse (2hrs 15mins).

(11) Turn left and be careful to cross to the other side of the road just before the signposts (Gap, Orange, Nyons) as the lefthand side has narrow verges and you can't see the cars coming round the corner.

(12) Cross the bridge over the River Ouvèze but be careful to cross on the lefthand side motor lane facing the traffic and where there is a proper footpath. Walk along the road (there is a good view of the old town of

Vaison-la-Romaine up left), past a large international camping centre right.

(13) Branch left onto a lesser road, the Avenue Cesar Geoffray, past a tall cement building on the right and later the hostel of the Centre Accord Joie left. When you cross a bridge the river is down on the left and as you get nearer town and the Roman bridge you can appreciate the ingenuity of the medieval builders as the rock on which the old town stands towers above the river (2hrs 45mins plus 15mins for visiting the castle).

Walk No. 30
LA GAMBADE - from Gigondas
(Dentelles de Montmirail)

Difficulty:	Easy with no great ups and downs, through woods and vineyards near the Dentelles de Montmirail - 10kms.
Time:	2hrs 30mins.
Height gain:	Negligible.
Maps:	Cartes IGN 3040ET Top 25 Carpentras/Vaison-La-Romaine 1:25,000.
	Editions Didier Richard No. 27 Ventoux 1:50,000.
Depart from:	Village of Gigondas.
Signposting:	Follow the red/yellow splashes of the local GR signs some of the way - otherwise no markings.

Observations:

A delightful easy walk round the side of the hills around Gigondas with maximum views to the plain just below and occasional glimpses of the famous rocky Dentelles de Montmirail. For a number of years there has been a race called La Gambade around this course during the last weekend of June with hundreds of participants. This was one of the first walks I ever did in Provence. I simply started before the runners and followed the conveniently placed yellow flags - easy! When I tried to do it again without the convenient markings I got hopelessly lost when the GR markings disappeared!

Gigondas, on the edge of the Dentelles de Montmirail, is a typical Provençal hill village; a huddle of houses winding up a hill to a château and church on the summit. The old church and medieval fortress with the vestiges of the old ramparts have been tastefully restored in recent years and the little community has taken on life and prosperity. For wine connoisseurs the name Gigondas conjures up the delicious red wine for which is the area is renowned. Wine producing started gaining ground after the frosts in 1929 killed many of the century-old olive trees. Now the region has more than 1200 hectares of vines and produces over 5 million bottles of wine per year.

How to get there (from Vaison-La-Romaine):
From Vaison-la-Romaine take the D977 signposted Avignon and after 9kms turn left on the D7 which goes through the village of Sablet. Turn left again on the D79 signposted Gigondas 1km. Park your car beside the new post office in the centre of the village.

Directions:
(1) Walk back over the little bridge and bear up right on a paved road just before entering the main square. Ignore a small path to the right as you walk up the hill (red/yellow cross).

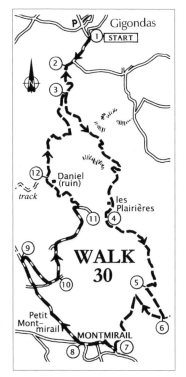

(2) At the top, where the road curls round left, follow the sign Montmirail to the right marked with yellow/red splashes (5mins). Almost immediately go left at a fork. This is a wide track going gently down through vineyards and then undulating through pines as it winds round the side of a hill.

(3) At a further fork keep left on the main path upwards (10mins). You will come in from the right on your return. The wide track meanders through pine woods with slopes each side. Soon there is a view of the attractive rocky Dentelles ridge on the left as the track starts to go upwards. Ignore a path to the right with a yellow splash and continue following the red/yellow markings. Reaching a crest (30mins) where the woods thin out there are again extensive views over the plain below to the right. The track goes down, past a small building called Les Plairières on the left and through vineyards. In front below is the village of Vacqueras.

(4) After the vineyards go up left (35mins) (cross on a stone to the right). This wide cindery jeep track passes a tall aerial on the right before bearing down to the left; you can see the path ahead wending around the contour of the hill (yellow and red splashes continue) and there is still a lovely view down into the plain. The path re-enters woods through attractive stunted pine trees with views of rocks over on the left. It then bears round to the right and down again.

(5) Keep left at the next T-junction (cross on right) and continue round on the wide smooth track (50mins). Go straight following splashes avoiding a path up left (55mins). There is a vineyard on the right as the track continues to follow the contours of the hill.

(6) At a T-junction at the end of the vineyard bear hard down to the right (red/yellow cross left). On the horizon over to the left is a long serrated ridge of grey rock. Stay on the main path which you can see ahead going round and down to the left through vineyards. It is clearly indicated with splashes. It is sandy underfoot slowly descending through vineyards interspersed with olive groves and tall cool pines, almost to the plain itself.

(7) When you reach a narrow road turn right at the splashes. Do not take the unsurfaced road on the extreme right which also has red/yellow splashes (1hr 10mins). Follow the road down through two rocky cliffs and go straight at a crossroads where the Hôtel Montmirail is on the right and the Domaine Vaubelle on the left. Further on the right there is a brown house, the grounds of the hotel (you can see the swimming pool through the trees) and a mini château complete with tower and an imposing statue in the garden!

(8) Just after the château leave this road and turn up right (1hr 20mins) on an even narrower one. **Here you leave the red/yellow splashes of the GR. From now on you are following no consistent coloured splashes though the road has a blue arrow on it from time to time.** You are now heading back towards Gigondas along the side of the plain with vines down on the left. The road passes by Petit Montmirail which consists of two large houses and through olive trees and vines - up to the right is a quaint old round tower which has been made into a private house.

(9) Follow the road round a U-turn to the right when you can look back where you walked and down on to the round tower house.

(10) Cross a dry watercourse and bear up left past the entrance to a Gîte Rural; from higher up this looks rather enticing standing isolated in a shallow vine-covered valley complete with swimming pool!

The road goes straight up through vineyards (northeast) with two aerials in front, the one to the right being that seen earlier on. After passing a large house on the left the paved road turns into a jeep track (1hr 55mins). Do not go up right, where there is some tarmac, but stay on the jeep track round to the left and into woodland.

(11) At the first intersection go down left (2hrs). There is a dark green arrow on a rock (light green arrow straight ahead). On the right is a small vineyard. A few minutes later avoid a path up right and keep bearing left (big green arrow on rock). The track curls round the hill southwest through pines past a ruined house on the right (Daniel Ruins on the map). Follow the contours of the hill and avoid two offshoots to the right (one just after the ruins and one in a clearing). The view opens up again down on the left with more vineyards.

(12) Bear right at a T-junction where the vineyard ends and then almost immediately take a narrow path to the left in a sandy intersection - do not take the one straight up. This is now a narrow track through woodland meandering around the contour of the hill - ignore branches going off right or left.

Where the path dips down just after crossing a narrow stream bed bear up right (red mark on rock) (2hrs 20mins). You have arrived at the turning you took on the outward journey (No. 3 on map). Turn down left and retrace your steps to the village (2hrs 30mins).

Walk No. 31
LES DENTELLES DE MONTMIRAIL

Difficulty:	Walk A. Medium - some scrambling around the Dentelles Sarrasines but much of this walk is on forest roads and walking along a valley.
	Walk B. Strenuous/Difficult - same as above but on a more strenuous path with some scrambling around the Dentelles de Montmirail. Not suitable for anyone suffering from vertigo.
Time:	Walk A - 4hrs 45mins
	Walk B - 4hrs 15mins.
Height gain:	167m.
Maps:	Cartes IGN 3040ET Top 25 Carpentras/Vaison-La-Romaine 1:25,000.
	Editions Didier Richard No. 27 Ventoux 1:50,000.
Depart from:	Col de Cayron, Nr. Gigondas.
Signposting:	Good except when you really need one! Blue and then yellow splashes.

Observations:

A truly delightful walk with splendid views of these curious peaks. For those who like a challenge the walk along the side of the Montmirail is exciting though not to be done in bad weather.

The Dentelles de Montmirail is a dramatic row of white limestone peaks which stick out like a lacy border over the surrounding Vaucluse plain and are said to be the foothills of the nearby Mont Ventoux. They were caused by the folding of the earth's crust which forced the limestone upwards. Centuries of wind and erosion have shaped them into needle-like peaks and ridges. They are a lovely sight at any time of the year but more so in May and June when the lower slopes are covered with yellow flowering broom. They have attracted many artists, climbers and walkers - the area is very popular and can be crowded in high season.

How to get there (from Vaison-La-Romaine):

From Vaison-La-Romaine take the D977 signposted Avignon and after 9kms turn left on the D7 towards Gigondas, passing by the village of Sablet. Turn left again on the D79 signposted Gigondas 1km/Dentelles de Montmirail/ Hôtel Les Florets. At a crossroads turn left (Gigondas is straight on) and then again almost immediately following the same signs (Dentelles de Montmirail/ Hôtel Les Florets). Continue up this road for 2kms past the Hôtel Les Florets and then on a rougher road to the Col de Cayron (Alt. 396m) which is a large open space with a car park. There are two large information boards.

Directions: Walks A and B

(1) From the car park take the narrow path to the right of the Forestry Commission notice (direction southwest), with blue splashes signposted Dentelles de Sarrasines. This is a clear sunken path with initially wide manmade steps through pines and boxwood going towards the serrated crests of the Dentelles de Sarrasines. Down on the left is an attractive valley of vineyards with a television mast beyond on top of the Crête de St. Armand. The path goes up medium steep getting rocky as it gains height.

(2) At a T-junction there is a signpost (15mins). Turn right following Col d'Aise/Rochers du Midi/Sentier face Nord. Continue on this path following blue splashes up towards sheer cliffs. Ignore a path to the left.

(3) At a fork go down right (30mins).

The path up left is a steep short cut which goes right over the cliffs and directly down the other side to the Col d'Aise, but should only be done by people who can cope with a vertiginous scramble. NOTE: It has not been done by the author and shortens the walk by about 30mins.

Continue along the flank of the mountain gradually gaining more height

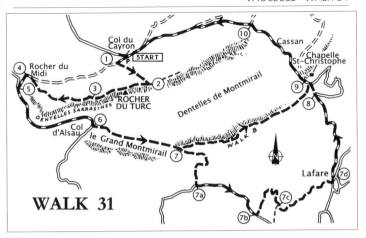

WALK 31

until you are right under the cliffs. After about 5mins look for a little path up to the left which goes to the crest between two rocks. From here there is a magnificent view over the other side to the vine covered valley below and another range of serrated rocks beyond, Le Grand Montmirail - the views on either side of the ridge are extensive and on the horizon north is the white crest of the Mont Ventoux - it is the perfect place for a picnic (40mins).

The path continues below these incredible rock formations. At a fork go either way which takes you to a spot where there is an impressive wide crack in the rock giving an extra dimension to your view over the plain. Bear down right being careful to follow the blue dots on the rocks. When the path comes to the end of the rocky range it starts to go down rather sharply over small patches of scree. At another fork following a small path of scree, take the upper path (blue dot) as there are a number of scree patches here and it is easy to lose the way (50mins). There are lovely open views of the plain dotted with villages as you pick your way down but don't gaze too long as you must watch your feet on the stones!

(4) The path meets an unpaved road (1hr 5mins) at a clearing with pines called the Rocher du Midi (curiously not marked on the map). It is worth following the sign to the right to the Belvédère Rocher du Midi (viewpoint) through pines and then up manmade steps to a lookout site and an orientation table. Straight ahead below is the village of Gigondas, to the right Sablet with a tower at the top of the huddle of houses, and further right Seguret.

Retrace your steps to the road (1hr 15mins) and go right. This track curls round the end of the Dentelles (direction southwest) towards the Col d'Alsau.

(5) Do not turn down right towards Gigondas (there are blue markings here also) and ignore a following road to the right. The steep short cut joins the road just before the col where there is a parking area with a new wall to the left (1hr 30mins).

(6) Continue past the parking area and, just after a right corner (indicating Tour Sarrazin) go up left on an equally wide road for a few minutes. This leads to the gates of a *domaine* (winery) called Clos Bois de Menge. Take the narrow path up left, marked by blue dots and yellow splashes, through stunted trees and bushes and later over patches of scree. There is a charming vine-covered valley down on the left with the Dentelles de Sarrasines behind so the route has done a complete loop - the jagged peaks of Le Grand Montmirail are looming ahead with the Mont Ventoux on the skyline behind.

Be careful to keep to the path with the blue dot and yellow splashes (at the first fork it goes left but after generally up right avoiding various left branches down into the valley). Continue on this clearly marked path which initially heads directly for the Dentelles de Montmirail but eventually bears down right (direction east) towards another valley below.

(Walk B diviates here on a more strenuous route [see below])

(7) Continue down, ignoring a path up left with blue dots/yellow splashes (1hr 50mins). There are occasional yellow splashes as the bushy path winds quite steeply down reaching a narrow road just below a small clearing where the marks seem to disappear (2hrs 15mins).

(8) Turn left down the road - this is a beautiful unspoilt valley with the wooded slopes and the rocky crags of the Dentelles to the left and rows and rows of vineyards and a large house to the right.

(9) Watch for a narrow road up to the left (2hrs 55mins) where blue and yellow markings sprout again and there is a round sign saying 8T (whatever that means). This is the last blue marking to be seen for a while - continue following yellow splashes (blue markings appear later but the yellow are more frequent).

(10) At a fork turn up left (right goes back down to the original more major road). Continue upwards fairly steeply with yellow splashes, avoiding branches usually marked with yellow crosses. There is a row of stately cypresses to the right and every piece of cultivated land seems to be covered with vines.

The road deteriorates as it winds down over a river by a bridge into the village of Lafare. Following yellow splashes turn into the village (3hrs

Dentelles de Montmirail, above Col de Cayron

10mins), there is a high wall to the left on the way up to join the D90. This is a typical Provençal hamlet with its huddle of houses - there are a couple of places where refreshment is available including a smart hotel.

(11) At the road junction turn up left and continue till you see a cement plinth with a small iron cross on top and a sign left, Dentelles de Montmirail (3hrs 15mins). This is a lesser paved road (direction north) which crosses the river again and continues upward with the Grand Montmirail over on the left. The Chapelle St. Christophe is high above on a rocky knoll. Continue till you reach a hairpin bend to the left by a ravine (3hrs 30mins).

(Walk B rejoins just before the hairpin)

(12) Watch for a narrow path marked with blue and yellow splashes going straight up. It is quite a steep scramble - follow the markings carefully over smooth rocks and then bear left, avoiding a miniature gully. The path goes over patches of scree (keep up right at a T-junction in the scree). Just before a telephone pole go left at a crossroads (blue signs) and meet the road again by a small parking area (3hrs 50mins).

(13) To visit the chapel, cross the road and go up the medium steep path for about 5mins. The chapel has been partially restored and is not normally locked. There is a crude altar inside but a dirt floor - it does not look as though it is used for worship. There is a lovely view here of Le Grand Montmirail range and the valley with the village of Lafare.

Retrace your steps to the road and turn right (4hrs). The paved road continues up gently (direction north/west) through vineyards to the large buildings of the Domaine de Cassam, suppliers of well-known wines such as Gigondas and Beaumes de Venise. This is a good opportunity to stop and indulge in some *dégustation gratuit* (free tasting) - they are highly recommended and it is worth tucking the odd bottle into your rucksack if you have the space!

(14) A few minutes later bear to the left towards Col de Cayron (4hrs 15mins) when the road deteriorates. You are entering a valley (direction west) with the rocky peaks of the Dentelles de Sarrasines on the left. Initially there are vineyards both sides of the road and then woods with a cleared area (probably for another car park) as the road goes steadily up to the large parking area and the start of the walk at the Col de Cayron (4hrs 45mins).

**Walk B: shorter and more strenuous (avoid this option if you suffer from vertigo; it is also not recommended after heavy rain or in bad weather).

(7) Bear up left following the blue spots/yellow splashes (1hr 50mins). This path goes much higher up and underneath the rocky crags of the Montmirail. It follows a rocky path where there are often bushes and stunted trees - there is some clambering in places as it goes across patches of scree and slabs of rock but the signs are very obvious and you should follow them carefully.

Where the blue dots go up left keep straight on the yellow splashes (2hrs 15mins) meeting up with the blue dots further on. The path swings down to the right and then left a few metres later, at a T-junction lower down.

The yellow flashes go right but take the blue spot going down left. The path can be quite slippery here and there are lots of loose stones before it bears left and becomes less steep. At a further T-junction go left (2hrs 35mins). The bushy way steepens again as it rounds the high rocky buttress at the end of the Montmirail rocks. There are lovely views into the valley below. Go right at a fork 5mins later following blue dots. You can now see the road running through the valley below. Bear right again by a cairn shortly after and continue down.

Careful at a sign which says Access Difficile. This is a short scramble sideways over a large slab of rock but there are numerous hand holes. If in doubt sit down and worm your way across and down. It is not technically difficult but it needs some care. The lower part is through pines but the path is rather stony and slippery and at the end there is a tiresome short eroded slope to reach the road.

At the road turn up left just before the hairpin bend and watch for the narrow path up left with blue and yellow splashes No. 8 (3hrs). Continue as for the longer walk A back to the Col de Cayron (4hrs 15mins).

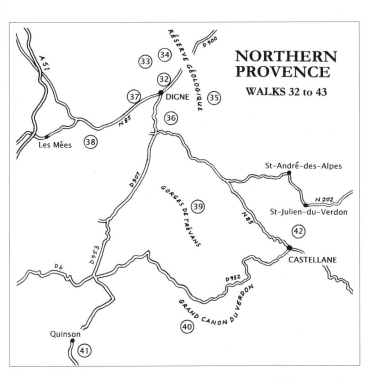

Northern Provence

WALK Nos. 32 - 43

This is the least known area of Provence and the wildest! There are fewer cosy little villages, the hills are higher, the plains more windswept, the gorges deeper and wider, the climate harsher, the population more dispersed. Because of its relative inaccessibility until fairly recently, it has retained the traditional rural way of life and is more "authentic" than the other regions. People tend not to choose this area to retire to or have holiday homes because of its rugged nature and climate, leaving its charms to be discovered by discerning walkers!

But tourism is expanding nevertheless, and areas are being opened up for walking, canoeing, rafting, hang-gliding and swimming. Walking is becoming more popular as the signposting and paths improve. There is also downhill and cross-country skiing in the Val d'Allos, around Barcelonnette and Seyne les Alpes.

The Alpes de Haute Provence region only sprang into official existence in 1971 when the general area of Provence was divided into specific *Départements*. This mountainous northern area stretches from the Gorges de Verdon in the south (see Walk No. 40) to the dramatic peak of Mt. Pelat (3050m) in the Mercantour National Park in the northeast. Southwest is the Valensole plain, one of the largest lavender-growing areas in Provence and a blaze of purple during the month of July.

The main artery through the region is the 305km long Durance River with its many tributaries. Once turbulent and capricious, it was used for floating logs down until 1908. It was finally tamed in 1960 with dams and a huge hydro-electric scheme creating the vaste expanse of water, now called the lac de Serre-Ponçon, in the north. This harnessing of the river has created employment and industries have sprung up, thus stemming the exodus of the rural population to towns in other parts of the country.

Faience (a particular type of china) comes mainly from the region around Moustiers-Sainte-Marie, a little village perched impressively between craggy rocks at the entrance to a ravine north of the Gorges de Verdon. The distinctive glaze on the pieces dates from 1679 when the first workshop was opened by Antoine Clérissy. The exceptional quality of the products came from the clay used from local quarries. Flourishing until the 18th century the industry went into decline, to be revived again in 1927. The village and workshops attract numerous tourists and the intricately painted highly glazed pieces are widely exported.

Agriculture still plays an important role in the region. Fruit growing in the rich alluvial soil of the Durance valley has grown to represent 30 per cent of the agricultural revenue, farms staying in the hands of the same families for generations. Lavender and its derivative Lavendin grows in the Valensole plain, providing 80 per cent of the world's needs. Other herbs are cultivated such as thyme, rosemary, sage and oregano. Bee-keeping was introduced at the end of the 19th century and honey is now a growing export.

Sheep rearing is the main activity in the mountainous areas, well known for the traditional *transhumance* when the sheep are taken in the spring to graze in the upland pastures and back in the autumn, sometimes a considerable distance from their home. This still continues but on a much smaller scale than in the previous century. Once vast flocks could be seen making their way through the countryside but now much of the transportation is done by truck. Goat rearing has expanded since 1950 due to the excellent milk they produce which is often used for medicinal purposes.

A favourite pastime in this area, though happily on the decline, is the trapping of small birds, particularly thrushes. *Pâté des grives* (thrush paté) is seen less and less on local menus. During the hunting season in October and November, the birds are attracted to the traps by fake bird-calls - imitating bird-calls is a typical Provençal skill dating back to the days when catching wild birds was a day-to-day activity.

Digne-les-Bains, at the confluence of three valleys (the Bléone, the Mardaric and the Eaux Chaudes), is the capital of the region. It is more of a working town, serving as the hub of a largely rural region, than a tourist oriented venue. Nevertheless, it has been famed as a spa since Roman times and hundreds of people (mainly French) come here to take a cure in the sulphurous springs every year. Digne was also the home of Pierre Gassendi 1592-1655, a well-known mathematician whose statue can be seen in the main square. A more recent inhabitant was Alexandra David-Neel, an intrepid traveller and explorer in Tibet who lived to be over 100 years old. Her house has been turned into a fascinating museum and Tibetan centre. Digne-les-Bains has displays of modern sculpture dotted around town (there is a big symposium every two years) and a flamboyant four-day lavender festival in August.

Dignes is also the terminus for the train des Pignes which runs on a 151km line from Nice through spectacular scenery. There are four journeys a day by electric train but the real train des Pignes is the renovated steam engine dating from 1909 which only operates on Sundays from May to October. There are many theories as to the name but the most prevalent is that, during the war, the train had to stop numerous times due to lack of coal, so the travellers had time to jump off the train to collect pine cones *(pignes)*.

North of Digne-les-Bains, in the Bès valley (see Walk Nos. 33 and 34) is the largest geological reserve in Europe. This was created in 1984 and is a mecca for geologists from all over the world. In a dramatic mountainous area of 665 acres are 18 protected sites, some of which can be visited by car, while others entail some walking. Guided visits can be arranged through the Tourist Office.

About 3 miles from the town centre on the D900A is the Geology Centre which makes a fascinating visit. It is open all year round Monday to Sunday (excepting public holidays) 09.00 - 12.00 and 14.00 - 17.30 (16.30 on Fridays). An informative leaflet is available in English showing the sites which can be visited. Do not miss the fascinating wall of ammonite fossils on a tall limestone wall just up the road. Continue on the D900A stopping at the sites and driving through the Clues de Barles (*clue* meaning narrow valley) - the dramatic rocks through this gorge-like traverse with the river one side are worth the experience.

As a tourist attraction Sisteron is probably the best known town in the region. Calling itself The Gateway to Provence its citadel, dating from the 13th century, dominates the town which clings to the banks of the Durance River. The old town is a pleasure to explore with narrow winding streets, some dating from Roman times, and striking wooden doorways built in the 16th century. In season there is a small train to whisk you up to the citadel, where there is a dramatic view plus dungeons, chapels and ramparts to discover. Little evidence remains of the extensive damage during the Second World War when Sisteron was bombarded by the allies to stop the Germans descending further south. Every summer since 1956 there has been a festival of music, theatre and dance called Nuits de la Citadelle.

Forcalquier and Manosque, both south of Sisteron and west of the Durance River, are interesting towns. Forcalquier, perched on top of a hill crowned by a ruined castle, has not changed much, but Manosque, whose name comes from the Celtic word meaning "people of the hills" has become an affluent little town. It is the site of France's largest nuclear research centre, inaugurated in 1963 and built in the grounds of the 15th-century Château de Cadarache. It was also home to the famous author Jean Giono 1895-1970 whose books evoke a rural romantic Provence which no longer exists today. His house in the Lou Parais district has been made into a museum.

At the extreme east edge of the region, on the border with Alpes Maritimes, is the town of Entrevaux, magnificently situated with its citadel atop a rocky outcrop 440ft above the quaint medieval town. It has a music festival in August.

Mention should be made of Barcelonnette in the Ubaye valley which is the town furthest north. Surrounded by snowy peaks, it looks as if it should be in Switzerland rather than in Provence but with a specific difference. Suffering from poverty many of the inhabitants emigrated to Mexico in the 18th century. Having made their fortune they returned and built sumptuous villas, giving the town a Mexican touch! Barcelonnette still suffers from a certain isolation but welcomes tourists and is the gateway to the Mercantour National Park.

Where to base yourself for walks as described in this book

The author was based in Digne-les-Bains and most of the walks are within an hour's drive of this town. It offers a number of hotels and two camping grounds, one two-star, one three-star. The Bureau de Tourisme in the centre of town is one of the most helpful in Provence (English spoken).

This region does not have the wealth of hotels that you find further south in the more affluent regions, but many villages offer accommodation (ask the

Tourist Bureau for a list). There are the usual Gîtes de France and Chambres d'Hôtes.

St. André les Alpes (see Walk No. 42), a charming village at the northern end of the Lac de Castellane, is a good centre. It has half a dozen modest hotels and two campsites, one on the lakeside. St. André is noted for its hang-gliding, the French championships being held here in 1991.

Walk No. 32
THREE CHAPELS WALK FROM DIGNE-LES-BAINS

Difficulty:	Easy although there is some climbing.
Time:	2hrs.
Height gain:	270m.
Maps:	Editions Didier & Richard No. 1 Alpes du Sud 1:50,000.
	Cartes IGN Série bleu 3440 Ouest Thoard 1:25,000.
	Cartes IGN Série bleu 3441O Digne-les-Bains 1:25,000.
	(This walk is spread between two 1:25,000 maps and is clearer on the 1:50,000).
Depart from:	Place du Général de-Gaulle, Digne-les-Bains.
Sign posting:	Very good - follow yellow splashes.

Observations:
This is an easy short walk from the town - the views are glorious and there is the added interest of the three chapels, two of which are due for restoration. For information on Digne-les-Bains see the Introduction to 'Northern Provence'.

How to get there:
Park your car in the Place du Général de-Gaulle in Digne-les-Bains.

Directions:
(1) Go down the Boulevard Victor Hugo (just off the Place heading north) and turn right on to the Rue du Capitaine Victor Arnoux to a roundabout. Take the first street left signposted PR les Trois Chapelles.

(2) After about 100m turn up right opposite the Institut St. Martin onto a paved lane which, after a house with green gates, turns into a wide stony track. Pass the gates of another house on the right as you wind up the hill through pines following the yellow splashes and reach a signpost (10mins) at a T-junction - right is the chapel of Notre-Dame des Lourdes and to the left Chapelle St-Vincent.

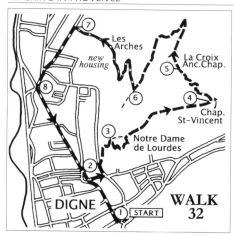

(3) Go right and then 50m later right again (here you get your first view over the town of Digne and surrounding hills). Almost immediately the path forks. Keep to the lower path which leads to the chapel. There is a primitive little grotto here with lots of artificial flowers and a tiny statue of the Virgin Mary. Then take the steps on the left going up to the chapel.

(4) The chapel itself is an empty shell, open at the altar end with a gaping hole in the roof. Unless it is renovated in the immediate future it is likely that the whole building will quickly fall into ruins. Retrace your steps or return to the junction by the upper path.

The area around Digne-les-Bains is the most northerly point of the Mediterranean climate and on this particular hill you will find Le Pin d'Alep (Aleppo Pine) recognisable by its pyramidal or rounded crown and egg shaped cones.

Retrace your steps to the first T-junction (No. 3 on map) and follow the sign up right to the Chapelle St-Vincent (20mins). Continue upwards by a small electricity pylon onto a wooded ridge and a pleasant undulating path through stunted oak trees. Beyond is a wide field which sweeps up to another wooded hill where you are heading. You emerge from the woods with the field on your left and straight ahead is the chapel of St. Vincent on a grassy knoll. There are glorious views of the surrounding hills from the front of the building, including the Cousson (Walk No. 36) on the right and straight ahead the Coard (Walk No. 35).

The Chapelle St-Vincent possibly replaced another edifice on the site which housed the remains of the first Bishop of Digne. Dating from the 12th century it was destroyed during the religious wars but reconstructed in 1597 and restored in 1950. The bas-reliefs dating from the 12th century, which disappeared at the end of the 19th century, are actually preserved in the chapel of the Maegt foundation at Saint Paul de Vence. This chapel also needs to be restored again rapidly as nothing remains but the walls.

190

Coard & Cousson mountains from Three Chapels walk

(4) cont. Cross the end of the field (north) to a signpost which you can see clearly from the chapel (ignore a path on the left shortly after the signpost) and follow the stony, winding path upwards until you come to the third chapel called La Croix. It consists merely of a small edifice of stones on the summit of the hill 870m (1hr).

(5) Follow the sign here to Digne on a pleasant path down the other side of the hill through the inevitable stunted oak trees. At a clearing on a ridge go left (there is a yellow cross on the tree ahead). You are winding round to the north side of the hill now and the air feels fresher. Down on the right you can see the outskirts of the town, the River Bléone and the radio mast at the summit of the Andran mountain on the other side.

(6) Do not take the smaller path to the left at a T-junction. Follow the main path round two further bends before coming to a road (not indicated on the map as it is a new housing development). Cross the road (yellow crosses to left and right) and continue down a narrow track with new houses to the right to another road (also not on the map).

(7) Turn right and then left into Rue Charles Grouiller following consistent yellow splashes. Continue along with houses on both sides to a crossroads. Here go straight on the Avenue des Arches.

(8) Turn left at traffic lights and go straight down the Avenue Victor Hugo till it reaches the Place Général de-Gaulle (2hrs).

Walk No. 33
L'ICHTYOSAURE FOSSIL
National Geological Reserve site

Difficulty:	Easy walk through a delightful narrow valley.
Time:	1hr 15mins + time to look at the fossil.
Height gain:	About 100m.
Maps:	IGN Série Bleu 3440 Ouest (west) Thoard 1:25,000.
	Didier Richard No. 1 Alpes du Sud 1:50,000.
Depart from:	Parking on D900A, 7kms from Digne.
Signposting:	The path is obvious, marked by the occasional wooden post marked with a green fossil.

Observations:
A delightful short walk within the capabilities of most people. It is a good idea to visit the Geological Museum (see Introduction to 'Northern Provence') before you visit the fossilised sites as this gives you background information about the area - see also Walk No. 34 ('Le Serre de l'Esclangon'). Information on the noticeboard in the parking area states: "These L'Ichtyosaure fossils date from 185 million years ago when the sea covered the entire region and was teeming with life including the enormous L'Ichtyosaure reptiles. In spite of strong currents which hindered fossilisation the skeleton of a 4-metre long specimen was partially preserved. This is one of the eighteen listed sites constituting the National Geological Reserve of Haute Provence. In 1981 a small 15 metre glass case was built on the site to protect the fossil."

How to get there (from Digne Les Bains):
Take the D900A out of town in the direction of Barles and follow all signs to the Geological Museum (see below) which is up left after crossing a cream bridge. Continue up the D900A until you come to the first geological site which is a large limestone slab containing ammonite fossils. Continue past a turning left to La Robine and watch for a new parking area left and a sign L'Ichtyosaure (7kms from Digne).

Directions:
Read the information given on the noticeboard in the parking area (in French and English).

A wooden post marks the start of an easy path which has been recently made (1998) along the righthand side of an attractive narrow wooded valley with stunted oak and beech trees. It runs level with a small stream on the left before climbing up higher and continuing along. The valley narrows and the stream drops into a gorge left where you see an attractive waterfall. The path becomes rocky and drops down to cross the stream by a slatted wooden bridge (20mins). It climbs up again the other side of the valley through denser beech trees and boxwood draped with moss - the river is now down on the right with a rocky slope on the other side. Keep to the main path.

The track comes out rather unexpectedly into a shallow grassy valley where there is a wooden post. On the other side are slopes of fissured black rocks which look like shale, softened by bushes and stunted trees. Up on the tree-covered slope right is a building (Le Pailler). Continue on the obvious path down the valley through scattered woodland. Ahead is the long tree-covered ridge of the Crête de Liman. Soon you reach the site of the Ichtyosaure fossil markings (40mins) at a low glass-covered edifice (resembling a large cold frame). Beneath is a rocky slab with the fossilised impression of this huge marine reptile - it is certainly an impressive sight and worth reflection that such huge creatures roamed the seas so long ago. On the back of the frame is a picture of an Ichtyosaure producing a baby and then swimming away to catch fish. There is also a notice with further information about these creatures which, although the exhibit is 4.2m long, could attain a length of 15m. They were very good swimmers and hunted shelled fish (such as the fossiled ammonites) but, like the whales of today, they needed to surface from time to time to breathe air into their lungs. It also mentions that this technique of protecting a fossil where it was actually found is the first of its kind in Europe.

Retrace your steps back to the car park (1hr 15mins).

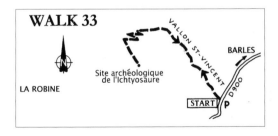

193

Walk No. 34
LE SERRE DE L'ESCLANGON
National Geological Reserve

Difficulty:	Medium/strenuous. A short steep walk. The path up is rocky and eroded in places.
Time:	1hr 45mins up and down (leave at least 45mins for exploring the village and walking to the end of the ridge).
Height gain:	340m.
Maps:	Cartes IGN Série Bleu 3440 Ouest Thoard 1:25,000.
	Editions Didier Richard No. 1 Alpes du Sud 1:50,000. (note: this walk is difficult to follow in detail on the maps).
Depart from:	Parking area on D900A just before bridge going into the Gorges de Pérouré.
Signposting:	Signposts and yellow splashes which are not always easy to see. There are also infrequent red dots.

Observations:

This walk is one of my favourites as I love exploring old ruins and cemeteries! As geologists come from all over the world to see the velodrome I cannot understand why they don't make the path easier to follow. The walk could be combined with a visit to the fascinating Geological Museum, 4kms out of Dignes on the same road.

If you have not driven through the Cluses de Barles gorges, then this is your opportunity! The word *cluses* comes from the Latin *clauses*, meaning shut. There has been a mule track through here for centuries but these rocky edifices not only represent a human barrier but a natural one too. South of the gorge the vegetation is Provençal but north it is alpine.

For a round trip continue on past the village of Barles and through further gorges (Clues de Verdaches), where there is a fossilised forest site worth visiting, to the village of Verdaches. After this village take a turning right on the D900 back to Digne-les-Bains (61kms). On this road there are five geological sites (see printed map in English which is given out free at the Geological Museum) indicated by large signposts at the side of the road so you cannot miss them. There is adequate parking in each spot.

How to get there (from Digne-les-Bains):

Take the D900A in the direction of Barles for 14.6kms. 2.2kms from Esclangon, and after a sign on the right indicating one of the fossil sites (*site à empreintes de pas d'oiseaux* - fossilised bird footprints), cross an iron bridge. Shortly after look for a parking area on the left before another iron

bridge. This is just before the road enters a gorge called the Clue du Pérouré. There is a signpost on the other side of the road indicating Vieil Esclangon but it is rather hidden by trees.

Directions:

(1) At the signpost there is a red arrow on a rock right. Take the fork right (there is a yellow splash further up). A few metres later at a T-junction turn right and then almost immediately left. The path is medium steep over rust coloured rocks and powdery rusty soil. **Note:** this path is stony and very eroded which makes it difficult to see.

Follow the infrequent yellow signs carefully all the way up over this bumpy rocky shoulder dotted with pines and bushes. The path flattens out (10mins) and goes parallel to the valley down below right before it turns a corner and goes up the side of a wide tree-covered ravine. It then winds up and away from the ravine over to the other side where there is another ravine. As you gain height you can see your destination, the rocky Serre d'Esclangon, up on the right while on the left is the long curiously white ridge of the Blayeul.

The path goes round the top of the ravine on the right, which has sort of split into two, over a slope of red cindery soil which could be slippery in wet weather. It continues up and then branches off to the left to the other side of the shoulder, looking down to the ravine on the left. Follow the infrequent yellow splashes as you zigzag up this rocky shoulder from one side to the other. Ignore a path to the left (yellow cross on rock) as you turn a corner (35mins) and go over the top of the ravine. The path eventually flattens out as you start to walk through cool woodland. Ignore another branch going back left, also with a yellow cross. Continue through attractive grassy glades dotted with hawthorn bushes and deciduous trees reaching open hillside.

Make for an imposing willow tree up on the left which you can't miss. Just beyond it you can make out the first ivy-covered ruin (the church although you don't recognise it as such) of the abandoned hamlet of Esclangon (40mins). *Here you can take time to explore the ruined buildings which make up the village. One can only speculate on how the inhabitants scratched a living in this remote area. Surprisingly, after such a rocky climb, it is a beautiful grassy area, very fertile looking with a considerable number of trees and presumably there must have been a water source nearby though you can see no streams. Just beyond the willow tree to the left is a faint grassy path which takes you to an overgrown cemetery surrounded by a wall. Go round on the path till you come to the entrance gate. Amongst the few remaining graves is a once elaborate but now rusty iron bower dedicated to Leydet Duvraz who died on 26th December 1934 aged 28 years old. There are some artificial flowers on the ironwork so it looks as though the grave is still looked after.*

From the willow tree go diagonally right across the grassy hill to a wooden post with a yellow top, then round and up through stunted blackthorn bushes past a signpost with the name of the village Vieil Esclangon and another ruin. After the signpost the path starts to climb through trees, then getting rockier, crossing a slab of smooth rock, up to the summit which is a delightfully flat grassy area ringed with lavender bushes.

(2) The view from the summit is spectacular (1hr). *To the right (west) is the geological phenomena called a velodrome which is an impressive swathe of lined and pleated rock curving round in the shape of a rainbow, caused by erosion. It sweeps down, the lower slopes covered in trees, and facing it in the ravine is the voile de Facibelle which is a curious long blade of grey rock rearing up. This rare rock formation is an impressive sight. Below is the valley with the road and Bès River winding through. To the east (left) is the long cream coloured arid ridge of the Blayeul mountain contrasting with the green meadows in the valley and around the ruined hamlet of Esclangon. There are Charollais cattle so this is obviously still used as a grazing area. Straight ahead right the valley snakes through the mountains with the road and the Bès River. Behind you more mountains descend into the gorge which is hidden.*

The ridge continues and it is possible to walk to a manmade cairn at the end but there is no defined path or yellow splashes. You go down with a bank of rocks on the left and then pass to the other side of it and pick your way along. Where there is a tricky ridge of rocks and brambles keep to the left below it. Continue along the ridge where there are rocks and grassy areas until you reach the cairn (15mins). There is an even better view of the Bès valley at the end and you look down on the new hamlet of Esclangon in the valley. From the cairn the ridge drops down and it is not worth going further.

When you retrace your steps to the hump you realise that you actually lost 50m in height and the way back is up! Retrace your steps back to the car park but be careful to go down left from the willow tree over the grassy hill to find the descending path. Follow the yellow splashes down as carefully as you followed them up as it is easy to miss your way (1hr 45mins) - (allow about 2hrs 30mins if you have done the extra walk along the ridge and stopped to explore the village).

Walk No. 35
SOMMET DE CUCUYON (1886m) or
SOMMET DE COUARD (1998m)

Difficulty:	Strenuous - stiff climb most of the way up to the Cucuyon though not technically difficult.
	Longer and stiffer climb to the summit of the Couard.
Time:	4hrs 30mins (Cucuyon) 6hrs (Couard).
Height gain:	967m (Cucuyon) 1079ms (Couard).
Maps:	Cartes IGN Série Bleu 3440 Est (East) La Javie 1:25,000.
	Editions Didier & Richard No. 1 Alpes du Sud 1:50,000.
Depart from:	Village of Archail - 919m.
Signposting:	Signposts and yellow splashes but sometimes difficult to see.

*The cliffs beneath
the Cucuyon*

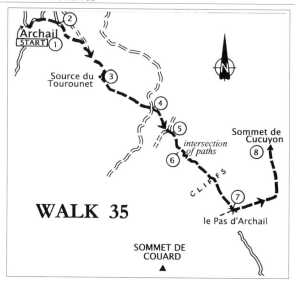

Observations:

A very satisfying walk despite the stiff climb up and down the same way. The curious shapes of the twin summits of the Couard and Cucuyon are a landmark in the surrounding area.

How to get there (from Digne-les-Bains):

Take the D900 from Digne-les-Bains signposted La Javie for 6kms turn right on the D22 signposted Archail and continue for 5kms until there is a further turning to the right indicating Archail. Go up this winding road to the hamlet (2kms) and park in the little square in front of the church.

Directions:

(1) There is a sign on the lefthand side of the square indicating Le Sommet du Couard 3hrs (an optimistic estimate). Follow the sign up on a narrow paved road to the left of the little church, immediately starting to gain height-there is a yellow splash on a tree.

(2) A few minutes later where the paved road becomes a jeep track, go through a chain across the road ignoring a path down to the left (there are signposts here). Follow the track round to the left past a small stone barn and then, after another wide turn, past a second one on the right. Continue straight up with a good view down right to the valley backed by marled black cliffs which are such a characteristic of this region. Looming ahead are the pointed rocky peak of the Cucuyon on the left and the more dramatic rocky mass of the Coard on the right, separated by the wide grassy Pas d'Archail. Go past a wooden cross to the right and cross over a stream.

(3) Just after crossing a second stream there is a high fence up on the left, surrounding a small reservoir, the Source du Tourounet (25mins). The track narrows as it goes up through intermittent woodland and small glades. Continue to a flat open clearing (40mins).

(4) Keep straight as the gradient gets steeper. About 5mins later, cross a wide jeep track up a short steep track which turns out to be a short cut (alternatively go right and then almost immediately first left where there is a yellow cross on a tree). Soon there is a signpost indicating Pic de Couard so keep up left where an overgrown track comes in from the right. The going steepens as you go straight up through tall pines before again reaching a wide smooth jeep track.

(5) Go straight across (1hr) where there is a signpost and a yellow splash. Continue on this wider track through pine forest bearing to the right and reaching an intersection of five paths (1hr 10mins).

(6) Take the narrower second track to the left signposted Couard. There has been a lot of logging along this path so there may still be piles of logs before you enter an attractive beech forest dotted with larch trees which get more frequent as you go higher. After passing a small gully the path turns sharp right (blue arrow on rock) and starts to wind up towards the rocky mass of the Couard. Tracing long zigzags through the forest, it crosses the wide scree bed of the Fournas gully several times, the result of a recent landslide. Watch out for one spot where the path doesn't cross the scree but turns sharply left. As the gradient steepens there is a stream on the right and later a waterfall flowing over the cliff.

Soon you reach the bottom of huge rocky cliffs and wonder how you are going to get round them! In fact the wide stony path winds up the rock face and across scree slopes with no difficulty. If you look down to the right you can see the reservoir in the woods and the villages of Archail and Draix far below. Back right is the distinctive Blayeul ridge with its aerial. The rock face ends in a small promontory where you can appreciate the incredible strata of the Cucuyon behind as the rocks fold over like waves and thrust out above the slopes below (1hr 50mins). Turn left into tall pine forest where there is a series of iron water troughs fed by a pipe, obviously for cattle. Beyond is the *source* (spring) with another water pipe and wooden trough. Continue straight up by the spring (there is a yellow mark on a tree).

(7) Suddenly the path reaches the wide grassy Pas d'Archail pass where there is a small wooden hut and two lots of smart signposts (2hrs). The right signpost indicates Pic de Couard right 1hr 15mins, the summit of the Pré d'Evèque left and Abri Publique (public refuge) straight ahead. You can see this small building in the trees ahead with a large corral beside it to shelter the animals. On the other side of the pass is a jeep track coming up which may explain why a car is stationed outside the refuge!

The left signpost indicates Pic de Cucuyon left 40mins. This sign is ambiguous as there are two peaks left, the Crête du Pré d'Evèques and the Cucuyon. The Cucuyon is the one on the far left.

Here you can go to the top of the Coard which you can see up on the right. It consists of a stiff climb to a shoulder and then up the ridge to the summit. Alternatively you can climb to the top of the more pointed rocky Cucuyon which is less steep and only takes 40mins.

There is no defined path to reach the Cucuyon though there is a yellow splash on a lone pine at the start. Bear left towards a ridge between the rounded hump on the right of the Crête du Pré d'Evèques and the final slope of the Cucuyon on the left - this takes you along the side of the hill by a shallow dip through scattered firs.

The dip is down on the left as you continue on to the top of the pass which does not appear to have a name (2hrs 15mins). From here there is another 120m stiff climb to the summit of the Cucuyon. Keeping right rather than left pick your way up carefully over grass, rocks, clumps of nettles and sheep droppings - obviously the sheep love this mountain too!

(8) At the top is a short ridge and then a cairn (2hrs 40mins). *The view from the summit is extensive. You can see the valley below (northwest) with the river winding through it and Digne-les-Bains just visible over on the left. The summit of the Couard looks even more impressive from this angle and there is also a good view of the double peaks of the Cousson to the southwest. Northeast is the long grim light brown ridge of the nearer Montagne du Cheval Blanc.*

Go back to the Col keeping to the easier side of the slope. From the pass retrace your steps to the village of Archail (4hrs 30mins).

Walk No. 36
LE COUSSON - Alt. 1511m

Difficulty:	Medium - one short stiff grassy uphill climb but nothing technically difficult.
Time:	4hrs 15mins.
Height gain:	510m.
Maps:	Cartes IGN Série Bleu 3441 Ouest (west) Digne-les-Bains 1:25,000.
	Editions Didier & Richard No. 19 Haute Provence Verdon 1:50,000.
Depart from:	Village of Entrages 1001m.
Signposting:	Some signposts, red/yellow splashes of the Grande Randonnée du Pays and then yellow splashes.

Observations:
A delightful walk with one stiff uphill climb. In fact the Cousson consists of two summits divided by a wide grassy pass. The lower one, by a few metres (1511 as against 1516), is the one more often climbed. From the wide ridge at the top there are uninterrupted views in all directions plus the interesting little church. An observatory was planned on this summit but abandoned as the lights from Digne are too bright.

Entrages is very pretty with its narrow twisting streets and a château built at the end of the 18th century, a big square building part of which is now a gîte! The church, of ancient origin, was enlarged in the 16th century and renovated in 1850. Every time the author did this walk some of the elderly villagers were sitting in the square playing a noisy game of cards and enjoying life!

How to get there (from Digne-les-Bains):
Take the D20 from Digne-les-Bains which goes past the Bains Thermaux (thermal baths) for 6.5kms. Then turn right on the D120 signposted Entrages for 3.5kms and go up the village to the square in front of the church.

Directions:
(1) Beyond the church there is a cross on a plinth dated 1866 and beside it is a large noticeboard with details of the village and area. Follow the wooden sign Digne/Le Cousson on a path by the noticeboard. This is a flat defined track along the bottom of a long ridge to the left. After a few minutes bear up left where it says Cousson and there are red/yellow splashes of the

Grande Randonnée du Pays.

The track now starts to gain height with bushes on either side. Ignore all branches off left. There is a beautiful view to the right of the village in the valley with an attractive coned hill behind and the mountains beyond, particularly the curiously shaped Couard peak. The track becomes grassy. Keep right at a fork (left ends up in a field). Almost immediately the path divides again (20mins).

(2) Go up left on a narrow path with yellow/red GR signs steadily gaining height. From time to time clumps of tall waving grass tickle your legs with their feathery ends as you walk along but apart from occasional low bushes the slopes of the mountain are bare and rocky. The path narrows, becomes somewhat rocky and eroded and then bears hard to the left before reaching a signpost 5mins later (40mins).

(3) Go right where it indicates Digne (straight on there is a cross and to the left it says le Cousson, the way you will return). After a few metres there is a small clearing at the Pas d'Entrages (no sign). Turn down left, following hard to see GR splashes. There is a narrower path straight on to the Tête de Clapière. The path descends about 50m through cool woodland and tall pine

202

trees to the deep valley you can see on the righthand side below with the path doubling back. It comes out at a T-junction between two cairns (50mins).

(4) Turn hard right on this wider track which penetrates deeper into the valley turning into a dry stream bed. The high rock face of the Tête de la Clapière is up ahead. *The vegetation is quite lush and there are lots of willow herb (more commonly called fireweed as it grows on disturbed ground) with young fruit trees to the left that look somewhat neglected.*

(5) Continue down through woodland, ignoring a branch left through the overgrown orchard (there is a red/yellow cross). Suddenly you hear the sound of a stream to the right - cross the stream at a ford (1hr 10mins) and a few metres later turn left and cross the stream again. *Careful* here as this is easy to miss - there are yellow/red splashes on a tree.

The path takes you up the other side of the valley (direction north/west) through woodland and pine trees, crossing small landslides and a spring. As you go steadily up there is a jeep track down on the right which you eventually meet (1hr 30mins).

(6) Bear up left on the jeep track past another abandoned orchard on the left, then levelling out before reaching an open area and crossroads called the Hautes-Bâties de Cousson, 1095m (1hr 45mins). There is an old house by three huge trees (two lime and one pine) and a water trough - very welcome on a hot day!

(7) Come off the jeep track and take the narrow path which goes straight up to the left of the water trough (there is a yellow/red splash on a rock). Continue for a few metres, then go left at a signpost to Le Cousson par le Pas de Boudillon. You now leave the yellow/red GR which goes straight on to Digne. **Follow yellow splashes.** This narrow path goes up and along the top of a ridge (direction south/west) through delightful woodland and pine forest. You can see the jeep track below on the left. Suddenly you come to eroded cliffs and your first view from the ridge of the town of Digne-les-Bains down in the valley with the Bléone River meandering through.

There are magnificent views in both directions all the way along this wide tree-covered ridge as the path rises medium steep to the top of a tree-covered hill where there is a stony clearing with tall pine trees (2hrs). Continue on a wider track which climbs up a further pine-covered hill.

(8) At a fork go right (yellow cross on tree to left). The path goes on the right side of this hill which is a north facing slope, so deliciously cool on a hot day. It undulates through delightful beech woods with a considerable drop to the right. After starting to gain height again, the trees thin out and there are extensive views over Digne and into the valley - you can also see the little village of Courbons and the mountain of La Bigue du Siron behind (Walk No. 37).

Suddenly the huge cliffs of the Cousson appear on the left (2hrs 25mins) and the path goes underneath them for a while - the slope drops vertiginously right, happily masked by vegetation. The path goes round the mountain, becoming rocky in places, reaching an impressive lookout spot at the Pas de Boudillon (2hrs 30mins). It then leaves the wooded mountainside, curving gently through scattered trees to an open area and a pine tree.

(9) Keep right up the grassy path (left is a fainter track). Behind is the slightly higher of the two summits (1516m as against 1511), and you can see a wide path winding up to the top. This is a popular hang-gliding jump-off spot. Continue on the grassy path up and across a wide ridge skirting left round a low hill. Rearing up ahead is the second summit with a large mass of scree on the right and a short steep grassy path to the top (it looks a long climb from below but actually takes only 10-15mins!). Go straight at a signpost indicating Le Cousson (right goes to Gaubert village and RN85) and continue up a grassy path (there is a wooden post halfway up to encourage you), which ascends 100m steeply to the summit. What a puff up but the view is breathtaking! (3hrs). On the top is another hang-gliding flag.

There is a magnificent view in all directions - the whole of northern Provence with the endless peaks of the southern Alps extending in all directions. North is Digne-les-Bains with the Bléone River meandering through the valley. South is the l'Asse valley with its river, road and villages. East is the long ridge of the montagne de Coupe with the distinctive peak of the Pic de Couard at the end, and west the long white shoulder of the Lure mountain.

(10) Turn left and walk along the glorious long wide rocky ridge (direction east) enjoying the continuing panorama all around. At the end, on a precipitous rocky promontory, is the little chapel of St-Michel de Cousson - one wonders how on earth they managed to build anything in such a spot!

The church bell is not on the top of the chapel but hanging in a small dell in front on what looks like a football net. The chapel is usually locked. You can see inside through small windows to a primitive altar but don't try to walk round the chapel as it is built on the edge of an eroded tall cliff with a precipitous ravine below. In fact erosion will cause the chapel to fall into the ravine before long.

Not much is known about the origins of the chapel although it is supposedly built on the ruins of an old monastery. Above the door are fragments of a sarcophagus which was found in a nearby necropolis (collection of tombs) - the originals are in the museum in Digne-les-Bains.

Retrace your steps to the grassy path and continue along the ridge for a few minutes and then away from the cliff edge to the top of a slope (another wooden post here). From here you can see the track curving left

Chapel St-Michel, Cousson

round the other side of the long mountain you climbed up from Entrages.

(11) Go down the open slope on a narrow stony path to a small bushy pass (3hrs 20mins) and keep going on the path seen from above, pleasantly flat bordered with herbs and low bushes. Down on the left is the valley walked through on the outward journey. The path descends through larches and deciduous trees and finally emerges on the shoulder of the mountain. It continues down a bushy ridge on a medium steep path where there are now views down into both valleys; soon Entrages comes into view down on the right. You come to the signpost (No. 3 on book map) where the path divided on the way up (3hrs 45mins). Head for Entrages and retrace your steps to the village (4hrs 15mins).

Walk No. 37
LA BIGUE DU SIRON - Alt. 1653m

Difficulty:	Medium/strenuous - no steep climbing though there is quite a height gain.
Time:	4hrs 40mins.
Height gain:	790m.
Maps:	Editions Didier Richard No. 1 Alpes du Sud 1:50,000.

Cartes IGN Série Bleu 3440 Ouest (west) Thoard 1:25,000.

Depart from: Hamlet of Courbons.

Signposting: Good - yellow splashes and then the yellow/red of the Grande Randonnée du Pays.

Observations:

A really satisfying walk with extensive views and no hard climbing. The village of Courbons used to belong to the Grimaldi family (of Monte Carlo fame) until 1862 when it became a part of Digne-les-Bains. The sunny slopes leading to the village are covered with herbs, vines and olive trees. It is one of the most northerly areas to have such vegetation and also the architecture of a typical Provençal hill village, namely a huddle of houses dominated by a rock with the ruins of a château. There are also vestiges of the fortifications erected in the 16th century, when the church Notre Dame des Anges was constructed. The village is still remembered for a tragic event on Christmas

Eve 1916 when a house on the side of the hill collapsed carrying away other houses and killing a number of people.

How to get there (from Digne-les-Bains):
Take the N85 towards Sisteron and at the first roundabout bear right signposted Gare (station). Opposite the station (on the left) turn up right on a narrow road signposted Courbons. Continue zigzagging steeply upwards for 5.4kms until you come to this attractive hamlet. Turn right in the village where there is parking alongside the road and a modern looking water trough.

Directions:
(1) Walk past the water trough and take the narrow road up to the left called Montée Grimaldi where there is a no entry sign for cars. This goes up round the side of this attractive hamlet (there is a beautiful view over the town of Digne-les-Bains to the right) and reaches the cemetery and church; up on the left are the few remaining ruins of a château which used to belong to the Grimaldi family - there is now a clock tower and a private house, but it is worth going for the view.

(2) Walk past the cemetery and the church (5mins) to a wooden signpost indicating La Bigue and Le Martignon straight on. This is a delightful undulating balcony path flanked by blackberry and rosehip bushes, curling round the mountain direction north/west, with the slopes of Les Roches Rouges to the right and open views over grass-covered slopes down the Durance valley with its meandering river to the left. Beyond is the pyramid shaped mountain called the Pic d'Oise. The path goes beneath a house marked La Gomar on the map and continues on with clearly marked yellow splashes, passing the occasional stately oak tree until it reaches a hang-gliding windsock on the left (20mins).

After the windsock the path starts to gain height as it goes left round the slopes of La Clapière mountain - look out for two outcrops of rock up to the right called Les Oreilles d'Ane which, with some imagination, do look like the ears of a mule! Look back from here and you will see on the slope further down the small stone edifice of a shrine dedicated to St. Barnabé. On the horizon back left are the two distinct peaks of Mt. Cousson (Walk No. 36). The path bears round to the right (30mins) where there is a yellow cross straight ahead. It becomes stonier as it gains height and makes a long zigzag before skirting round two small gullies, continuing upwards alongside a third and much wider gully with the higher peak of the Clapière Haute straight ahead.

(3) Just before the pass of the L'Aire des Chiens at the top of the gully (55mins) the path bears round to the left (yellow splash on a stone) through a small pine grove and along the edge of a pine forest on the left (there are posts with a green stripe on a white background from time to time on the trees along here). You can see the radio mast on the L'Andran mountain over on the right and the imposing Pic de Coard on the left. The pine forest ends with the path on the edge of a steep slope before the trees start again briefly. You can see the track ahead curving round the Gomberge mountain. Proceed with care round the top of an eroded gully (1hr 15mins) where there has been a landslide (1hr 15mins) and follow the contour of the mountain and up a grassy slope to signposts at another pass (1386m), between the peaks of La Gomberge (1490m) to the left and Martignon (1430m) to the right (1hr 30mins). This is where the Grande Randonnée des Préalpes comes in from the right from Dignes-les-Bains (the direction taken on the return journey). From now on the signs are red and yellow until the path turns off up to the summit of the Bigue.

(4) Turn left signposted La Bigue on a path which goes round the right side of the Gomberge, direction north/west. It passes initially through beech trees and then becomes quite rocky. There is an impressive ridge called Le Bouichard descending down right into a ravine with the valley and river beyond. On the skyline is the long Blayeul ridge.

The balcony path goes through a green metal barrier and a delightful beech wood (ignore a branch to the right), before reaching another very attractive grassy pass called Le Darau (1hr 45mins).

The Gomberge is now behind and up ahead left are three peaks - (from left to right) La Blache, La Collerette and Gueride. After the pass the path gains altitude and a multiple intersection. Go left (there are crosses on the other paths so you can't go wrong). Here you get your first view of the summit of La Bigue which has a television aerial on the top.

(5) Continue along the contour of the mountain and then go right at a fork (cross on left). There are lots of offshoots along this slope but continue on the top path with the yellow/red splashes which starts to climb (there is also the occasional cairn). At a T-junction go right (cross on left) and then swing up to the left, following the markings. At a grassy clearing bear right at yellow splashes and make for a signpost at the top of a shoulder (2hrs 10mins). There is a good view ahead of the two rocky summits of Les Cloches de Barles.

(6) Go up left signposted La Bigue and follow yellow splashes - you are now off the Grande Randonnée. The path continues medium steep through scattered pine trees and low broom bushes. It is undefined in places so watch for a line of white-topped stones going up the slope. The TV mast at the top is clearly visible so there is no drama if you lose the path! The path comes to a small hump (called an *anticime* in French) and then across to the shoulder of La Bigue. Bear right along the top of the shoulder and then up the final medium steep slope to the summit at 1653m (2hrs 30mins).

The summit itself is rather an anticlimax as the TV aerial is surrounded by nettles and the droppings of sheep and goats! However, the views are extensive so the climb is worth the effort - down in the valley northeast is the village of Robine near the icthyosaure fossil (Walk No. 33). Southeast is the Martignon and the aerial on the L'Andran summit. Northwest is the village of Thoard nestling in its valley with the white summit of the Lure on the horizon. To the north is the jagged ridge of the Géruen.

Retrace your steps carefully passing the first signpost and joining the yellow/red GR markings, again direction Digne. At the Col de Darau (3hrs) remember to take the left path down and a few minutes later fork upward to the right, following the GR markings.

At the second signpost - No. 4 on book map (3hrs 15mins) take the path straight ahead marked Dignes-les-Bains (you came up from the right). This goes up and along the wide top of the Martignon, with sweeping views all round. Go down the shoulder on a long steep stony path where you have to watch your feet, through stunted broom and box bushes to a pass called Basse des Chatières in a lovely wide grassy area where there is a signpost (4hrs).

(7) Leave the GR path which goes straight on to Dignes-les-Bains and bear right down this grassy slope signposted Courbons. There is no defined path, especially if the grass is high, but make for the ruin on the right called Les Chatières and a yellow hut (what for one wonders!). There is a yellow splash on one of the ancient cherry trees which surround the tumbledown farm.

(8) At the bottom of the grassy meadow look carefully for the path by a wooden post with a yellow splash. It goes over a dry stream bed surrounded by bushes, then takes you down over rocks into the shallow ravine called Riou. Cross a stream bed and continue down the lefthand side. The path is rocky and eroded. Traverse the stream for the third time and emerge into a little clearing. Cross a rivulet coming down from another larger ravine on the right and continue straight on the path up the hill. You now go along a wide rocky balcony path climbing gently. The narrow ravine is down on the left with some really impressive cedar trees at the bottom and the grassy slopes on the other side have a curiously unusual pleated appearance. Quite suddenly you come to the end of the mountain (Rochers Rouges) at a cross and below is the hamlet of Courbons. The rocky path ends in front of the church where you set off on the outward journey. Retrace your steps to where you parked the car (4hrs 40mins).

Walk No. 38
LES ROCHERS DES MEES

A spectacular row of rocks standing in columns over 100m high and 2km long, this is one of the most interesting geological features of the region.

Difficulty:	Medium - the slope to the summit of the rocks is fairly steep and eroded; it should not be attempted in wet weather in which case you should keep to the road in the valley.
Time:	Shorter route 1hr 35mins.
	Longer route 2hrs 30mins.
Height gain:	370m.
Maps:	Editions Didier & Richard No. 28 Haute Provence 1:50,000.
	Map given out by local Syndicat d'Initiative (not very precise).
	IGN 25,000 map currently out of stock.
Depart from:	Main square of Les Mées village.
Signposting:	Wooden signposts and infrequent yellow splashes.

Observations:
These fascinating columns are made out of resistant puddingstone, a mixture of shingle, pebble and sandstone formed by erosion thousands of years ago. They have a romantic legend dating back to the 6th century when some local lords attacked and overthrew the Saracens who had invaded and installed themselves in the region. When they took over the garrison they were surprised to find seven beautiful Moorish ladies who begged for mercy. It was decided to send them down the River Durance to the town of Arles where the authorities would decide their fate. Meanwhile one of the lords kept them in his castle and was himself captivated by their charms. This came to the ears of the local prior who was outraged and threatened to excommunicate the lord if he did not send the ladies immediately down the river under the eyes of the whole village of Les Mées. Unfortunately the community of monks from the nearby monastery heard of this and decided to watch the exodus from the hills behind the village. When the ladies appeared the monks were captivated by their beauty and stood in a row with eyes aglow and hearts beating with passion. From the other side of the Durance was a crusty old hermit called Saint Donat. When he saw how the monks reacted to this procession of beautiful women he was thrown into a rage. To protect them further from their sinful thoughts he turned them there and then into stone. Well, with a bit of imagination they do look like a row of monks in their brown robes!

Les Rochers des Mées

How to get there (from Digne-les-Bains):
Take the N85 from Digne in the direction of Sisteron for 18kms and then, at a roundabout, look for a sign (second right) to Les Mées 8kms. As you go along this road you will see the spectacular column of rocks to the left. Park in the main square of Les Mées which is up left at a roundabout.

Directions:
(1) At the top of the square (Place de la République) there is a map of the various walks in front of a small Casino supermarket. There are also several signposts in the square but follow the one to the Sentier des Rochers (on the lefthand side of the map) which is straight ahead on the Rue Clovis Pichon.

After a few minutes ignore a sign to the left indicating Aire des Pénitents coté nord des Rochers (this is the way you will return) and continue straight past the old washhouse dated 1902 on the right. Further up is a sign left to the Chapelle St. Roch. *It takes about 5mins to climb the steps to this chapel which was originally built on Roman foundations. There is a good view down onto the village which has attractive tiled Provençal roofs not so common in this area.* Continue straight past an old chapel on the right until you reach the entrance to the Municipal Camping at the top (5mins).

(2) Keep right on the paved road by the side of the campsite following a fence. When it starts to bend left look for a sign on a tree and yellow arrow indicating a narrow path along a wall at the back of the campsite (10mins).

211

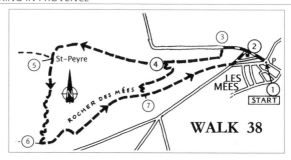

(3) Bear left at the end of the wall, where there is a tunnel to the right with a pipe issuing from it. Zigzag up this path keeping to the yellow splashes and ignoring all offshoots (two have yellow crosses and lead to the Chapelle St. Roch but should not be taken as they are very eroded). The path winds gradually up the hill which is south-facing and coastal Mediterranean in character. It is stark and arid, dotted with pines, and there are delicious smells from the numerous thyme and lavender bushes. You have to be careful where you put your feet in places as the hillside is made of puddingstone (see explanation below) and is very eroded. Down to the right is a narrow valley (Ravin de la Mort) and beyond are tree-covered slopes.

(4) The path reaches an attractive clearing with pines (40mins) where there is a magnificent view into the valley with the busy Route Napoléon and the Bléone River on its way to meet the wider Durance flowing south from Sisteron (see below for further details). Here there is a choice of direction.

Short walk:
The second left turn is the shorter but more panoramic route which goes directly round the back of the rocks. To the right is the longer route along the ridge of the mountain with lovely views. Do not take the path immediate left with a yellow cross as it is not maintained. Go down the path signposted Les Pénitents through woodland (this slope is north-facing so the vegetation is lush and bushy, quite different from the one you have climbed up). After winding sharply it reaches a fork a few minutes later. Take the signposted fork up right (left is a shorter way down) which goes up steps made out of logs and soon reaches a promontory where you get a first rear view of the rocks.

From now on this attractive path undulates along the back of these magnificent rocks with log steps to help when on the up or downward slopes. After 10mins you are directly behind your first "Pénitent" and you can see right down the precipitous cliffs which are made up of the curious stone

212

formation called puddingstone, essentially lots of small stones held together by a glue of sandstone! In all there are six places where the path goes up close to the top of these fantastic columns and you can appreciate their bizarre rock formation and their enormity as you peer down at the valley below. After the last rock on the lefthand side, you start to go down steeply and surprisingly quickly, considering the height of the rock faces. At the bottom you reach the path at point No. 7 running along the front (25mins from No. 4).

From now on you are on the same path as the longer walk so continue from ** to the end.

Longer walk:
(4) From the clearing go right along the ridge signposted San Peyre initially upwards through attractive pine trees with views on both sides. Then go through woodland and into the open, gaining height all the time. After a short stiffer height ascent you reach an open clearing with panoramic views all round (1hr). The path becomes a wider track as it bears right undulating along the top with trees each side. As it starts to gently lose height you can see ahead a path going round an amphitheatre of hills with three small pylons on them - this is the longer La Haute Montagne walk. Shortly after you pass the ruins of the Chapel St. Peyre on the left, little more than fragments of walls hidden in ivy and bushes. The track reaches San Peyre, a confluence of paths and a lone pine (1hr 10mins).

(5) Turn down left signposted Les Mées par Bel Air (the Haute Montagne path is to the right and straight on is a lookout point). The path traverses a wide bush-covered shoulder to a promontory where there is a strategically placed bench to admire the panoramic circular view of the valley below with its rows of fruit trees and a rather nasty looking industrial site. To the east are the mountains north of Digne-les-Bains. There is as yet no sign of the Pénitent rocks which are hidden by the tree-covered slopes of the ridge (1hr 20mins).

Take a narrow path down medium steep through stunted oak forest (there are no yellow splashes at the start but infrequent ones on the way down). *The trees are widely spaced which lets the sun dapple through delightfully and the view of the valley comes and goes, particularly of the wide Canal du Moulin right below which seems to disappear into the side of the mountain (if you look at a map it indeed tunnels beneath the Pénitent rocks and emerges at the other side of the village of Les Mées - what an engineering feat!).* The path continues to wind down through woods and grassy clearings and finally along a balcony path getting nearer to the canal and the busy road to Les Mées. It reaches a wide jeep track at a T-junction (1hr 45mins).

(6) Turn left signposted Les Mées along a wide flat jeep track which narrows to a pebbly path through a low barrier (the track has eroded here) and then widens again. Here you get your first view of the Pénitent columns. The track also discreetly crosses the canal. Just before you reach the rocks, the shorter path down from Les Pénitents joins the jeep track from the left (2hrs).

** Both itineraries are now the same.

(7) Suddenly the sheer pebbly brown wall of the first Pénitent looms above quite alarmingly - the path continues along the bottom and you get dizzy peering up at the pointed peaks high above and wondering if anyone has dared to scale them, they are so smooth. The floodlights along this path makes these peaks look spectacular at night. Ignore all branches going up left. The track undulates slightly downwards and through another barrier (2hrs 20mins) where it meets a road. Turn left - along here the cliffs are even more spectacular with the dark holes of caves and smaller indentations, a nesting ground for the swallows which are darting in and out.

At a fork go left (no signs) leading to the outskirts of the old part of the village with the steeple of the village church on the horizon. Keep straight till the first Aire des Pénitents signpost, then turn down into the village square (2hrs 30mins).

Walk No. 39
LES GORGES DE TREVANS

Difficulty:	An easy walk through a gorge - some height gain.
Time:	3hrs 15mins (time includes detour to ruins).
Height gain:	420m.
Maps:	Cartes IGN Série Bleu 3441 0 (ouest) Digne-les-Bains 1:25,000. Editions Didier Richard No. 19 Haute Provence Verdon 1:50,000
Depart from:	Parking on the D667 5kms east of the village of Estoublon.
Signposting:	Good, with red, green and finally yellow splashes.

Observations:

If the Gorges de Verdon sound too challenging then try this delightful walk round a gorge covered in Mediterranean vegetation such as juniper and boxwood on the southern slopes, a variety of mosses in the canyon bottom and sombre tall Austrian pines which were planted by the Department of Forests. The area is said to be rich in bird and animal life. If you are lucky you may see an eagle, green lizards or even a chamois!

How to get there (from Digne-les-Bains):
Go out of Digne-les-Bains on the N85 direction Nice (Route Napoléon) for
11kms. Then turn right at Châteauredon on the D907 direction Mézel and
continue for 9.8kms to the village of Estoublon. Just before the bridge over
the River Estoublaisse turn left at a sign Gorges de Trévans and then turn right
on the Chemin Presbytère at the entrance to the village (no sign here but
there is a bottled gas advertisement) - the road goes past a church on the
right. Continue along this narrow road, the D667, past a house displaying an
amazing collection of sculptured figures in the garden (with a sign Sculpteur
Cippolini) for 5kms until you reach a small parking area on a righthand corner
with a shabby green sign saying Gorges de Trévans. Nearby is a smart
wooden cross with the following inscription: "Camp Josette, Maquis de
Trevans, April 1944 - April 1945".

Directions:
(1) Take the wide jeep track which descends to the Estoublaisse River. Just
before the track ends at the bottom of a field go right (the way is rather
hidden in bushes) and over a concrete bridge with black railings where the
river below tumbles over small boulders (5mins). On the other side is a large
wooden board with a map of all the different footpaths that can be taken
in and around the gorge. If you look carefully on your return you will see that
the walk described here (red-green-yellow) is in fact a small one on the map
so some of them are really long. You are warned not to go up the Pont de
Tuf without ropes!

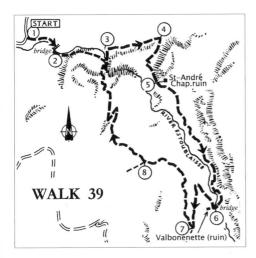

(2) Following the
red splashes go left
on a defined path
through woods -
there is a further sign
indicating you are
entering the Forêt
Dominiale de Mont-
denier, Gorges de
Trévans. The river is
on the left as the
gorge goes through
narrow rocks before
widening and then
narrowing again.
The path goes under
some high cliffs and

there is quite a drop to the river below.

(3) Shortly after the cliffs turn down left at a fork (the right fork has yellow splashes and is where you will come back) and cross over a wooden bridge at an attractive spot where the river rushes over big boulders coming from another gorge on the right (15mins).

A few minutes later cross the river again and continue up the other side towards a high cliff. Before the path reaches the cliff it bears right and starts to climb seriously for about 10mins going round the lefthand side of a large rocky cliff in another small gorge. At the top you can again see the main gorge on the right (25mins). The path goes up briefly and then flattens out before descending through tall pines and stunted oaks all the way to the bottom of the gorge at a dry river bed.

(4) Go right, indicated by red markings, down the dry river for a short distance and then cross another stream at the Pas de l'Escale where there are two wooden bridges. The path doubles back right along the gorge and goes upwards through tall pines - there is also a lot of spagnum moss around as in other places near the river along this walk. Keep to the main path (there are occasional offshoots to the side of the gorge only) as it continues to go higher and round under a tall cliff face. The slope down to the right is quite steep but covered in bushes. After a while the rocky path flattens off as it continues round the cliff, then goes gently up again before undulating into woodland. The gorge becomes wider at this point.

(5) Just after a sign on the left (not easily seen) saying Gîte de Valbonnette there is a path left up to the ruined chapel of Saint André (55 mins). *It is worth a half hour detour for the magnificent view of the gorge from the ruin.*

Detour:
Take the path sharp left signposted Chapelle St-André/Pas Romaine and follow the yellow splashes. As you go up this path medium steep you can see the ruins on the rock ahead. You are going back round the rock you circumvented but higher up. After 10mins you come to a flat area with pines where there is a sign ahead to Pont Romaine 30mins. However, take the path up left (yellow splash) which goes up fairly steeply for 5mins until it reaches the large ruin (15mins). If you go round the back and climb up there is a magnificent view. To the right you can see the path you will be taking down the other side of the gorge. Retrace your steps to the sign and turn left, back onto the main path (1hr 25mins).

It continues gently upwards far above the river down on the right, and then starts to descend gently, crossing a number of scree slopes where the track is sometimes eroded. Surprisingly quickly you reach the river again (1hr 40mins) at a very pretty spot where there are some large flat rocks - an ideally tranquil place for a picnic and the opportunity to take off your boots and refresh your feet in the cool rushing water!

(6) Cross the River l'Estoublaisse by a rickety wooden bridge. Double back on the other side. There is an attractive grove of trees (another ideal picnic spot) with the small hut of the Valbonnette gîte up on the left (the "gîte" (shelter) is a complete shambles inside!). Later on the path goes through some ruins. At the gîte turn right and continue upwards through tall pines around the head of a ravine coming in on the right.

(7) At a T-junction at the head of the ravine leave the red splashes which go up left and go right over a minuscule dry river bed following green splashes (2hrs). Here the vegetation is denser with moss and larch trees. Five minutes later you pass what looks like a primitive bread oven on the left and then there are a couple of ruins covered in ivy and bushes - this was originally the hamlet of Valbonnette. Continue on for a few minutes to a small promontory with a pine tree where you can see the way you came up the gorge.

Still undulating upwards with the river far down on the right there is an impressive rock face on the other side of the gorge which was not so noticeable when walked around earlier though you can see the path taken clearly. Continue round the curving hillside. After passing the rock face the path seems almost level with the Chapelle St-André on top of its rocky summit. Behind is the Montagne de Beynes with a road running along its lower flank.

(8) At a fork go down right leaving the green splashes to the left and from now on follow yellow splashes (2hrs 20mins). The path goes down through tall pines, beech and oak which thin out in places where it is quite sandy. It curls round two densely wooded ravines, then starts to zigzag down quite steeply on stony and eroded ground, becoming rockier as it loses height.

The gorge narrows and the rock face navigated on the outward journey gets nearer as the path continues to zigzag downwards towards the river. There is a pleasant sound of water rushing over boulders. The path goes under an overhanging rock with a sharp drop to the river on the right. Take a look back here for a good view of the water rushing through this narrow part of the gorge. Ignore a rickety bridge crossing an eroded slope and keep to the main track back to the fork on the outward journey (No. 3) and the red splashes (3hrs). Retrace your steps to the big wooden map and go over the bridge back to the car park (3hrs 15mins).

Walk No. 40
THE VERDON GORGE - Sentier Martel

Difficulty:	Strenuous (14kms) but within the capability of regular experienced walkers. Not suitable for anyone suffering from vertigo. One long steepish ladder and two tunnels. **Take a torch and plenty of water.**
Time:	5hrs (allow 6-8hrs for looking at views, picnic etc.).
Height gain:	The path descends 640m into the gorge - the way back up is 400m but more gradual.
Maps:	Cartes IGN 3442 OT Gorges du Verdon 1:25,000.
	Editions Didier Richard No. 19 Haute Provence Verdon 1:50,000.
Depart from:	Refuge de la Maline 893m on the D23 (more details below).
Signposting:	A linear path on the GR4 - you can't go wrong!

Observations:

A spectacular walk for reasonably fit people who do not suffer from vertigo. Personally the author found it less demanding than she had been led to imagine!

The 21km long Verdon gorge, which forms a natural boundary between the Var and northern Provence regions, is the longest and most dramatic gorge in Europe, where the Verdon River (a tributary of the Durance) cuts its way through limestone rock at depths of between 250m and 700m.

The gorge was not properly explored until 1906 when the Agricultural Ministry, wanting to know more about local water resources, asked the geologist Edouard Martel (1859-1938) to study the region. In 1930 the French Touring Club opened the first walk along the gorge, naming it after Martel. In 1936 the Refuge Maline was built.

The tour of the gorge by car is very popular and the complete round trip of 130kms takes a whole day. It is a narrow mountainous road with lots of hairpin bends. In high season the cars are nose to tail all the way as they crawl round, stopping at the many *belvédères* (viewpoints) for spectacular views of the gigantic cliffs plunging into the sinuous gorge below.

Important information:

A walk down the Verdon gorge needs careful planning. Select a day when the weather forecast is good and try to avoid the weekends. This is a very popular walk and can get very crowded which is no fun. As the path is linear it is easier to do with two cars but otherwise there are two alternatives.

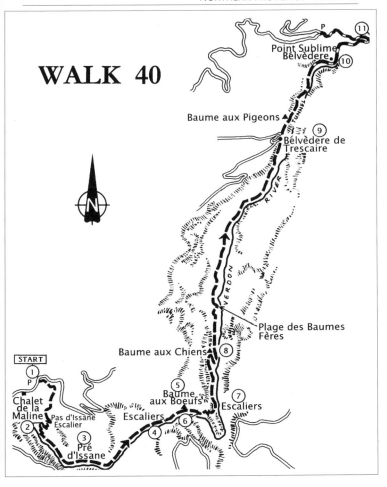

During the season (1st July to end August) there is a bus service from La Pointe Sublime to Refuge de la Maline. The bus leaves Point Sublime at 16.00 so you must start the walk early so you do not miss it. (current cost is FF18). Taxis are also available.

It is suggested that walkers ring the Verdon Information Service in

Castellane, Tel. (33) 04.92.83.67.36: Fax (33) 04.92.83.73.11 (English spoken), to make sure the bus service is operating. They also have helpful documentation in English.

How to get there (from Castellane):

Take the D952 from Castellane to the village of La Pallud sur Verdon (25kms). Then take the narrow winding D23 (Route des Crêtes) for 8kms to the Refuge de la Maline, belonging to the French Alpine Club, where you park your car.

Directions:

There is a big noticeboard near the refuge with a map showing the walk in detail all the way to the Point Sublime (says 6hrs).

(1) The path starts quite flat just below the road along the top of the gorge which looks a long way down on the right. You pass a noticeboard with instructions about walking in the gorge, including a **warning that the level of the water can change abruptly!**

The path descends gradually direction southeast. The upper part of the cliffs on the other side are covered in trees, then become bare grey and brown rock as they plunge vertically down for hundreds of metres to the river below.

Keep to the main path zigzagging downwards, following the red/white splashes of the GR4. The path is built up in parts with artificial steps but is otherwise stony and bouldery. The vegetation consists mainly of boxwood and stunted oak.

After about 15mins there is a sign saying *sens unique* (one way only) where you start down a series of steep steps with a chain to hold on to, through the Pas d'Issane Escalier. Continue over small patches of scree and past the enormous bole of an oak tree to a T-junction (40mins). Go left following the signs Sentier de Martel/Point Sublime and *attention danger*. As the path gets lower the vegetation becomes more abundant and there are a number of stately oak trees. You start to detect the noise of the Verdon River and shortly after get your first glimpse. *The water level depends on the amount of rain which has fallen in recent weeks. When we did the walk in June 1998 there had been a dry winter so there was relatively little, hence extensive banks of shingle.*

There are a number of eroded short cuts but basically choose the easiest way - they all head towards the river.

(2) At the bottom of the gorge go left at a T-junction (45mins), unless you want to go right to the river's edge for a swim! The water looks enticingly clear and very green. The path continues along under some tall cliffs. If you look up you can see a restaurant on the lip of the cliffs opposite. This is on the D71 which winds round the other side of the gorge. You are about 100m above the river as the path meanders through dense woodland.

(3) You come to a sign Pré d'Issane, *pré* meaning field though there is no sign of one. There is access here to a beach. *If you look carefully you will see that the deep rocky pools harbour enormous trout and in fact the largest trout ever caught in France was fished out of this river!* Through the trees you can peer up to the towering cliffs which are so high that you crick your neck trying to see the end of them! The path passes a bivouac to the left - people sometimes sleep in the gorges although this is not officially allowed. Further on there is a cave in the cliff wall.

The path undulates, sometimes high above the river, and then descends almost to the edge. Look up to appreciate the numerous caves in the cliff walls on the other side and a series of square holes which are not caves but the road passing through a tunnel in the rock face - what an engineering feat!

Care is needed at a place where the path has eroded (1hr 15mins) before another camping spot, almost at river level. In many places the rocks are shiny and slippery and this is because the path is walked by hundreds of people every year.

(4) High above the river there is a scramble over rocks (both hands needed) followed by some iron steps with a notice saying Guègues (probably the name of the place), followed by a small area of scree and then two further lots of steps. ***Careful*** - there has been a small landslide after the steps so there is a short haul over vertiginous scree hanging on to a stout rope (1hr 35mins). *You are now one third of the way to the Point Sublime.*

(5) At a fork go left (right goes to the river) close to the tall cliffs and then under an impressive rocky overhang called La Baume aux Boeufs (1hr 45mins). The path becomes rocky and there is some clambering over boulders as it gains altitude.

(6) You arrive at signposts (2hrs). Up left indicates Point Sublime 3hrs, and down right La Mescla 30mins. The latter is a path to a peninsula jutting out into the gorge with a good view where the Artuby River flows into the Verdon from another narrower gorge. The way there and back would take approximately 45mins (not done by author).

Continue up left with some more rocky scrambling to signs saying one way only and Brèche Imbert (*brèche* meaning gap or opening). If you wish you can scramble up the rock to the right for a view of the tall cliffs in this narrow part of the gorge called the Baumes Fères.

(7) Soon after there is a long series of iron ladders (240 steps, taking about 5mins!) going down fairly steeply (2hrs 10mins). It is easier to go down them backwards and care is needed, especially in wet weather. Then continue down steeply to an attractive promontory (2hrs 20mins) where there are extensive views of this magnificent gorge.

The path is now high above the river with trees towering above. It goes right underneath rocky overhangs beneath towering cliffs with precipitous drops on the right *(in high summer this section of the walk can be very hot)*.

(8) The path turns to the right and starts to descend quite steeply towards the river over patches of scree (2hrs 40mins) - there are one or two tricky bits which require a scramble but nothing difficult if you are agile - long legs are a help!

As you get nearer the river you can hear the gurgling of the water which is music to the ears! The path reaches a signpost indicating Plage des Baumes Fères (3hrs) at some stately birch trees. The short descent to the *plage* (beach) is eroded so take care. *This is an idyllic spot to have a picnic as the river flows attractively under a steep rock wall in front, creating a pool deep enough to swim in - the beach is covered in small shingles. You can relax a bit as you have already done two-thirds of the walk!*

From here the path goes up rather steeply and then levels out before going upwards again. It goes under a serrated rock edge and across patches

of scree and rocks where you have to watch your feet. Sometimes you need both hands to get over the rocky boulders. *You can see the river far below, a deep enticing green as it rushes along over boulders between banks of shingle. There are caves in the cliffs above the other side.*

The path becomes flat and bushy as the gorge starts to narrow. Do not take the entrance to a tunnel on the left where there is a red/white cross (lovely wafts of cold air coming from it which is a relief on a hot day). There are

Cliffs, Verdon Gorge

old rusty rail lines coming out of it as this area was once quarried for building stone (3hrs 50mins). Continue along the gorge crossing another patch of scree and then climbing up again to a rocky area where there is a large boulder to be negotiated. *The author found it easier to walk round the back rather than the front. Care should be taken as the scree and rocks are slippery from over use. This is the most dramatic part of the gorge as it has narrowed and the immense cliffs tower above you.*

(9) Go down to the right after the rock; shortly after there is a sign indicating Taurs de Trescaire which is a lookout spot (4hrs). The path descends again and there are more iron steps (you can see another attractive bathing area). Ignore the entrance to another tunnel on the left with old railway lines issuing from it. *Look down at the river which looks particularly attractive, rushing over boulders with what looks like another torrent joining it from behind an island. The cliff faces are particularly serrated and riddled with caves; bushes and stunted trees cling to the indented rocky surfaces.*

You arrive at the tunnel de Trescaire which is 100m long (4hrs 10mins), but quite wide and you can already see a glimmer of light from the other end. A torch is necessary if you want to avoid wet feet from the puddles! This is shortly followed by a longer tunnel of 670m which is very dark but pierced by three entrances in the rock wall which have grilles over them. The first entrance shows a ladder going down the side of the gorge to the Baume aux Pigeons. Access to this was closed in 1995, because it became dangerous after heavy floods.

After the tunnel there are concrete steps descending to the right becoming wooden and then iron! The path bears round left (4hrs 20mins) where the river bank is strewn with large boulders. The road comes into view up ahead with cars parked on it. Clamber down more concrete steps to river level and then along on a man-made concrete path. After more steps the path crosses the Bau stream, a tributary of the Verdon, by a wooden bridge with green iron railings. The steps continue up the other side and then bear round to the left - avoid the path ahead marked by a red/white cross.

(10) Shortly after the path meets the wall enclosing the Samson parking area (4hrs 35mins). You have finished your walk along the Verdon gorge! If you have a car here you are lucky. If not continue up the road following the sign Point Sublime. It is quite a relief to be on a smooth concrete road after so much scrambling. *There is a GR splash to the left and what looks like a steep short cut; not tried by the author.* The road bears round left on a hairpin bend by a sign Belvédère Couloir Samson (another viewing point) to meet the D23 road.

(11) Turn left and continue up to the Point Sublime where there is a large parking area with a café - one of the points where a short walk takes you to a splendid view of the gorge (5hrs).

The *navette* (bus) normally leaves at 16.00 pm. to take you back to your car at the Refuge Maline (this journey takes about half an hour).

Walk No. 41
THE LOWER VERDON GORGE

Difficulty:	Medium - some short ladders and walking along tops of wide walls. This walk is not suitable for young children. Take a torch for the tunnel.
Time:	3hrs 15mins.
Height gain:	220m.
Maps:	Cartes IGN Top 25 3343 OT Gréoux les Bains 1:25,000.
	Editions Didier & Richard No. 19 Haute Provence Verdon 1:50,000.
Depart from:	Car park in front of the Mairie in Quinson village.
Signposting:	Excellent - yellow splashes and then the red/white splashes of the GR99.

Observations:

A very attractive walk, shorter and less vertiginous than the main Verdon gorge. Here the water is still and sluggish, quite different from the rushing clear water higher up.

The lower Verdon gorge is situated between the village of Esparron de Verdon and the dam which creates the Lake of Sainte Croix. The area is of great archaeological interest as the numerous caves and grottoes have served as dwelling places for primitive man and also as refuges in troubled times up until the Second World War.

The Barrage de Sainte Croix, built in a narrow vertiginous gorge where the cliffs rise to a height of 300m, was not completed until 1974. The dam is 95m high and retains the immense waters of the Sainte Croix lake. To accomplish this delicate engineering enterprise it was necessary to move and reconstruct the village of Salles sur Verdon.

The 82km long Verdon canal was started in 1865 principally to provide water for Aix-en-Provence (the first water arrived there 10 years later). Numerous secondary branches were added over the years but it slowly fell into disuse and was finally abandoned in 1981 in favour of new installations on the Provence canal.

The village of Quinson, meaning chaffinch in Provençal, is strategically positioned between the Valensole plain and northern Var. It was founded, as legend goes, by five Roman families and in the 14th century was fortified

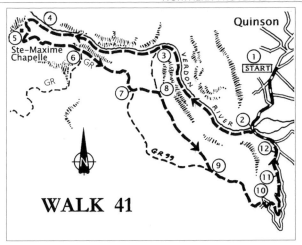

Quinson

WALK 41

by walls, of which a few traces remain. The old part of the village is situated on a rocky outcrop and dominates the entrance to the lower gorges - it has a number of charming fountains dating back to the time when a nearby spring of the Verdon was used to bring water to the village.

How to get there (from Digne-les-Bains - 62kms):
Go out of Digne-les-Bains on the N85 direction Nice (Route Napoleon) for 11kms. Then turn right at Châteauredon on the D907 direction Mézel/Riez, through the villages of Mézel and Estoublon. At the hamlet of La Bégude Blanche the road becomes the D953 (the D907 bears off right) and starts to climb up to the Plateau de Valensole (14kms from the turnoff). Continue for 16kms to Riez and then on the D11 for 21kms to Quinson. Go in to the village and park in front of the Mairie at the end.

Directions:
(1) Walk down the road (D15) which meets the D11 below the Mairie, past the signpost indicating Camping and Barjols 22kms. Go past a Logis de France hotel on the right and round a corner when a charming little lake opens up to the left, not really a lake at all but a widening of the Verdon River before it narrows and goes through the gorges. There are picnic areas along the banks and a sports centre with canoes and kayaks on the other side. The road passes a bar/restaurant on the right with a pleasantly shady terrace on the left - all rather charming on a sunny day except in high season when there are lots of people!

225

(2) Cross a bridge over the river and then look carefully for a signpost about 50m further on to the right indicating PR St. Maxime par les Gorges (10mins). Following the yellow splashes the path climbs up rocks with steps cut into them and gains height rapidly. It reaches a dry wide ditch on the left which is an old canal. This canal winds all the way along the side of the Verdon River, sometimes disappearing into long rock tunnels - an amazing feat of engineering

The path curves round parallel to the road with a wonderful view down to the right of the big expanse of water before it turns and enters the gorge. The slow moving water is a deep sinister green contrasting with the towering brown rocks it is winding through. The path goes down steps hewn out of the rock with a rail at the side (there are helpful rails most of the way along this gorge, though sometimes they are broken). It goes right underneath the rock face on a wooden bridge almost level with the water (20mins) and then starts to ascend again quite high above the gorge continuing along the old wall of the canal.

Undulating along the side of the gorge with the old canal left and the Verdon down on the right, the path is clear but eroded in places. From time to time it leaves the edge of the gorge and there are tree-covered slopes but the canal is always on the left and much walking is along the wide old stone wall.

(3) Do not go left over a small wooden bridge scanning the canal, signposted Malasoque (40mins) but continue straight. After the bridge the river curves left and the path is flat but then goes along the canal wall with considerable drops each side. Continue up and down rocky steps, along the canal wall, then below the wall under overhanging rock to the water level. The reflections of the rocky cliffs in the still green water are particularly clear at this point.

Cross a small wooden bridge over an inlet and up steps under an overhanging rock where there is a metal ladder (11 rungs) and the protection rail has broken. Shortly after turn up sharp left (50mins) on a rough rocky path (straight is a yellow cross). You reach the wall of the canal again which you walk along with steep drops on each side for around 200m - there is not always a railing so be careful here! There are three further stretches of walls and then the path goes down again and under the wall towards the river on a rocky eroded path (55mins).

Go back up to the wall, along a section which is crumbly in places and needs some upkeep. When the river starts to bend to the right, the canal disappears into a tunnel by a small *cabane de surveillance* which is a small hut full of rubbish which one can presume is used as a refuge in case of emergency (1hr 10mins). Take the ladder going down the canal wall (further along you can see the original descent, four rocky projections of which the top one has broken off!). Turn right and go through an eerie tunnel about 200m long - you can see the other end but it is wise to use a torch to avoid the dirty puddles! At the end of the tunnel there are high walls and a ladder to climb back up on the left (10 rungs).

(4) Bear left away from the edge of the gorge into a narrow very bushy (mainly boxwood) valley called the Vallonet de Sainte Maxime (1hr 15mins) where you glimpse tall cliffs each side. About five minutes later go left at a fork where there are yellow splashes (1hr 20mins). This is a pebbly and then steep rocky, narrow path which would be slippery in wet weather as some of the rocks are flat slabs. At the summit is the chapel of Sainte Maxime (1hr 35mins), a simple square building which has been renovated in the past. Inside are a rickety altar and a statue of Our Lady. (We were lucky on one occasion as, at the exact moment we reached the chapel, the heavens opened and there was a terrific thunderstorm - we sheltered in the church eating our lunch till the rain let up.)

(5) The rounded flat area in front of the church is called a *croupe* (rump) and it looks as though there was originally some sort of building here. With your back to the door of the church continue to the end of the rump and turn left, looking carefully for a yellow splash on a tree which is not immediately evident (don't take the path on the right in front of the ruin). There are various yellow crosses in places telling you where not to go! As soon as you round the corner the path is clear and sets off down the slope.

At a small promontory you can see gorges coming in to the right and left. There is a last view of the Verdon River far below showing brown patches of algae on the dense green-coloured water; it makes you realise how far you have climbed!

The path turns sharp left and skirts a rocky hill (*mamelon*) through stunted mossy oak trees, then into denser woodland, going back along the top of the gorge.

(6) Just before a large strangely shaped rock the GR99 joins from the right so the markings are now red/white instead of yellow (1hr 45mins). The wide path is still climbing gently and you can see the tops of the cliff gorges left. At a T-junction go up right away from the gorges on a wider jeep track where the woodland thins.

(7) Just after a ruin take the path to the left with yellow splashes (2hrs). (The GR goes straight on and will meet up with the yellow path later, an alternative route but less interesting.)

(8) The path goes down for about 5mins to a T-junction at a cairn where you take the right turn (left says Le Pont des Vaches and goes down to the bottom of the gorge). The terrain is reasonably flat through attractive woods and bushes reaching the GR99 again at a jeep track (2hrs 20mins).

(9) Turn left and continue on the jeep track ignoring a branch to the left. Shortly after at a T-junction keep left (red/white signs on a tree) and start to go down with a view below of rolling cultivated countryside and mountains in the distance. At a fork shortly after go left (signs again); on the other side of the valley there are cliffs with pylons and a huge dam to the right called the Barrage de Quinson which controls the rushing waters of the Verdon as it emerges from its upper gorges. The village of Quinson looks very near at this stage.

(10) A few minutes later the path (an old mule track) crosses the jeep track and then again shortly after. It becomes quite stony, winding down in large loops, and you have to pick your way carefully.

(11) Turn left when it meets a jeep track (2hrs 50mins). Shortly after there are houses over on the right and a barrier over the track to stop cars coming up.

(12) On joining the D13 road, go left for a few metres before branching off left on a narrow path just after the canal goes underneath the road. This takes you high above the road on the right with the dry canal down on the left. It meets the road again where you scramble down a short slope (3hrs 5mins). Go past the signpost PR St. Maxime taken on the outward journey and retrace your steps to Quinson (3hrs 15mins).

Walk No. 42
LE SOMMET DE CRÉMON - Alt. 1760m

Difficulty:	Strenuous - do not do this walk in bad weather or fog as the summit is a series of promontories and it would be easy to lose your way.
Time:	4hrs 45mins.
Height gain:	860m.
Maps:	Cartes IGN Série Bleu 3542 Ouest (west) Castellane 1:25,000. Editions Didier & Richard No. 19 Haute Provence Verdon 1:50,000.
Depart from:	Parking on D955 (direction Castellane) 1km after Saint-Julien-du-Verdon.
Signposting:	New yellow splashes and signposts up to the shoulder of the mountain and then they disappear! However from there the way is evident.

Observations:

A very dramatic walk with wonderful views in all directions. The way up is long but through cool woods on the north side of the mountain. There is usually a fresh breeze along the top even on a hot day. The signposting and markings are good until the start of the ridge walk. Only do this walk in good weather!

Lac de Castillon - This is an artificial lake 14km long which has brought much needed water to the area. In flooding the valley the village of Castillon disappeared and all that remains are a few old houses clinging to the banks of the lake. Work was originally begun in 1924 by the Germans as reparation for damage inflicted on the region during the First World War. But in 1932 it floundered due to lack of funds, only to be restarted in 1938 and again abandoned due to the Second World War. It was finally finished in 1949 by the EDF (Electricité de France) and was the first dam created in the region. The strange platforms floating in the lake which look like oil rigs are in fact underwater sound research centres.

The creation of the Castillon lake has turned the ordinary little village of Saint Julien de Verdon into a charming lakeside resort sitting on a promontory with suberb views and possibilities for numerous water sports. It boasts an ancient church dedicated to Notre Dame de l'Assomption, renovated in the 18th century. There is an interesting painting in the chancel of the Virgin Mary with St. Julien painted in 1660 by Jean André whose works of art grace many churches in this region.

How to get there (from Digne-les-Bains):

Take the N85 (Route Napoleon) to Barrème and then turn left on the N202 passing through St. André-des-Alpes to St. Julien-en-Verdon (the village is up on the right).

Turn right on the D955 signposted Castellane and continue for 1.5kms until you see a parking area on the right and a signpost on the left at the start of the walk, 51kms from Digne-les-Bains.

Directions:

(1) From the parking area cross the road and follow the signpost Sommet de Crémon/Demandolx/Vergons and yellow splashes. This is a defined path going up medium steep through pine forest (picnic spot to the right). After a few minutes there are further signposts. Go right direction Sommet de Crémon/Col de Demandolx (left goes to the village of St. Julien-de-Verdon). Continue on this wide path winding up through tall pines and boxwood. At a grassy T-junction (5mins) bear left (*careful* as you could easily miss this turning) and shortly after right underneath the wires of EDF pylons. You are now on an overgrown jeep track for a few minutes before branching off left

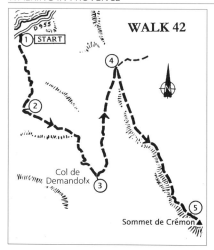

WALK 42

START

Col de
Demandolx

Sommet de Crémon▲

(yellow splashes) on a narrower path which starts to climb up medium steep past further signposts.

The path crosses another jeep track (15mins) - could be the same one but no jeep tracks are indicated on the map! It goes through delightfully spaced out woodland consistingly mainly of pines. Through the trees down right you catch glimpses of the long Castillon lake.

The path curls round the side of a mossy, vegetated ravine where there is a an attractive row of larches, then undulates upwards and comes out onto yet another smooth jeep track (25mins). Go right, following signpost Sommet de Crémon (yellow sign on tree) for around 100m, then up left on a narrow path indicated by a yellow splash on a stone. A small rocky island comes into view in the lake below.

(2) The path goes up the left side of another wider ravine mostly covered in pines with some shale slopes on the other side and the jeep track just below. Further on, at a little promontory, you can see down into a (normally) dry watercourse. The ravine narrows and you cross the watercourse and up the other side medium steep. The path zigzags up with the ravine still down on the left and reaches the Col de Demandolx, Alt. 1336m, where there are more signposts (1hr).

(3) Go left on a wide track which swings round (north) in a loop back the way you have come but higher. There is now an uninterrupted view of the long jagged Crémont ridge rearing up ahead and the lake down left. The track, restfully flat for a short while, crosses the top of the dry watercourse and skirts the top of forested ravines as it curls round the base of the Crémon.

Watch for a signpost and yellow splashes (1hr 15mins) onto a path up right which runs parallel to the jeep track for a while, across a stony slope and through pine trees. As the path gradually diverges from the jeep track there is a view of the village of St. Julien-de-Verdon and the Retenue de Chaudanne (where the sinuous Verdon widens again after the Castillon-Demandolx dam).

(4) Look for a signpost going sharp right indicating Crémon (1hr 30mins) (straight on goes to the village of Vergons). Now the path starts to gain height through boxwood bushes, juniper and pines which thin out as you go higher. Five minutes later there is a small cairn on the path and others higher up which you should continue to follow - strangely enough the smart new yellow splashes disappear at this point but the way towards the summit is obvious. *If the mist is coming down at this point do not continue.*

Look back and the village of St-André-les-Alpes is now visible. The path becomes less defined but there are still pines on the left with boxwood bushes and lavender as you ascend the grassy shoulder which flattens off as you go over it and onto another grassy ridge following occasional cairns. *Over on the right is a clear view of the little village of La Baume perched on the side of the hill and to the left a lovely valley with the village of Vergons.* You are now on the top of the first ridge (2hrs) on the mountain proper. *You can see the winding D102 which goes to the village of Demandolx and a clearer view of the Retenue de Chaudanne.*

Continue along the edge of the mountain looking down to the Col de Demandolx and the long track traversing the bottom of the slope. There are promontories where there would be a real risk of falling over in foggy weather! The ridge becomes stonier, dropping sharply on both sides at some points. You can skirt the overhanging edges by walking lower but then you would miss the incredible views on all sides. The first overhangs are stony and rocky but further on they become grassier. There are lots of interesting alpine flowers but be careful of the clumps of nettles which look rather out of place in such a spot! In the distance you can see the summit (although curiously it looks lower from afar). It consists of two piles of stones and some sticks standing up. Make for this point, crossing some rocks and walking over grassy slopes.

(5) At the summit, Alt. 1760m, there is a flat ordnance survey marking between two piles of rock and a mini-gorge to the left (2hrs 45mins). Looking back across the ridge you can now see that you have crossed six jagged promontories - not apparent when you were actually walking over them! *The panorama of the surrounding peaks and the two lakes is fantastic, plus an even clearer view of the dam and the winding gorge called the Couloir (corridor) Samson. The outskirts of the town of Castellane can just be glimpsed at the end of the Retenue de Chaudanne.*

To make the return a bit shorter keep below the overhanging promontories. There are paths which come and go. However do not go too low or you will miss the way down. If in doubt veer up to the crest when you think you are at the end of the ridge and the way down is then clear. The path down is the same as the way up (4hrs 45mins).

Appendix A
MAPS

The maps used in this guide are as follows:

Maps 1:25,000 (1cm = 250m) - show the paths more clearly.

Alpes Maritimes

Cartes IGN 3643 ET Top 25 Cannes/Grasse/Côte d'Azur - (Walks 1, 3, 4)
Cartes IGN 3642 ET Top 25 Vallée de l'Estéron - (Walks 2, 5)
Cartes IGN 3543 ET Top 25 Haute Siagne - (Walks 6, 7)
Cartes IGN 3544 ET Top 25 Fréjus/St. Raphaël - (Walks 8, 9, 10)

Var

Cartes IGN 3245E Série Bleu Aubagne/La Ciotat - (Walk 17)
Cartes IGN 3244E Série Bleu Trets/Montagne Ste-Victoire - (Walk 16)
Cartes IGN 3345 OT Top 25 Signes/Tourves - (Walks 11, 12, 13, 14, 18, 19)
Cartes IGN 3344 OT Top 25 St-Maximin/La-Ste-Baume - (Walk 15)

Vaucluse

Cartes IGN 3142 OT Top 25 Cavaillon/Fontaine-de-Vaucluse - (Walks 20, 21)
Cartes IGN 3243 OT Top 25 Pertuis/Lourmarin - (Walks 22, 25)
Cartes IGN 3242 OT Top 25 Apt - Parc de Luberon (Walks 23, 24)
Map from booklet *Découverte du Colorado Provençal* by F. & C. Morenas (in French, available from local book shops)
Cartes IGN 3040 ET Top 25 Carpentras/Vaison-la-Romaine - (Walks 26, 29, 30, 31)
Cartes IGN 3140 ET Top 25 Mont Ventoux - (Walks 27, 28)

Northern Provence

Cartes IGN Série Bleu 3440 Ouest Thoard - (Walks 32, 33, 34, 37)
Cartes IGN Série Bleu 3440 Est La Javie - (Walks 35)
Cartes IGN Série Bleu 3441 Ouest Digne-les-Bains - (Walk 36, 39)
Cartes IGN Série Bleu 3441 East - NOW OUT OF STOCK
Cartes IGN 3442 OT Top 25 Gorges du Verdon - (Walk 40)
Cartes IGN 3343 OT Top 25 Gréoux-les-Bains - (Walk 41)
Cartes IGN Série Bleu 3542 Ouest Castellane - (Walk 42)

Please note that the Série Bleu are being phased out and replaced by the Top 25 series. It could be that some of the maps are out of stock but the new ones not yet published.

Maps 1:50,000 (1cm = 500m) These are useful for a broader perspective.

Editions Didier Richard No. 26 Pays d'Azur
Cartes IGN Var - L'Arrière Pays Toulonnais*
Editions Didier Richard No. 14 Du Luberon à la-Ste-Victoire
Editions Didier Richard No. 27 Ventoux
Editions Didier Richard No. 19 Haute Provence Verdon
Editions Didier Richard No. 1 Alpes du Sud

Editions Didier Richard No. 28 Haute Provence
*Note: Editions Didier & Richard IGN Nos. 24 & 25 (Var region) are at present OUT OF STOCK.

Maps 1:100,000 (1cm = 1km)

Vaucluse Carte Touristique - gives good general view of whole area including the Luberon and Mont Ventoux.

Maps 1: 200,000 (1cm = 2km)

Provence/Côte d'Azur - good map of the whole of Provence.
Most large English bookshops with a travel section should sell these maps.

Specialist shops are:

Stanfords, 27A Floral Street, London WC2 9LP
    Tel: 020 7836 1321
    Fax: 020 7836 0189
    Email: Sales@Stanford.co.uk
Stanfords have the largest selection of guides and maps in England. Anything they do not have in stock can be ordered (delivery delay 2-4 weeks).

The Map Shop, 15 High Street, Upton-upon-Severn, Worcs WR8 OHJ
    Tel: 01684 593146
    Fax: 01684.594559
    Email: Themapshop@btinternet.com
A wide selection of maps and guides.

France Magasin, Digbeth Street, Stow-on-the-Wold, Glos GL54 1BN
    Tel: 01451 870920
    Fax: 01451 831367
Everything appertaining to France (books, videos etc.) including a quarterly magazine.

    Local newsagents and bookshops in Provence also stock maps and guidebooks (the latter mainly in French). The big supermarket chains in most towns also stock local maps (often cheaper).

Appendix B
TOURIST OFFICES AND SYNDICATS D'INITIATIVE
(relevant to places named in the book)

The prefix from outside France is: 0033 + 9 digits (omit first zero)

General information on Provence

Comité Régional de Tourisme Provence-
    Alpes-Côte d'Azur
    Espace Colbert, 14 Rue Sainte-Barbe
    13231 MARSEILLE Cedex 01

Tel: 04.91.39.38.00
Fax: 04.91.56.66.61

General information on the Alpes-Maritimes region

Comité Régional de Tourisme
  Riviéra Côte d'Azur
65 Promenade des Anglais
BP.602, 06011 NICE
  Tel: 04.93.37.78.78
  Tel: 04.93.86.01.06

Office de Tourisme
22 Cours Honoré Cresp
BP.98, 06130 GRASSE
  Tel: 04.93.36.66.66
  Fax: 04.93.36.86.36

Office de Tourisme
8 Place du Grand Jardin
BP.131, 06140 VENCE
  Tel: 04.93.58.06.38
  Fax: 04.93.58.91.81

Office de Tourisme, Place Tour
06620 LE BAR-SUR-LOUP
  Tel: 04.93.42.72.21
  Fax: 04.93.42.92.60

Office de Tourisme, BP.14
1 Boulevard Courmes
06530 ST. CEZAIRE SUR SIAGNE
  Tel: 04.93.60.84.30
  Fax: 04.93.60.84.40

Syndicat d'Initiative, BP. 15
8 Rue Soucare
06640 SAINT JEANNET
  Tel: 04.93.24.73.83

Office de Tourisme, 10 Place Tour
06460 ST. VALLIER-DE-THIEY
  Tel: 04.93.42.78.00

Office de Tourisme, 5 Route Vence
06140 TOURETTES-SUR-LOUP
  Tel: 04.93.24.18.93
  Fax: 04.93.59.24.40

General information on the Var region

Comité Départemental du Tourisme du
  Var (C.D.T.)
l Boulevard Maréchal Foch, BP.99
83300 DRAGUIGNAN Cedex
  Tel: 04.94.50.55.50
  Fax: 04.94.50.55.51

Office de Tourisme, Place Hôtel de Ville
83470 ST-MAXIMIN-LA-STE-BAUME
  Tel: 04.94.59.84.59
  Fax: 04.94.59.82.92

Office de Tourisme
2 Cours Général de Gaulle
83860 NANS-LES-PINS
  Tel: 04.94.78.95.91
  Fax: 04.94.78.60.07

Office de Tourisme, Square Reda-Carré
83640 ST-ZACHARIE
  Tel: 04.42.32.63.28

La Maison du Tourisme, 29 Rue Pasteur
83870 SIGNES
  Tel: 04.94.90.83.53

General information on the Bouche du Rhône region

Comité Départemental du Tourisme des
  Bouches du Rhône
13 Rue Roux de Brignoles
13006 MARSEILLE
  Tel: 04.91.13.84.13
  Fax: 04.91.33.01.82

Office de Tourisme
2 Place du Générale de Gaulle
13100 AIX-EN-PROVENCE
  Tel: 04.42.16.11.61
  Fax: 04.42.16.11.62

Maison du Tourisme du Pays d'Aubagne
Imm. Les Marronniers, Av. Antide

Boyer13400 AUBAGNE
   Tel: 04.42.03.49.98
   Fax: 04.42.03.83.62

General information on the Vaucluse region

Comité Départemental du Tourisme du
   Vaucluse
12 Rue Collège de la Croix
BP.147, 84008 AVIGNON Cedex 1
   Tel: 04.90.80.47.00
   Fax: 04.90.86.86.08

Service du Tourisme, Mairie
Place Bouquerie
84400 APT
   Tel: 04.90.74.03.18
   Fax: 04.90.04.64.30

Office de Tourisme, 41 Cours Jean Jaures
84000 AVIGNON
   Tel: 04.90.82.65.11
   Fax: 04.90.82.95.03

Office de Tourisme des Pays de
   Mt. Ventoux,
Rue Portail Olivier 84410 BEDOIN
   Tel: 04.90.65.63.95
   Fax: 04.90.12.81.55

Syndicat d'Initiative
Chemin de la Fontaine
84800 FONTAINE-DE-VAUCLUSE
   Tel: 04.90.20.32.22
   Fax: 04.90.20.21.37

Office de Tourisme, Place du Portail
84190 GIGONDAS
   Tel: 04.90.65.85.46
   Fax: 04.90.65.88.42

Office de Tourisme, Le Château Place
84220 GORDES
   Tel: 04.90.72.02.75

Office de Tourisme
Avenue du Chanoine-Sautel
BP.53 84110 VAISON-LA-ROMAINE
   Tel: 04.90.36.02.11
   Fax: 04.90.28.76.04

General information on the Alpes de Haute Provence region

Comité Départemental du Tourisme et
des Loisirs des Alpes de Haute Provence
19 Rue de Docteur Honorat, BP.170
04005 DIGNE-LES-BAINS Cedex
   Tel: 04.92.31.57.29
   Fax: 04.92.32.24.94

Office de Tourisme
Rond Point du 1 Novembre, BP.201
04001 DIGNE-LES-BAINS
   Tel: 04.92.36.62.62
   Fax: 04.92.32.27.24

Office de Tourisme
Place Frédéric Mistral
BP.4 04400 BARCELONNETTE
   Tel: 04.92.81.04.71
   Fax: 04.92.81.22.67

Bureau d'Accueil, Porte Royale
Places Charles Panier
04320 ENTREVAUX
   Tel: 04.93.05.46.73
   Fax: 04.93.05.43.91

Office de Tourisme
Intercommunal du Pays de Forcalquier
Place de Bourguet
BP.15, 04300 FORCALQUIER
   Tel: 04.92.75.10.02
   Fax: 04.92.75.26.76

Syndicat d'Initiative
2l Blvd. de la République
04190 LES MÉES
   Tel: 04:92.34.36.38
   Fax: 04.92.34.31.44

Office de Tourisme
340 Avenue Jean Monnet
06210 MANDELIEU LA NAPOULE
   Tel: 04.92.97.86.46
   Fax: 04.92.97.67.79

Office de Tourisme
Place du Docteur Joubert
04100 MANOSQUE
   Tel: 04.92.72.16.00
   Fax: 04.92.72.58.98

Office de Tourisme, Mairie
04500 QUINSON
   Tel: 04.92.74.01.12
   Fax: 04.92.74.00.03

Office de Tourisme
Place Marcel Pastorelli
04170 ST-ANDRE-LES-ALPES
   Tel: 04.92.89.02.39
   Fax: 04.92.89.19.23

Appendix C
MARKET DAYS

Alpes Maritimes

Daily except Monday:	Antibes, Cannes, Grasse, Nice (in different areas of town)
Monday:	St-Cézaire-sur-Saigne
Tuesday:	Vence
Friday:	Théoule-Sur-Mer, Valbonne, Vence
Sunday:	Vence

Vaucluse

Monday:	Bollène
Tuesday:	Beaumes-de-Venise, Gordes, Vaison-la-Romaine
Wednesday:	Malaucène
Thursday:	L'Isle sur la Saorge, Orange
Friday:	Carpentras
Saturday:	Apt, Bollène, L'Isle sur la Saorge, Pernes-les-Fontaines

Var

Tuesday:	Mazaugues, St-Tropez, Toulon, Aubagne (Bouches du Rhône)
Wednesday:	Brignoles, Draguignan, St-Maximin-La-Ste-Baume
Thursday:	Forcalquier
Friday:	Entrecasteaux, Tourves
Saturday:	Draguignan
Sunday:	Forcalquier, Nans-Les-Pins

Northern Provence

Monday:	Barrême, Forcalquier (not 1st Monday in month)
Tuesday:	Les Mées, Seyne Les Alpes
Wednesday:	Barcelonnette, Digne-les-Bains, La Palud-sur-Verdon, Riez, Saint-André-les-Alpes, Saint-Croix-du-Verdon, Sisteron, Thoard (Wed. afternoon), Valensole (2nd Wed. in the month)
Friday.	Entrevaux, Les Mées, Moustiers-Sainte-Marie, Quinson (summer)
Saturday:	Barcelonnette, Castellane, Digne-les-Bains, Manosque
Sunday:	Thoard, Valensole

Appendix D
A GLOSSARY OF PROVENÇAL WORDS

Baou or Bau	A rocky outcrop which dominates the surroundings
Baume	A grotto or large cave with a narrow entrance
Balme	An overhanging rock creating a shelter underneath (used as dwellings by ancient man)
Bories	Small oval shelters made out of stone
Clapier	A large mass of rocks
Doline	A round depression due to breaking down of the limestone subsoil (used by primitive man as areas of cultivation and often ringed by stones)
Embut	(Provençal) Swallow hole (*aven* in French) These holes are seen on the rocky cliffs, particularly in the gorges
Mourre	Muzzle - a projection of land
Oppidum	A vague circle of jumbled rocks - the remnants of strongholds of ancient Ligurian tribes
Puy	(Provençal) Summit of a hill or mountain
Roubine	(Provençal) Rock fall or scree on a hillside at the entrance to a gully

OTHER CICERONE GUIDES TO FRANCE AND THE ALPS